D1400442

COLLABORATE TO COMPETE

DRIVING PROFITABILITY
IN THE KNOWLEDGE ECONOMY

ROBERT K. LOGAN • LOUIS W. STOKES

Praise for Collaborate to Compete

"This book is a reference model and a major step forward for organizations that need to master collaborative work. Logan and Stokes paint a rigorously compelling vision for collaboration as a competitive advantage. They back it with a precise roadmap and an effective diagnostic tool for avoiding common mistakes and focusing on the tried and true."
— *William Mougayar, Author of* Opening Digital Markets, *and Fortune 500 Consultant*

"The impediment to knowledge sharing has always been the ability of the organization's leadership to create a collaborative environment where every employee truly believes that his or her future is intimately linked with successful knowledge sharing with all other employees. Stokes and Logan in their new book provide hands-on answers and a roadmap on how to successfully create a collaborative environment in today's technology-focused workplace."
— *Howard Firestone, Director of Marketing, iPerceptions Inc.*

"Logan and Stokes have cut to the heart of [the issues surrounding] Knowledge Management's failure to deliver promised returns. The solution may not be achieved overnight, but we will not succeed in a knowledge economy until we heed their message."
— *Robin L. Athey, Consultant, Deloitte Research*

"This book not only makes explicit the major *raison d'être* for Knowledge Management, but draws from it important lessons for the meaningful and successful implementation of KM. Your first reaction is 'but of course, why didn't I put two and two together so eloquently?', and then you read the book for its important insights and lessons learned."
— *Michael Koenig, Dean & Professor, College of Information and Computer Science, Long Island University; Frequent contributor to* KMWorld, *and Co-editor of* Knowledge Management for the Information Professional, *and* Knowledge Management: Lessons Learned, What Works and What Doesn't

"Teamwork without collaboration is a façade. Now that managers have access to powerful computers, networks and the Internet, there are no longer any technical restrictions to information and knowledge exchange. Stokes and Logan in their new book deal with the interaction of employees and how to create a collaborative environment made more powerful through technology. They demonstrate and illustrate this through informative and thought-provoking case studies."

— *Peter Duffield, President, Capability Snapshot Inc.*

"Logan and Stokes create a brilliant business case for the essential change of the 21st century mindset. Competition is inevitable, but enterprises—public and private—that do not master the art (and science) of collaboration are destined to extinction. The authors effectively provide us with the rationale, case story examples, and practical strategies for implementation. As technical systems and social networks abound, collaboration—complete with the new value-set outlined in this book—will be more essential for optimal company performance, national economic development, and global stability. It is only a matter of time."

— *Debra M. Amidon, Founder and CEO of ENTOVATION International Ltd., and Author of* The Innovation SuperHighway

"Bob Logan and Louis Stokes have truly captured the spirit of the times and in [*Collaborate to Compete*] have given us a powerful lighthouse to find our way within the new seas of change."

— *Charles Savage, Author of* Fifth Generation Management

"The core message of *Collaborate to Compete* seems counter-intuitive, yet it is one of the underlying principles for success in a knowledge economy. Bob Logan and Louis Stokes have thoughtfully and carefully traced the roots of this intriguing concept and compiled a compelling collection of practices, anecdotes, and resources that demonstrate how much the business climate has changed in the last few years. If you are one who appreciates the breadth and depth of the business transition we are experiencing, you will find *Collaborate to Compete* to be a valuable guidebook for emerging management practices and new business thinking."

> — *Verna Allee, President and Founder of Verna Allee Associates,*
> *and Author of* The Future of Knowledge: Increasing
> Prosperity Through Value Networks

"*Collaborate to Compete* offers up a compelling, well designed, and very helpful bridge to the promise of profitability in organizations that pursue knowledge as a key strategic capability. Robert Logan and Louis Stokes introduce a new lens through which we can view our work in organizations."

> — *Charles Armstrong, President and CEO, S.A. Armstrong Ltd.;*
> *CEO and Founder of Know Inc.*

"Collaboration is indeed the key to bringing together knowledge, learning, and experience. And technology is finally positioned to be an effective enabler for that process."

> — *Bob Blondin, Vice President, Learning Strategy and Assessment*
> *Services, Intellinex LLC*

National Library of Canada Cataloguing in Publication

Stokes, Louis
    Collaborate to compete : driving profitability in the knowledge economy / Louis Stokes, Robert Logan.

Includes index.
ISBN 0-470-83300-9

    1. Interpersonal relations. 2. Strategic alliances (Business)
3. Psychology, Industrial. I. Logan, Robert K., 1939- II. Title.

HC79.I55S74 2003   658.4'095   C2003-905252-4

Production Credits
Cover & interior text design: Interrobang Graphic Design Inc.
Photo Credits: Louis Stokes by Movie Alive Media
Printer: Tri-Graphic Printing Ltd.
Printed in Canada
10 9 8 7 6 5 4 3 2 1

To Maria
(RKL)

To Beverly, Jason & Sandra
(LWS)

Contents

Acknowledgements

The process of writing this book has been a true collaborative venture and we would like to thank our collaborative partners for their ongoing support and ideas and for allowing us to use their material to support our arguments. In particular we appreciate the contributions of: Verna Allee, President and Founder of Verna Allee Associates, and author of *The Future of Knowledge*; Debra Amidon, author of *The Innovation Super-highway*; Charles Armstrong, CEO of S.A. Armstrong and founder of Know, Inc.; Charles Savage, author of *Fifth Generation Management*; and Karl Erik Sveiby, author of *The New Organizational Wealth*.

The following people generously shared their collaborative business and organization experiences with us: James I. Mitnick, Senior Vice President, Turner Construction Company; Ted Graham, World Wide Director of KM Services, Hill & Knowlton, Inc.; Scott Shaffar and Jerry Garcia, Project Managers, Knowledge Management, Integrated Systems Sector, Northrop Grumman Corporation; and Aaron Hurst, Founder and President, The Taproot Foundation; and Mick Majid, Senior Partner, BDStrategies, Inc.

We are grateful to the individuals and companies that provided assistance in our case study examples: Accenture; Sharon Dratch,

Public Relations Manager, Centra Software; Irv Christy, Director of Marketing, CoCreate Software, Inc.; David De Jear, Senior Manager, Corporate Communications, Documentum, Inc.; Laura Heisman, Public Relations, iManage, Inc.; Brian Wick, Vice President of Marketing, Intraspect Software Inc.; Shannon Kelly, Senior Corporate Communications Strategist, J.D.Edwards (PeopleSoft, Inc.); Larry Rudolf, Vice President, Marketing Development & Corporate Affairs and Nancy Mancini, Director, Product Marketing, Hummingbird Ltd.; Margaret Dobbin, Director, Public Relations and Lisa Dekker, Reference Relations Specialist, Open Text Corporation; Barb Killam, Marketing Department, Primus Knowledge Solutions, Inc.; Clay Helm, Senior Public Relations Manager, Siebel Systems, Inc.; Heidi Gabrielson, Vice President, Marketing, SiteScape, Inc.; and Tim May, Marketing Manager, Vignette Corporation.

We would also like to thank The Conference Board in New York for the opportunity to present our ideas at *The 2003 Conference on Knowledge Management and Organizational Learning: Collaborating Beyond Boundaries to Create Value*. The valuable participant feedback we obtained there helped make this a better book.

Special thanks go to our publishing consultant Malcolm Lester of Malcolm Lester and Associates for his collaborative participation in helping initially to shape our different business and academic perspectives on and experiences of collaboration into a unified book. And we certainly owe our thanks to our collaborative Wiley business team, whose members brought their professional expertise to the book's development: Karen Milner, Editor; Elizabeth McCurdy, Project Manager; Robert Hickey, Project Coordinator; Gayathri Baskaran, Marketing Manager; Michelle Bullard, Copyeditor; and Valerie Ahwee, Freelance Editor.

On a more personal note, Bob Logan would like to thank his wife, Maria Ielenszky Logan, for all her help and loving support.

Louis Stokes extends a special thanks to Beverly Stokes for her wholehearted support during the writing of this book—it was a more than sufficient *quid pro quo* for enthusiastically supporting her while she wrote her book. Reciprocity certainly is the cornerstone for continuing collaboration success! Thanks also to Jason Stokes for his sharp-witted encouragement and the sharing of his collaborative business experiences in the burgeoning world of Internet marketing in Silicon Valley—he exemplifies the critical importance of a collaborative mindset for business success and success in business.

Special thanks to to our collaborative business partner, Jon Wagner, with whom we have formed Collaboration Associates Inc. in order to exploit the ideas and methodologies we developed in this book.

In the spirit of an ongoing dialogue on collaboration the authors would welcome the readers' ideas, comments, and inquiries as they implement collaborative processes in their businesses and organizations. The authors can be reached at info@collaborationassociates.com.

The Dawning of a New Era

Internet, Knowledge and Collaboration

Rationale

> "Collaborate or die—the writing is on the wall. Collaboration
> is the key to profitability in the New Economy."
> —*J.D. Edwards*

> "Organizations and individuals must be competitive to collaborate
> and at the same time they must **collaborate to compete**!"
> —*Logan & Stokes*

With the unprecedented growth of the Internet as the medium of communication, knowledge has become the new source of wealth and the
co-creation and sharing of knowledge through collaboration, the key to
the success of today's organization. Unfortunately, the mindset of most
business people is not one of cooperation, but of competition. This
all-too-pervasive attitude is the major barrier to conducting business
effectively in a networked world and, in particular, to the successful
implementation of knowledge management (KM) systems. In this book,
we address the critical question of how to create a collaborative organization and foster a spirit of cooperation among co-workers, suppliers
and customers. We believe that since the Internet has served as a natural environment for collaboration without any management input or

central controlling agency that there are lessons to be learned from the use of this medium. We therefore use the Internet as a model or metaphor for collaboration and examine how this technology can be used to promote collaboration. Our focus throughout this study, however, will be on the human-human interaction and not the technology.

The first quote above, found on the Web site of the software vendor J.D. Edwards, is more than just an advertising slogan. It reveals a fundamental truth about today's Internet-configured economy, one that can no longer be ignored. *Collaborate to Compete: Driving Profitability in the Knowledge Economy* is informed by this truth: The ideas expressed in our book are, we believe, a major step forward in establishing collaboration as the new business paradigm. In addition, we believe that we have developed a strategy for the most effective application of Internet technology to business and to the role it can play in the development and the implementation of an organization's collaboration strategy.

Our approach to developing an understanding of collaboration and the role it plays in the knowledge economy is to focus on the way in which personnel work with each other within the context of a networked world, and hence our concern with emotional intelligence and how it relates to the use of knowledge networks. In addition to our focus on the human issues of knowledge sharing and collaboration, we also take into account the technical issues as embodied in the use of information technology (IT), knowledge management (KM) techniques and human resource (HR) issues such as organizational development, training and education.

Other books on the topic of collaboration seem to focus on either the technical issues, such as Skyrme (2001), or the human resource issues (Straus, 2002; Beyerlein et al., 2003). We believe our book is unique in that we treat all aspects of collaboration and bridge the gap between HR on the one hand and IT and KM on the other hand. As a result this book will be of interest to IT personnel who want to build information systems that foster collaboration, as well as human resource personnel who want to use IT that will promote collaboration. In addition, it will be of interest to those charged with developing the KM strategy for their organization and want to make it work, realizing that collaboration is the missing link between IT and KM. The main purpose of the book is not to focus on the problems of any particular sector of the organization such as IT or HR, but rather it is intended for all members of the organization concerned with the success of their organization. Collaboration is not the concern of any one department or some specialized working group; rather it is the concern of every member of the organization from the CEO and CFO to the salesforce, to the marketing team, to the R&D group, to the shipping department. Collaboration is everyone's business and every business's concern.

Our book, co-authored by an academic and a business consultant/organizational psychologist, is in a certain way a response to the challenge posed by Bertels and Savage (1998) who called for KM research in a number of diverse areas: "We need an approach where academia and business work closely in what might be called an 'action research learning and implementation' approach." We have chosen to explore the role of collaboration in KM and to develop what we call a collaborative knowledge management approach.

The Transformation of Commerce by Information Technology

Computers and other forms of information technology have transformed the nature of manufacturing and commerce. The Industrial Era has given way to the Information Age in a transition that began about 50 years ago with the introduction of the mainframe computer into the world of business. The Information Age really took off, however, with the widespread use of microcomputers about 20 years ago, especially when they became networked to the mainframes. Although we now find computers are indispensable for our work, one of the ironies of their widespread use is the productivity paradox. The essence of the paradox is that the long-awaited increase in productivity that computers promised to deliver has never really materialized. Instead of a reduction in the number of hours worked per week there has been an actual increase in the number of working hours since the introduction of personal computers.

At first it was thought that this was because computers were merely automating out-of-date business processes left over from the Industrial Era. Hammer and Champy (1993) suggested that by reengineering these business process and restructuring organizations, primarily by downsizing, that computing's promised increase in productivity would be realized. After almost 10 years of restructuring and reengineering it is clear that the resolution of the productivity paradox will not be achieved by improving strategies of information or work flow or by developing more effective forms of information technology alone.

This realization led us to the formulation of what we call the technology paradox, which states: **The more complex and sophisticated the technology, the more important are the human behavioral issues of attitude, cooperation and motivation, as well as the training, education and learning of all members of the organization.** The lack of better results from improved IT and the implementation of business process reengineering or KM initiatives is because issues concerning the personnel and their attitudes have not been properly addressed. **The soft issues are the hard problems.** Even in an area of KM as mundane as data warehousing, Michael Kull of the firm Running Light reported, "In the course of delivering data warehousing services to clients...most of the challenges were about process, people and change management issues."

If there is not a spirit of trust, sharing and collaboration, no amount of IT, business process reengineering (BPR) or KM techniques will create an organization that can tap fully into its own knowledge. We must remember that an organization's knowledge is not owned by any particular person or small group of people, but is distributed throughout the organization and requires the cooperation and collaboration of all to be accessed and utilized. One of the themes of our study is that the Internet and in particular the World Wide Web bring a human dimension to IT which facilitates collaboration. This is no accident that, as according to the words of one of its developers, Tim Berners-Lee (1999, p. 123), it was designed precisely to do this job: "The Web is more a social creation than a technical one. I designed it for a social effect—to help people to work together—and not as a technical toy."

With the collapse of the dot.com bubble there came some well-deserved skepticism as far as the use of the Internet goes. We want to make it perfectly clear to our readers that we are not Internet "evangelists" who believe that the Internet is the solution to every business problem that arises or that the Internet is a panacea that will so revolutionize commerce that all of the traditional ways of doing things will become obsolete. Not at all! We believe that the basics of commerce will remain much the same but, at the same time, that the strategic use of the Internet will be absolutely key if a company wants to be competitive in today's networked economy. The Internet has become a basic business tool just like the telephone or the computer. Any firm that ignores this technology does so at its own peril.

It is only through collaboration, through knowledge sharing and knowledge co-creation that an organization can tap into all of its knowledge held collectively by all its members, its customers, its suppliers and its business partners. It is only through collaboration that the executives, the managers and the staff of an organization can tap into each other's knowledge and the knowledge of their counterparts in customer and supplier organizations. In order for these things to happen there are two conditions to be met.

One is technical and fairly straightforward to achieve. It involves creating an Internet- or browser-based environment that is linked to the organization's email system, groupware applications, document management system, data warehouse and any other applications being used. It also involves structuring the network so that it operates as a knowledge network, in which information and knowledge can be communicated, shared, stored, organized and created. This is the work of an IT department, where the emphasis is usually on the day-to-day operations of the organization and on information rather than knowledge.

The second condition is the creation of an environment of trust, teamwork and collaboration and the promotion of emotional intelligence. Trust is something that is built slowly but can be destroyed very quickly, either by deception intended or not, or even by carelessness. Trust entails developing a new style of learning—one suited for collaboration and not just individual achievement. This is the work and responsibility of every manager and every employee in the organization, for there is no technical solution for developing trust and teaming. It is the role and responsibility of the human resource department to provide the corporate enterprise-wide support necessary for creating an environment conducive to collaboration. Learning styles cannot be imposed from a central agency but rather must emerge from the experience of each member of the organization.

As a result of the failure of BPR it has become clear that knowledge, not information, and people, not technology, are the keys to increased productivity and the creation of wealth. And by knowledge we do not mean a stock of information but rather the ability to use information to achieve one's business objectives. The challenge is then seen to be how to take advantage of IT so that people can create, share and utilize knowledge more easily, especially those technologies that promote interconnectivity as represented by the Internet and the World Wide Web, as well as intranets, groupware, local area networks, wide area networks, video conferencing and even the telephone. In particular the Internet is creating a communications revolution on the same scale as the one created by the printing press. The Internet in general has done for computing what Gutenberg did for writing.

When we refer to the Internet as in the above statements or in other remarks we make about this revolutionary technology we are including the World Wide Web, email, intranets and all of the forms of IT that support interconnectivity and facilitate the exchange of both information and knowledge. The Internet, as we will shortly document, has had a major impact on the way business is conducted. In addition, it has become the ideal medium for the implementation of KM. "Information is a relatively small component of the Web experience. A much more important component is and will be collaboration: people working together toward some goal" (Weinberger, 1999a). KM represents a major improvement over BPR in that it is based on the notion that knowledge has overtaken information as the principal source of wealth.

In fact, one can say that the Information Age, after a very short reign, is over and has been replaced by the Knowledge Era, in which the focus has shifted from data processing and management information systems (MIS) to KM systems. Although many people are now beginning to adopt the term, "the Knowledge Era", we believe that "the Collaboration Era" is an equally apt term or even the Collaborative Knowledge Era. We will stick to common usage, however, and refer to the newly emerging era as the Knowledge Era as most other authors do. When we use the term "Knowledge Era" though, the term "knowledge" refers to the collaborative process by which knowledge is shared and co-created, because knowledge is a process and not an object or a stock. And when we speak of "knowledge management" we are speaking of collaborative knowledge management but we will not always insert the adjective "collaborative" before knowledge management. But if one considers collaboration as the essential element for successful KM we can avoid the unnecessary debate about whether or not knowledge can be managed. Collaboration, as we will see, in the next sections, is the missing element or link that has prevented KM from being more successful.

The Internet and Knowledge Management: Collaboration Is the Missing Link

The Internet and knowledge management function as catalysts or stimuli for each other. The Internet provides a physical medium for the organization's sharing and co-creation of knowledge. As we will show later it also acts as a catalyst for the cultural shift in attitudes, which encourages cooperation and collaboration among all of the players in the activities of an organization including co-workers (by co-workers we mean all the members of the organization regardless of their status), suppliers, customers, business partners and in some cases even among competing firms. Knowledge management, on the other hand, requires a medium like the Internet for the distribution, facilitation and promotion of knowledge transactions. The Internet is reshaping collaboration and therefore one of the goals of this book is to understand how this is taking place and how we can take advantage of it.

Not only has the Internet functioned as an excellent medium for the practice of KM by speeding up the pace of innovation and the tempo at which commerce is conducted, but it has also been a driving force for bringing knowledge to the fore as today's principal source of wealth. In the age before computing and the Internet, when change was not so rapid as it is today, all players had more or less the same opportunity to acquire the knowledge to conduct business. In today's rapidly changing environment the ability to access and create knowledge is absolutely essential to success and, hence, the emergence of KM. When KM first appeared some 10 years ago it was skeptically regarded by many as just another management fad like BPR and total quality management (TQM). Even today there are still some holdouts, but it is safe to say that KM has altered the mainstream of business practice and is regarded by many if not most organizations as an essential part of their organization and operation.

The practice of KM has certainly led to many improvements in the way organizations share their information and knowledge, but if the truth be said, KM has not quite lived up to all the expectations that its promoters and practitioners led us to initially believe were possible. It is the thesis of our study that the reason for this failure of KM to deliver on its early promise is the lack of a desire by co-workers to share their knowledge, and for those with a desire a lack of the skills required to collaborate. We believe that collaboration is the missing link, which explains why KM has not enjoyed more success to date. The purpose of this book is to focus on this missing link by identifying how emotional intelligence, value sharing, trust, community, as well as the hard skills associated with KM can create an environment conducive to collaboration and hence the whole KM program of knowledge sharing and co-creation. We believe that the development and successful implementation of an effective collaboration strategy would lead to robust knowledge co-creation and the better management of an organization's intangible knowledge assets, namely its intellectual or knowledge capital and, hence, a final resolution of the productivity paradox. In other words, an effective collaboration strategy would allow an organization to access the potential of each and every individual's knowledge and experience to create new knowledge.

We believe that to develop a collaboration strategy to facilitate the goals of KM, it is necessary to understand the way in which the Internet has changed business. We also need to understand the dynamics of the Internet, collaboration and KM. It is obvious to any observer of today's business environment that the Internet has radically changed the practice of commerce and will continue to do so for the immediate future. Perhaps less obvious is the fact that the Internet has been the most successful medium for collaboration in the history of the human race with the possible exception of writing itself, which is subsumed by the Net. One of the theses of this study is that if we are able to understand how organizations can develop collaboration strategies, we must understand what underlies the success of the Internet as a collaborative medium, a success, by the way, that was not managed, but rather developed spontaneously.

> There are the people who have figured out that the company intranet is actually a pretty great way to ignore the organizational hierarchy, cut through the red tape and join with other motivated people to get some real work done....Project teams form consisting of people who have found one another, not people invited because someone higher up has to be made to feel useful or loved....The Web itself is the largest, most successful unmanaged collaborative project since the species voted to walk upright. (Weinberger, 1999a)

As a consequence we regard the Internet as both a medium for and a model of collaboration. And it is with that in mind that we have crafted our study to describe the nature of a collaborative organization and, more importantly, how to build one.

What Is a Collaborative Organization?

A collaborative organization is one that has the following characteristics:

1. The values and objectives of employees and management are aligned,
2. A climate of mutual trust and respect exists,
3. The knowledge of all the staff, customers and suppliers is shared and pooled to optimize the organization's operations and opportunities,
4. Decision making is more decentralized than it is in most current organizations and more stakeholders in the organization play a role in defining the direction in which the organization moves, and
5. Hierarchical structures are kept to a minimum. The company is managed democratically by consensus rather than by command and control. (By consensus we do not mean that every member of the organization is in agreement with every decision, but it does mean that all members of the community are heard and their views are taken into account by those responsible in the organization for making decisions.)

Collaboration has far-reaching implications for the enterprise-wide culture of an organization. Collaboration, as contrasted to the more circumscribed concept of teamwork, cuts across organizations, divisions, departments and working groups. It also involves more than just cooperation; it requires the ability and willingness to creatively share ideas and knowledge and to create new knowledge with others. And this is the crux of the problem, because it is hard for individuals to do this when they still believe that "knowledge is power" and they hoard their knowledge.

The Challenge of Collaboration

In the collaborative organization, the workplace is a community where people trust each other, share similar values and respect each other. Given the realities of today's corporate environment, our definition of collaboration creates a major organizational challenge. But we are confident that by embracing the paradigm of collaboration companies will experience improved efficiencies and greater profitability. Here's one example of how:

> The Documentum content management system is making it easier for DuPont engineers, designers, contractors and others, both inside and outside the enterprise, to perform their jobs effectively and to collaborate efficiently with one another. The end result is faster time to completion for new plants and other projects, which contributes to competitive market advantage and significantly increased cost savings for the company's bottom line. (www.documentum.com, 2003)

We predict that companies that do not become more collaborative with their managers, employees, customers, suppliers and alliance partners will not survive in the Internet era. We realize that the sophisticated reader has already heard something like this before, when similar claims were made for TQM, BPR and other formulae that turned out to be just another fad. So why do we think this is different? The answer is that the essence of a company is collaboration, as opposed to individuals working on their own. It is interesting that it is only within the past few years that people have begun to recognize the importance of collaboration and how it incorporates the whole spirit of commerce or doing things together.

Why the Internet Creates a Natural Environment for Collaboration

The Internet affects business today in every sector in ways that are only beginning to be understood. The foundational relationships between a business and its customers and suppliers, other businesses and even its competitors, has already evolved through radical changes that weren't even conceivable just a few short years ago. And more significant changes are coming, brought about by the use of the Internet as the new, ubiquitous language medium of two-way communication between any business and its customers and between businesses themselves.

Companies are using the Internet to realize new efficiencies that lower costs, thereby making them more competitive, and to increase their level of customer support, hence increasing the level of their collaboration with their customers. Customers now have the expectation that they should receive immediate answers to questions they have about the supplier's services and products, online information, online support and the facility for online ordering. Some customers would like to participate in the design of the next generation of products or services of their supplier (customer as customizer). Companies are using the Internet to create new business opportunities for themselves by pooling their knowledge and interests with the knowledge and interests of their customers.

The creation of a collaborative culture within an organization makes collaboration between businesses and organizations more feasible. But, because the rapid improvement of the technology is so dazzling, we are often blinded to the critical psychological and organizational cultural issues to which the new media give rise. These are the areas on which we focus our analysis in this book; these are also the areas that lead us to the conclusion that the Internet not only makes collaboration possible, it demands that a company be collaborative to succeed and thrive in the burgeoning Internet world of knowledge-savvy customers.

The Obstacles to Collaboration

Knowledge management systems have been organized to achieve the collaborative goal, but have only met with partial success as documented by Lucier and Torsilieri (2001): "Knowledge management fails to deliver significant results. Across the 108 companies we studied, we found no correlation between systematic management of knowledge and improved bottom-line performance. That is, we found that companies with extensive knowledge management programmes were not more likely to achieve bottom-line performance than companies without extensive knowledge management initiatives." These researchers did find some companies where KM initiatives did pay off. "Buckman Labs captured value by identifying and measuring relationships between investments enabling collaboration and sharing, time spent with customers, rapid problem resolution, sales from new products and overall growth." In other words a focus on collaboration, especially with customers so as to meet their needs, results in KM initiatives having a positive impact on the bottom line.

In terms of technology, it is not all that difficult to set up a knowledge network to facilitate knowledge sharing and knowledge co-creation. The challenge is to get managers, employees, suppliers and customers to actually use these systems. The problem is one of company culture, especially trust and the attitude of employees, often attitudes the employees bring to their organization based on their prior experiences.

Traditionally our education system has emphasized individual accomplishment and learning in a highly competitive environment in which students are graded and ranked. For most students their ability to find satisfactory employment and enjoy financial success depends on their ability to do well in school, which does not necessarily entail deep learning, but rather scoring well on tests and competing successfully with their classmates. Once these former competitors are employed they find themselves in a similar environment of competition. Now they must compete with their co-workers for the prestigious, more important and higher salaried positions within their organization. They quickly discover that personal knowledge and information is power, and that if they wish to advance their careers it is probably better to keep what they know to themselves.

Not only does the competitiveness of the former students add to an environment of mistrust, the organization itself, through its actions, adds to the level of mistrust. This is partly due to the nature of a free market economy in which the organization must think in terms of defending itself from its competitors. This adversarial mind-set adds to the general lack of trust within the organization. Another factor adding to mistrust in the business world is the massive amount of downsizing that has characterized most organizations in recent years, which has contributed to employees' mistrust of their employers. As a result, employees often put their own personal career goals way ahead of the needs of their company. This is reflected in the large staff turnover that many companies experience. The lack of trust operates in both directions. Because of the difficulty in retaining staff, companies create, and then exacerbate, a vicious cycle by not investing enough in their employees' professional development, which would build a greater atmosphere of trust.

The lack of trust, endemic in the culture of most companies, is the single biggest obstacle to creating a collaborative organization. Rodgers and Banerjee, in a white paper written for J.D. Edwards, concur with our judgment: "Although technology shortcomings are a significant hurdle to true collaboration, the biggest medium-term barriers to evolving a collaborative commerce strategy will be cultural and organizational. At an organizational level, successful collaboration is built on the principle of trust." (www.jdedwards.com, 2003)

When a climate of trust is created within an organization, by no means an easy thing to do, the cultural barriers can be overcome. It is for these reasons that the focus of this book is on the human issues of trust and cultural adaptation, and not on the technical issues of the deployment of IT. Technology will not be ignored, but where we do talk about the technology, it is to show how technology can be used to create community, trust, the alignment of personal and corporate values and objectives, and a spirit of collaboration within the organization.

Not Collaborate or Compete, but Rather "Collaborate to Compete"

The title of our book is intended to resolve the apparent paradox between collaboration and competition. We believe there is no conflict between collaboration and competition and that in fact, to compete in today's networked knowledge-configured environment one must actually collaborate to be competitive, even to merely survive. There are two senses in which we believe an organization can compete by collaborating. One is through the internal collaboration between the organization's managers and employees. The other is external, through collaboration with other organizations beginning with customers, suppliers and business partners, but even including competitors if the circumstances are right. This second form of collaboration is known as collaborative commerce or c-commerce.

The roots of the conflict between collaboration and competition can be traced back to the Industrial Era and Adam Smith's notion of the invisible hand of the marketplace. According to Smith, each person in the market economy was to act in his or her own narrow self-interest and allow the invisible hand of the marketplace to determine the value of labor or the products he or she was able to produce. The whole system was built on the notion that unbridled competition would rapidly determine the correct values in all exchanges and therefore if each person only looked after his or her own selfish needs, a fair and equitable system would emerge. We do not dispute the power of the marketplace to effect a basically fair exchange of goods and services, and in light of the failure of the planned economy model know of no better system. Yet, we believe that as is the case with all human systems and technologies, they provide both service and disservice and one must always try to strike a balance between the positives and negatives of all systems. It was only natural that in a competitive market-based economy that there were and are bound to be excesses. Hardin illustrates this point with his famous parable of the "Tragedy of the Commons," where he points out how the purely selfish behavior of the herdsmen results in the overgrazing and destruction of their commonly held pasturage.

The Eight Key Messages of the Book

1. The foundation of a profitable business culture is characterized by a robust spirit of collaboration between:
   - employees and management,
   - internal departments or divisions, and
   - the organization, its customers and its suppliers.
2. A collaborative environment best enables staff to align their professional goals with the objectives of the organization and to implement strategies and tactics to realize these objectives.
3. In order for a KM strategy to be successful, it must include a strategy for collaboration.
4. The Internet and the World Wide Web provide a powerful paradigm of collaboration for any organization.
5. There are cognitive, emotional and motivational dimensions to collaboration.
6. The book provides a number of practical recommendations for tools and processes that will help develop a culture and psychological environment of collaboration.
7. A unique assessment instrument, the Collaboration Quotient, measures the readiness of individuals and their organization to collaborate. This tool, created by the authors and introduced for the first time in the book, is also used to monitor the organization's progress in developing collaboration.
8. An Internet-based knowledge network dramatically facilitates knowledge sharing and co-creation. The book introduces a detailed design for a practical and effective knowledge network.

Each of the eight key messages forms the subject, respectively, of the eight chapters of our book:

Chapter 1 - The Impact of the Internet
on Business: The Need for Collaboration

This chapter describes the way the Internet is changing the nature of business and, as a result, the organizational structure of business. The Internet provides a medium for aligning and integrating the operations of an organization's activities. We give examples of this by examining the impact of the new media on certain organizational activities, including sales and marketing; customer relations and product support; and human resources activities including training, education, recruiting and retention of managers and employees. The impact on procurement is covered in Chapter 2. One of the objectives of our study is to show how these diverse functions can be made to work together more effectively and profitably in a collaborative organization.

We conclude this chapter by showing how the use of the Internet has contributed to the realization that knowledge, not information, is the ultimate source of wealth. We carefully define the difference between information and knowledge and describe the emergence of KM. We identify the lack of trust and collaboration as the factors that have limited the success of KM.

Chapter 2 - What Is a Collaborative Organization?

We survey the nature of and/or the lack of collaboration in the pre-industrial, industrial and post-industrial eras. We describe the difference between a hierarchical, command-and-control organization and a collaborative one. We present a historical review of commerce to explain the roots of command-and-control management. We then describe the cultural change in business as hierarchical organizational structures began to break down and shift towards collaborative ones brought about in part by three technological breakthroughs: namely the introduction of 1. mainframe computers, 2. personal computers, and 3. the Internet. We examine the collaborative nature of EDI (Electronic Data Interchange), e-commerce and e-procurement (i.e., electronically configured supply chains) and of the new phenomenon, collaborative commerce, or c-commerce, in which business partners and allies come together to create and share a common enterprise.

Chapter 3 - The Treatment of Collaboration in the Knowledge Management Literature: The Missing Link?

We review the recent work of management experts who have partially addressed the question of collaboration. We will specifically explore the role of collaboration vis-à-vis a number of ideas that have been developed in the management literature in the past 10 years, including the notions of business reengineering (Hammer and Champy, 1993); the learning organization (Senge, 1990); knowledge capital (Sveiby, 1997); Charles Armstrong's (2002) enterprise capital model; knowledge creation (Nonaka and Takeuchi, 1995); knowledge networking, dynamic teaming, knowledge management and value sharing (Savage, 1996); and the nature of collaboration in the scientific community and its analogy with knowledge sharing in the business community.

We close the chapter with a survey of some of the very recent works that look at collaboration explicitly, namely Allee (2003), Amidon (2003), Beyerlein et al. (2003), Saint-Onge and Wallace (2003), Skyrme (2001) and Straus (2002).

Chapter 4 - The Five Collaborative Messages of the Internet, a Medium for and a Model of Collaboration

In Chapters 1 and 2 we illustrated how the Internet and KM are changing the nature of commerce so that for businesses to be economically effective, they must transform themselves into collaborative organizations. In Chapter 3 we reviewed a number of pertinent approaches to KM and collaboration. In this chapter we set out our own comprehensive approach to the development of the collaborative organization in which knowledge is co-created and shared by all the members of the extended organization, which includes customers, suppliers and business partners, as well as executives, managers and employees.

In order to develop our approach to collaboration we demonstrate that the Internet also serves as a model or metaphor for collaboration and thus plays a central role in the creation of a collaborative organization. We make use of the insights of Marshall McLuhan, with whom one of the authors (Dr. Robert K. Logan) worked. McLuhan showed that a medium has a certain effect on its users independent of its content, which he expressed with his famous aphorism, "The medium is the message." We show that the Internet, which is a hybrid technology of telephony and computing together, with the World Wide Web, which marries the Internet to hypertext, has a unique set of five properties or characteristics ("messages" if you will) that, taken together, make it the ideal medium for collaboration and knowledge networking. They are:

- The two-way flow of information,
- The ease and speed of access to information,
- Continuous learning,
- Alignment and integration of common objectives, and
- The creation of community.

No other communication medium prior to the Internet possessed all five of these properties to the same extent (although certain media possess some of these properties), all of which, as we show in this book, are necessary (and sufficient) for creating a successful collaborative organization. This is what makes the Internet the ideal vehicle for collaboration.

We then show how the five properties or "messages" of the Internet create both an environment and a spirit of collaboration that allow the qualities of trust, shared values and the formulation of common objectives and strategies to flourish within a collaborative organization. Out of this discussion we develop the Logan-Stokes model, a model of collaborative knowledge management.

We conclude the chapter by discussing the role of values in promoting collaboration and introduce the idea of the organization value web in which collaboration encourages group cohesiveness, which encourages loyalty and retention, which encourages excellence and passion. The end result of harnessing the five collaborative messages of the Internet and the value web is a successful collaborative organization that maximizes the intelligence and innovation of its entire human resource population to best meet the challenges in today's and tomorrow's global competitive business world.

Chapter 5 - Three Psychological Dimensions of Collaboration: Cognition, Emotional Intelligence and Motivation

Since the human dimension, rather than the technical dimension, of collaboration is the greater challenge, we examine the nature of

emotional intelligence and motivation and their impact on successful collaboration. (This has been a central theme in the practical
consultative work of one of the authors, organization development
psychologist Dr. Louis Stokes.) We explore the relationship between
emotional intelligence and motivation on the one hand, and leadership and trust on the other hand.

For an organization to become successfully collaborative, executives, managers and employees must learn to become more aware of and
manage their own feelings and emotional reactions about collaboration
within the business environment, and how these internal forces impact
their self-motivation and their ability to understand and relate to others, which is the foundation of building trust with another individual.

We will show the reader the importance of better understanding his
or her own intrapersonal reactions to people and events and how their
emotions within the business context, if intelligently managed, positively affect their collaborative relationships with others. Based on this
foundation of self-knowledge, managers can then learn to increase their
interpersonal skills so they can communicate their ideas more persuasively, create the organizational environment to support better team
relationships, deal with conflict more effectively, and create a more
empowering work environment by assisting others to be more collaborative, which, in turn, encourages the diversity of innovation necessary
to be a leading-edge company.

Chapter 6 – Practical Steps in Building the Collaborative Organization

In this chapter we provide a number of practical recommendations to
implement the ideas presented in the book. We develop ideas for
everyday activities to promote collaboration and increase trust to support the organization's objectives. In particular, we examine how to
transform a command-and-control organization (or a partial command-and-control organization) into a collaborative one. We also
address the question of how to maintain and increase collaboration
once an organization has minimized its hierarchical barriers.

We examine ways to increase the overall trust within the organization, which includes the employees' trust of each other and of their
managers, as well as the managers' trust of each other and their
employees. We recommend ways to increase the number of individuals in an organization who are self-motivated and ready to accept the

responsibility of carrying out the organization's important objectives. We argue that within a collaborative organization with motivated employees, the amount of time devoted to supervising and managing staff is greatly reduced, which can result in significant cost savings and thereby allow managers to focus on creating new business.

The organization's resource systems and processes must support the individual's development of collaborative behavior. We identify what processes and tools are necessary to support collaboration. We address the issue of leadership and employee initiative. We suggest that an organization in which decision making is more decentralized, but aligned, empowers and motivates its employees and at the same time achieves the organization's overall goals and objectives. We'll examine how the organization can find ways to reward and encourage collaboration so that both managers and employees willingly align with the company culture of collaboration and commit themselves personally to collaboration. We also answer the question: Where does the "buck" stop in a collaborative organization? Answer: It stops at everyone's desk.

The discussion of this chapter is framed in terms of seven collaborative building blocks needed to make the transformation to a collaborative organization. They are:

1. Vision,
2. Leadership,
3. Trust,
4. Goals,
5. Strategies,
6. Tactical objectives, and
7. Action and implementation.

Chapter 7 - The Collaboration Quotient (CQ): Measuring the Collaborative Capacity of an Organization and Its Personnel

This chapter describes the Logan-Stokes Collaboration Tool, which includes the Collaboration Quotient and is a suite of collaborative knowledge management measuring instruments that allows an assessment of an organization's readiness for collaboration. The information gathered using this tool makes it possible to make the appropriate decisions for building a collaborative organization. The suite of collaboration tools consists of the following four elements:

1. The Collaboration Quotient (CQ), which measures the willingness and ability of individual employees to collaborate in co-creating and sharing knowledge.

2. The Manager's Collaboration Quotient (MCQ), which measures the level of support and encouragement for collaboration from senior executives and the middle managers.

3. The Organizational Collaboration Quotient, which measures the degree to which the organization's current systems, policies, procedures and infrastructure support collaboration.

4. The Collaborative Commerce Quotient, which measures the organization's readiness to enter into collaborative relationships with customers, suppliers and potential business partners.

The Collaboration Quotient (CQ) specifically measures the capability of individuals to engage collaboratively in knowledge co-creation and sharing. We identify three key factors that allow an individual to enter into collaborative relationships with their co-workers, customers, suppliers and business allies. They are:

1. The cognitive factor, which embraces analytic, communications and learning skills and includes such specific skills sets as the ability to formulate goals, devise strategies, develop objectives and implement action plans, and which we identify with IQ,

2. The emotional intelligence factor, which includes interpersonal and sociological concerns, such as trust, integrity, vision, agility, responsibility and the ability to share, and which we identify with EQ, and

3. The motivational factor, which includes psychological concerns, such as motivation, self-actualization, drive and willingness to share, and which we identify with MQ.

We formulate the equation $CQ = IQ \times EQ \times MQ$, where IQ is a measure of business-relevant cognitive skills, EQ is a measure of emotional intelligence and MQ is a measure of the level of motivation. The reason that CQ is the product of EQ, MQ and IQ is that people can be totally brilliant on the technical level, but if they do not have the proper social skills or motivation their collaborative contribution is ineffectual. Conversely, a well-motivated person with great social skills, but without strong strategic thinking skills or intellectual competencies has very little to contribute to a collaborative effort. Therefore it is our basic premise that emotional, motivational and intellectual competencies are all required for successful collaboration.

Based on the results of the CQ and the other collaboration tools, one can identify gaps in the organization's resources and processes that should support collaborative behavior, and what blockages are hindering collaboration. As a result of this analysis, certain systems, processes and procedures may need to be modified or eliminated, which, in turn, may entail significant changes in the company's organizational development and culture.

Chapter 8 – The Logan-Stokes Collaborative Knowledge Network (LSCKN)

One of the themes of the book is that a browser-based knowledge network is an ideal environment in which knowledge sharing and collaboration can take place. We describe the design of a typical knowledge network based on our experiences working with former clients, namely the Logan-Stokes Collaborative Knowledge Network, which is comprised of three basic elements: a learning system, a sharing system and a measuring system. The primary functions of the knowledge network are:

1. A medium for the development of a knowledge community through internal dialogue and information and knowledge sharing,

2. A knowledge management tool for the development of the organization's human resources,

3. A delivery mechanism and brokerage for online training and education, and

4. A medium for storing organizational memories and hence enriching the organization's culture.

The Impact of the Internet on Business

The Need for Collaboration

The Internet and Commerce

In this chapter we will review the impact that the Internet has had on business. The Internet was developed in the United States as an alternative backup communication system in case of a breakdown of the regular communication system due to war or natural disaster. Its first users were the military and the scientists and engineers who helped create it. The next cohort of users were academics, primarily scientists and engineers once again, who used it to facilitate their research activities, mainly through the use of email and the transfer of data and software files from one computer to another. The Internet proved to be an ideal medium for scientific and other scholarly research because science has always been a collaborative activity in which scientists have shared their data, their ideas and their results freely.

The World Wide Web was developed by the experimental physics community at CERN under the leadership of Tim Berners-Lee as a way of communicating and sharing visual and numerical/textual data at the same time. With the release of a commercial Web browser by Netscape in 1994, the general public and business community discovered the Internet and its potential for the dissemination of information and ideas. The scientists' ethos of sharing ideas, information and data, however, still dominates the use of the Internet by other communities. This gives the Net and the World Wide Web its unique character as an open medium of communication, which is no accident since it was purposely designed in this manner.

Now the use of the Internet is considered as indispensable to doing business as the telephone, the computer or the fax machine. In fact, many firms, among them Ford, demand that their suppliers conduct certain aspects of their commercial transactions via the Internet. "Jacques Nasser, [then President and CEO of Ford], always reminds us that leveraging the Internet in the 21st century is as critical to the company's future success as pioneering the moving assembly line was to our success in the previous one. Bipen Patel – Director Management Systems – Ford" (www.documentum.com, 2003).

The Internet is a benefit to organizations both large and small. For large firms it permits vastly improved communication among its staff, particularly those that are not co-located. It is also valuable for small-to medium-sized organizations who, for example, need to support a worldwide customer base or wish to expand their reach. "One Space Technology has become central to Harbec's (a plastic injection molding company) growth strategy. The company previously offered services regionally. But thanks to tools like One Space Collaboration, they can reach customers or partners efficiently regardless of their location" (www.cocreate.com, 2003). Using the same collaborative software Harbec was also able to reduce 50% of its tooling design time by exchanging 3D CAD data with customers and suppliers. The Internet is also impacting legal practices. "The way in which law firms are providing services is changing," said Knapp. "Clients are starting to expect the accessibility and collaborative features provided by portal solutions like Hummingbird Portal" (www.hummingbird.com, 2003).

The importance of the Internet to business grows as more and more commerce is either taking place directly online or as offline commerce is supported by Web sites that provide customers with all kinds of information, from product support to the location of dealers. The Internet, through the use of intranets and groupware, is also essential for the organization of a company's activities for a diverse number of functions, including the internal communication and coordination required to conduct business, information sharing, KM, budgeting, planning and product development and support. There is no doubt that the Internet is having a major impact on business particularly as new tools are developed. Many business people like Jim Mitnick

(2003), Senior VP of Turner Construction and the creator of a knowledge network for his company, are extremely optimistic about the
possibilities that the Internet holds for future development. "What we
have achieved today with the Turner Knowledge Network would not
have been possible five or six years ago. Internet technology is driving
a lot of the things we are doing. Our creativity and our imagination far
exceeds the capability of the Internet today, but we are solving age-old
problems by utilizing current technology and it's just going to get better and better."

Internet Culture

As the use of the Internet for commerce increases, the culture of the
Internet is having more and more of an effect on the way business is
conducted. Although media guru Marshall McLuhan never experienced the Internet, he had a number of insights about the nature of
electric information that have turned out to be pertinent for understanding Internet culture. McLuhan coined the phrase "global village"
in 1964, a phrase that is a perfect description of the Internet. It was for
his prescience that *Wired* magazine adopted McLuhan as their "patron
saint." In their inaugural issue they published the following quote from
McLuhan's 1967 book *The Medium is the Massage*:

> The medium, or process, of our time—electric technology—is reshaping
> and restructuring patterns of social interdependence and every aspect of
> our personal life. It is forcing us to reconsider and re-evaluate practically
> every thought, every action and every institution formerly taken for grant-
> ed. Everything is changing—you, your family, your neighborhood, your
> education, your job, your government, your relation to "the others." And
> they're changing dramatically.

In the Industrial Era information and knowledge were protected
and treated as a private good. Happily the spirit of sharing knowledge
developed naturally in the Internet environment without any overall
direction or management from any quarter. The World Wide Web, in
fact, as one of its original architects, Tim Berners-Lee, declares, was
designed for the free exchange of information:

> Whether inspired by free-market desires or humanistic ideals, we all felt
> that control was the wrong perspective. I think its clear that I had designed
> the Web so there should be no centralized place where someone would

have to 'register' a new server, or get approval of its contents. Philosoph-
ically, if the Web was to be a universal resource, it had to be able to grow
in an unlimited way. Technically, if there was any centralized point of control, it would rapidly become a bottleneck that restricted the Web's growth,
and the Web would never scale up. It being out of control was very important. (1999, p. 99)

Despite the freedom of the movement of information over the
Internet co-workers within the same organization for the large part still
remain ironically protective of their knowledge and information, which
they regard as a source of security and power. This has been one of the
barriers to the success of KM initiatives within organizations. Members of an organization often find it easier to find out what is going on
outside their company than it is to find out what is happening inside.

The Internet is a double-edged sword. At the same time that it is
retrieving some of the cooperative patterns of an earlier era when the
pace of commerce was considerably slower, it is also accelerating the
pace of business by creating the expectation that information can be
made available instantaneously. It has been gaining acceptance in the
business world at a phenomenally rapid rate reminiscent of how microcomputers took hold in the early '80s. Like microcomputers, the
Internet at first was used at strictly the grassroots level in a more or less
random manner by individual employees who had discovered that they
could enhance their performance at work by using this communication
channel. The same chaos that followed the introduction of microcomputers repeated itself with the Internet and in many organizations
continues to do so. A number of companies have begun to develop
company-wide Internet strategies including the use of intranets. Many
of these companies are making use of the Internet largely to realize the
cost savings in communications that the use of this technology affords,
rather than to realize some overarching organizational objective.

The value of the Internet to business is just beginning to dawn on
the community as a whole now that the pioneers have demonstrated its
many uses for commerce. Because the orientation of businesses,
whether they are members of the information, service, or manufacturing sector, is the provision of a greater level of service, direct
communications is one of the key ingredients for commercial success
today.

It is worth noting here at this juncture that, as those of us who had been bit by the dot.com craze well know, not all the applications and services that were attempted with Internet technology were a roaring success. The fact that the dot.com bubble burst does not reflect badly on the technology itself; it has had many stunning successes. It has always been the case that every time a new technology emerged there was a major shakeout and many false starts until the appropriate uses of the technology were discovered. What made the dot.com bubble so big before it burst was the unprecedented rate at which the technology caught the fancy of both the general public and computer aficionados. Another factor was that there were actually many instant successes with the Net, leading to a band wagon effect and a great deal of speculation that allowed some unscrupulous venture capitalists to take advantage of unsuspecting investors.

Communities of Practice (COP)

One of the most successful uses of the Internet has been the emergence of informal knowledge communities known as a community of practice (COP) or a community of interest. A COP is an environment usually outside of conventional organizational structures, where people can converse with each other about the common problems they face in their workplace or in their professional life, a common passion for some subject or a common mission. Most COPs are contained within a single organization (an intramural COP) but sometimes they cross institutional boundaries (an extramural COP). One should ask if the staff in one's organization are encouraged to join extramural COPs. If not, one's organization is like an insular walled medieval town and is cut off from multiple sources of possible new knowledge.

A COP does not necessarily have to be transacted solely on the Internet and in fact the most successful ones almost always have a face-to-face meeting component to them. As good a tool as the Internet is, it can never replace the intimacy and fullness of communication of face-to-face meetings of individuals. The importance of the Internet to a COP is that it provides a link beyond the times when people can physically meet and hence sustains the group. It also permits a COP to develop among people who are not co-located.

The importance of COPs to activities of commercial enterprises has been described in a monograph on collaborative knowledge networks by Robin Athey:

> When linked electronically into collaborative knowledge networks (CKNs), these communities enable rapid knowledge sharing that accelerates many important business processes: They can help companies rapidly respond to new and changing customer needs, improve supply chain efficiency, streamline product development processes and facilitate a wide range of special projects. Taking advantage of connectivity throughout the extended enterprise, CKNs make it possible for people and communities to collaborate freely across geographic and organizational boundaries. What's more, CKNs have the potential to drive key processes faster and more effectively than traditional structures. (2002, p. 1)

As effective as COPs are to a company, they cannot be managed or supervised. They flourish best when left alone as pointed out by Athey (2002, p. 7): "But before you start thinking of communities as things you can manage, understand that they often operate best when spared managerial intrusion."

Athey (2002, p. 1) reported that as of September 2001 Chevron had 100 COPs, Daimler Chrysler 140, Siemens 345 and the World Bank 120. Athey also reported an interesting COP created by Oracle that is really a community of developers.

> The Oracle Technology Network (OTN) was originally launched as a site where Oracle developers-both inside and outside the company—could download the latest tools, take skill-building tutorials, post messages on bulletin boards and discuss concepts and problems. Within two years, hundreds of thousands of members worldwide signed on to receive free software and technical information.
>
> The draw of the site served as a great basis for firms and Oracle-skilled freelancers to find one another. Recognizing an opportunity, Oracle launched the OTN Xchange in Fall 2000. Positioned as a service to the developer community, OTN Xchange serves as an online marketplace where developers can buy, sell and auction technical services. It helps Oracle to combat its own shortage of skilled IT professionals, as well. No longer restricted to finding programmers in their immediate area, companies now contact and hire talent from Silicon Valley to China to India and beyond. The site adds further value by allowing users to collaboratively manage individual, corporate, or open source development projects online. (ibid., p. 5)

Alignment: A Strategy for Connectivity and the Use of the Internet

The Internet provides an organization with the potential for total connectivity with all of its customers, suppliers and business partners and, hence, permits the integration of a number of its key business functions, such as marketing, advertising, sales, order fulfillment, distribution, customer support, market research, market feedback and product design. The cost of this type of connectivity to date has not been cheap but the price is coming down thanks to the use of XML and Java and will continue to become more affordable for smaller firms.

For the activities listed above to work well together, they must be coordinated and aligned so that they are working coherently together within a strategy to achieve the overall objectives of the organization. The alignment team must therefore consist of experts in marketing, communications and information technology.

Alignment goes beyond business process reengineering (BPR) and takes the process of integration represented by BPR a step further. BPR redesigns business processes so that the efficiencies of using computers can be maximized. Alignment takes those reengineered processes and aligns them to maximize the flow of information that arises from the connectivity of the Internet, electronic data interchange (EDI), or any other network that connects the firm to its markets and suppliers. Alignment is to the Internet and connectivity what BPR is to computing.

Internet as a Marketing Tool

Analysts often make the mistake of judging the value of the Internet solely in terms of its contribution to direct sales, an increasingly important aspect of the Internet with the proliferation of e-commerce and portal sites. Direct sales, however, are only one way the Internet can help an organization achieve its goals and hence should not be the only criterion for judging its usefulness. The Internet is just as strong as a communications, marketing and customer-support tool as it is as a sales tool. By fulfilling these other functions, however, it can increase sales, particularly if its use is guided by an Internet strategy that is aligned with the company's overall objectives. With a strategy, other benefits, such as the more efficient operations of the different functions of the organization, will also ensue. For instance, companies spend too much time generating information internally and do not take advantage of existing information that they could gather on the Net. The Net has to be used wisely, however. It is like a dragnet that pulls everything out of the sea and unless a strategy is in place to filter the data collected, time and effort will be wasted.

The Internet is an excellent marketing research tool. "Well informed employees can spot marketing opportunities, the emergence of new competition, unmet customer needs...but only if the company has organized its internal information sharing structure to incorporate their insights" (Cronin, 1994, p. 17). With an Internet strategy, firms will be able to take full advantage of the Net. But the strategic use of the Internet will require the cooperation and coordination of the whole organization and hence will require the reengineering of key business processes, especially those concerned with marketing and customer support, as well as a modest amount of personnel reorganization and training. All levels and aspects of a company's organization can benefit from the use of the Internet.

For further discussion of the role of the Internet for marketing and sales the reader is invited to read Appendix 1 – Internet as a Marketing and Sales Tool: Further Considerations.

Customer Relations and Product/Service Support

One of the areas where the Internet is having a huge impact is in customer relations and product/service support. In today's fast-moving world, customers no longer have the time to learn how to use or fix a product or service they have purchased. They want and demand instant product support and they are receiving it thanks to Internet Web sites that provide users with the vital information they need to realize the full potential of the product or service they have acquired. By developing an interactive two-way communication link with customers, companies are able to support their customers' information needs and at the same time tap into their customers' knowledge to learn how their products or services are being used and how they can be improved.

RCG IT, a company that consults on IT issues, built a Web-based best practices knowledge-sharing facility for its staff and its clients. Not only did it increase the productivity of its staff but it improved the level of customer service. As Leon Kish, an analyst with the firm, observed: "Having a central repository where the data is online, on time, accessible to clients, broadens the contact. It gives our clients real-time access to what's going on....And it gives us an edge over consulting groups that aren't doing it, because clients want to know where they're spending their money" (Haimila, 2001b). A number of other companies in the past two years have instituted Web-based information and knowledge sharing systems that their customers can access as a way of collaborating with and better serving their customers. The list includes companies from many different sectors, for example, Catholic Mutual Group, an insurance company; Honeywell Performance Polymers & Chemicals; Owens Corning, a manufacturer of glass fiber insulation; Regence BlueCross BlueShield of Oregon; Snelling and Snelling, a personnel firm; the Union Bank of Switzerland and Hill & Knowlton, an international public relations firm.

The following information was gathered in an interview with Ted Graham, Director of World Wide Knowledge Management Services, who shared with us his views on the importance and benefits of Hill & Knowlton (H&K) developing a stronger collaborative culture through their implementation of HK.net. Hill & Knowlton is an international public relations agency that regards its employees' knowledge and expertise as a vital company asset. With account information scattered across 71 offices in 32 countries worldwide, H&K has had to struggle to capitalize on its vast knowledge resources. The work of more than 1,900 employees resided in individual email inboxes and hard drives, making it impossible to manage and share with others. Whenever an employee left the company, some of that knowledge was lost. H&K needed a way to preserve knowledge and make it instantly accessible to others across the extended enterprise. As part of an effort to streamline account management and provide greater value to clients such as Compaq and Procter & Gamble, H&K worked with Intraspect Software to develop HK.net, a customizable intranet and extranet that allows employees and clients to collaborate online and save knowledge for future reuse.

Not only did H&K's efforts at collaboration pay off in increased efficiencies and lower costs but it also helped to attract and retain accounts, as Ted Graham pointed out to us:

> We are a global company with offices spread around the world. When we have a product launch or some intensive PR campaign going on there will be a lot of collaboration because we have to. Often our clients are in the same situation. For example, one client, Ernst & Young, was particularly interested in our collaboration capability because we were helping them

with their world entrepreneur of the year awards. The head of Ernst & Young public relations certainly thought our internal collaboration ability was a critical differentiator for us. We were the only ones among our competition who could back up the claim by demonstrating that we would be able to collaborate with our colleagues world-wide to better help Ernst & Young achieve their goals.

As part of H&K's goal of attracting more international business, HK.net has helped to demonstrate the agency's ability to work quickly and effectively around the globe by allowing project teams to collaborate with clients across organizational structure and geographic boundaries and by enabling immediate access to time-sensitive information.

We really use our expanded collaboration ability to reinforce what we can do when we pitch new business. We can show the client that they are not only drawing upon the experience of the one office that they may be local to, but here's the advantages they are getting by being able to collaborate with many of our consultants in different time zones around the world. That has certainly helped in the sales cycle. By establishing a single point of contact for business critical information and enhancing account collaboration and coordination, HK.net has also enabled us to dramatically improve the intimacy between our clients and the agency.

It also helps us to make best use of our human resource base in the way we staff assignments. We get the best kind of leverage, matching senior practitioners with more junior members, and using things like time zones to optimize our 24-hour service to a client's issues management situation and even managing it based on cost of labor. You might have something that does not require someone local to be doing media clippings when somebody else around the world within your organization can do that at less cost. So that kind of collaboration changes the economics somewhat and if you can do it effectively, you can beat a lot of your competition in terms of how you can budget for the assignment.

H&K has realized a significant ROI, reporting a considerable benefit in new employee productivity and in developing deeper relationships with clients. By measuring HK.net intranet/extranet use, asking clients why they chose Hill & Knowlton and tracking which documents are most frequently reused to determine how much time is saved in recreating content, we have determined the extent to which HK.net has contributed to the organization.

Specifically, new client acquisitions are integrated two times faster and new business processes require only two-thirds of the usual time. New hires become productive three times faster, as they get up to speed

on certain client engagements than they did the previous way. Previously, when someone had left, the new person didn't know when the last
budget was approved, they weren't sure when the last customer review
had happened and they had to root around for all sorts of documentation
and paperwork. Now we've been able to prove that using this kind of collaboration system yields much more touch points so that individuals new
to the project could direct themselves to find out what was happening.
And that was a true return on investment for us because the faster people
get up to speed the faster we can bill them out. This training time we typ-
ically absorbed into our budget, but now that the consultants quickly
understand what the work is about, we can start billing them out sooner
at the appropriate rate. (Graham, interview, 2003)

Conclusion—We have discussed a number of the positive impacts that
Hill & Knowlton have enjoyed as a result of the collaborative culture
they developed and the collaborative knowledge network, HK.net, they
implemented. In addition to the advantages we have just enumerated
they also improved the level of trust within their organization and with
their customers, they found ways to incentivize their employees,
improve employee retention, make better use of their strategizing with
customers and improve their vision of themselves as an organization.
We will return to these positive aspects of the collaborative culture they
created as we come to these topics in the course of our narrative.

Collaborative Product Development and Manufacturing

Not only has the Internet reshaped the marketing and sales activities
of business but just as importantly it has transformed product development and manufacturing for many organizations into collaborative
processes and an example of collaborative commerce. Ford Motor
Company employs collaborative product development team members
from across its various divisions plus engineers from Volvo, Jaguar,
Land Rover and Ford Europe, and major suppliers from across the
world. They make use of a Web-enabled collaborative tool, eRoom,
"for sharing and collaborating on product documents and maintaining
project history, as well as tracking and resolving issues" (www.docu-
mentum.com, 2003).

   Another example is provided by the collaboration of Elkay Manufacturing, a leader in the manufacture of sinks, water-coolers and
drinking fountains, and APTEC, a product development company.

Because Elkay wanted to bring a new home water-cooler to a trade show in an extremely short time frame, they contacted APTEC to collaborate with them on the new design. They made use of the collaboration tool OneSpace Collaboration, which "lets teams communicate over the Internet, sharing 2D and 3D design data and much more. Elkay and APTEC achieved a remarkable breakthrough. Together they cut prototype development time for the new water cooler by more than 75%, from Elkay's typical timeline of 18 months" (www.cocreate.com, 2003).

APTEC had a similar success using the same collaborative technology with Teleflex Electrical, which creates products for the automotive, marine, industrial, medical and aerospace industries. Together Teleflex and APTEC redesigned a watercraft speedometer/tachometer that reduced assembly time and reduced the failure rate. Patrick Mills, Senior Mechanical Engineer for Teleflex, commented on the project saying, "I can't imagine developing a product the old fashioned way with faxes and emails. We're now ahead of the planned re-launch schedule. The best part is, we can apply this awesome product concept to most of our future products" (www.cocreate.com, 2003).

Eli Lilly and Company came up with an innovative use of the Internet "to reduce cycle time for new drug development and increase the hit ratio for successful drugs" by forming a subsidiary InnoCentive. Participating drug companies post on the InnoCentive Website which medical issues they are targeting, along with relevant background information. Individual scientists can then go to a virtual project room set up on the site that contains more specific information, including product specifications. These scientists then take on the task of trying to come up with solutions for the drug companies, motivated by a reward that can be as high as $100,000" (www.Accenture.com/Outlook, 2002, #2).

There is a trend in today's world of manufacturing to have the components of the system one manufactures produced by a third party. This is almost standard in the automotive and computer manufacturing sectors. The ability of companies to communicate, co-create and co-develop together using collaborative technologies like those of Accenture is accelerating this process. According to Accenture's Allen Delattre, "Manufacturers always have relied on suppliers for raw materials and base components, but today the relationship is changing: the supply base is doing more of the actual production. In some cases, the 'manufacturer' now produces nothing at all. That means that some of the most successful manufacturers—many of which are actually the most successful product designers or marketers—may not manufacture at all. It also means tomorrow's competitive landscape is less likely to be dominated by the company with the best manufacturing than by the company with the best manufacturing capabilities" (www.accenture.com, 2003).

Another example of the importance of collaboration with customers in product design comes to us from Altera, a world pioneer of system-on-a-programmable-chip (SOPC) solutions. The company makes programmable logic devices (PLDs) that incorporate embedded software into integrated circuits.

A critical success factor for Altera is the ability to collaborate effectively with its customers. "Our relationship with our customers is really more of a partnership," explains Bill Levesque, CIS Program Director of Altera. "We work very closely with our customers [such as Motorola, Cisco and Alcatel], both in helping them leverage PLDs for their current and future-generation products and in getting their input about features they would like to see in future Altera products. To be successful, we need to closely coordinate our activities with each account so we stay in lock-step with the customer from the early design phase to production."

Given the importance of collaborating closely with customers, Altera recognized in the late '90s that it needed to implement a more robust customer relationship management system. "The advantage of the Siebel eBusiness solution," explains Levesque, "is that it provides an enterprise solution across sales, marketing and service, so we can retain all customer information in a single repository. This enables us to better coordinate our customer-focused activities across the globe" (www.siebel.com, 2003).

Knowledge Management and the Internet

All large organizations have a strategy for the management of their information, but most lack a strategy for the management of their knowledge. The team at Siemens AG, headquartered in Munich, which developed their intranet-based KM tools, had a saying that succinctly sums up this dilemma: "If Siemens only knew what Siemens knows." A recent study conducted by the Delphi Group revealed that "nearly 88% of a company's knowledge resides in the minds of its employees, but most companies lack an efficient system to tap into that knowledge in ways that provide a strong return on investment" (KM World Editorial, 2001d). The only way to tap into that knowledge is with a successful KM strategy, which requires the use of information technology especially the Internet. Software solutions exist such as AskMe, which Procter & Gamble has installed, that aid in this process and which "will enable users to locate, catalog, transfer and maintain employees' knowledge (as well as) identify qualified individuals with relevant expertise, to submit questions or business problems to individuals, to receive solutions from colleagues and to respond immediately and effectively" (ibid.). The real challenge with systems like this, however, is the participation of personnel and motivating them to share their knowledge, to co-create new knowledge and utilize the knowledge of colleagues from other working groups, i.e., overcoming the not-invented-here syndrome.

Two recent trends, the Internet and KM, which have surfaced only within the past 10 years, are currently reconfiguring and transforming communication, learning and commerce in today's workplace. They are at the vanguard of a shift of emphasis from information to knowledge. These two trends are parallel and support each other's mutual development and are responsible for the transition from the Information Age to the Knowledge Era. One indicator of the way in which the Net and KM reinforce each other is the large number of Internet-based "knowledge management-related products and services" that have emerged. *KM World* (Taylor, 2000), in its May 15, 2000 issue, listed what in its opinion were the top 100 "providers of KM-related products and services," almost all of which were Internet-based. The problem *KM World* had was limiting the list to just 100, as it was able to identify more than twice the number of providers. This large number indicates that KM and the medium of the Internet represent two new major management tools that have had and will continue to have a major impact on the way in which business is conducted. Neither is a fad which will be short lived. *KM World*'s list of the top 100 product and service providers is updated yearly and published on its Web site (see www.kmworld.com/100.cfm). It is interesting to note that new companies and their products or services have been added to the original list and some of the older ones have fallen off. Other lists of KM service and product providers have been compiled (Tiwana, 2000; Mertins et al., 2001) and can be consulted to make comparisons with the *KM World* list.

The Internet and KM both embrace the notion that knowledge is an abundant resource that can be openly shared and co-created, and that it represents today's principal source of wealth. Economist Peter Drucker reached this conclusion in 1993 a year before the release of Netscape: "The basic economic resource—'the means of production,' to use the economist's term—is no longer capital, nor natural resources (the economist's 'land'), nor 'labor.' It is and will be knowledge" (Drucker, 1993, p. 8). Marshall McLuhan came up with a similar idea published 29 years before Drucker when he wrote: "The very same process of automation that causes a withdrawal of the present work force from industry causes learning itself to become the principal kind of production and consumption....The peculiar and abstract manipulation of information [is] a means of creating wealth" (McLuhan, 1964, pp. 351, 354).

In the era before computing and the Internet, when the rate at which knowledge changed was slow, most learning was done by rote. Very little distinction was made between knowledge and information. With computing and Internet, the rate of change of knowledge greatly accelerated, as did the speed with which information is transmitted from one user to another. Having access to information in today's supercharged environment is no longer sufficient to survive in the marketplace. Knowledge is much more than just being informed. One must, among other things, possess the ability to cut through the information glut and discern what information is of importance and know what to do with it. The nature of knowledge has changed as well as its relation to information and data because of the impact of information technology.

One might well ask if it is a coincidence that the Internet, KM and the Knowledge Era emerged at more or less the same time. It is no coincidence according to the thinking of Marshall McLuhan, who coined the phrase, "The medium is the message." Each new medium creates a revolution in the way in which information and knowledge relate to each other and the way in which commerce is conducted.

The invention of writing and mathematical notation grew out of the commercial activities in the ancient city states of Sumer by accountants keeping track of agricultural commodities. Writing and mathematics led to formal education, scholarship and eventually science, and had a major effect on commerce. The printing press led to the Renaissance and the modern scientific revolution and also had a major direct impact on commerce through the development of double-entry bookkeeping and other text-based tools, such as gazetteers and almanacs. The greatest impact it had, however, was paving the way for the Industrial Revolution and mass production. "The invention of typography confirmed and extended the new visual stress of applied knowledge providing the first uniformly repeatable 'commodity,' the first assembly line and the first mass production" (McLuhan, 1962, p.153).

Just as the printing press led to the Industrial Era, so did computing create the Information Age and a new pattern of or relationship between data and information. Computers could process raw data into an infinite variety of combinations and thereby generate new information. Information and data share certain similarities. The distinction we make is that information is structured data and data are the raw facts. This is why computing was able to transform large amounts of data into information from which new patterns emerged. This is another example of how a quantitative change makes a qualitative change. This is the way computing changed the relationship between data and information and the Internet has changed the relationship of information and knowledge.

Data, Information, Knowledge and Wisdom

> "Where is the wisdom we have lost in knowledge?
> Where is the knowledge we have lost in information?"
> —*T.S. Eliot*

It is important that we have a clear understanding of what we mean by knowledge and not confuse it with information. In the Information Age the focus was on the processing of data into information and the control of the flow of information, but in the Knowledge Era there is a shift in focus to knowledge because of the recognition that knowledge is now the primary source of wealth. Given the importance of this shift it is essential to understand the distinction between information and knowledge, which are often confused for each other. It is also useful to understand the way in which they relate to data and wisdom. We therefore offer the following definitions of these terms:

• Data are the pure and simple facts without any particular structure or organization, the basic atoms of information,

- Information is structured data, which adds meaning to the data and gives it context and significance,
- Knowledge is the ability to use information strategically to achieve one's objectives, and
- Wisdom is the capacity to choose objectives consistent with one's values and within a larger social context.

These definitions lead to our definition of KM:

Knowledge management is the collaborative organizational activity of creating the environment, both attitudinally and technologically, so that knowledge can be accessed, shared and created within an organization in a way that all of the experiences and knowledge within the enterprise, including that of all its staff, customers, suppliers and business partners, can be organized to achieve the enterprise's objectives and reinforce its values.

Knowledge, Value and Values

"Structuring or processing data to convert it into information gives that data added meaning and added value. Data is not information until it is processed. Information is not intelligence until it is efficiently communicated" (Vine, 2000). In the same way that information structures data, knowledge structures information, giving it additional levels of meaning and providing it with utility. Information by itself, without knowledge, does not have utility. Wisdom augments and guides knowledge through values. Knowledge by itself does not create well-being. In fact, knowledge by itself can be very destructive and can be and has been used for evil ends. For example, at the root of our environmental crisis is the blind use of scientific and technological knowledge without the guidance of ecological wisdom. The laissez faire use of science, unmoderated by concern for human values, creates disservice in the long run. The instantaneous access to information that computers provide encourages the use of knowledge to achieve short-term goals without concern for the long-term effects. Wisdom and prudence buffer us from this impulse. At the core of the environmental challenges facing us today is the fact that data is transformed instantaneously into information and that the knowledge needed to exploit that information can be developed much faster than the wisdom that is needed to guide the use of that knowledge.

Knowledge: The Tacit and the Explicit

In order to create an environment of collaborative learning we must learn to distinguish between explicit knowledge and tacit knowledge and to recognize the importance of emotional intelligence. One way to describe tacit knowledge is in terms of intuition. Tacit knowledge is personal, intuitive knowledge, whereas explicit knowledge is the kind of knowledge that can be learned from a book. There is a vast difference between book learning—explicit knowledge—and experience-based learning—tacit knowledge.

Intuition is defined in *Webster's New World Dictionary* as "the immediate knowing of something without the conscious use of reasoning." There are times when we know something to be true but we do not know why or how we arrived at the understanding. One form of intuition arises because we know something so well and so thoroughly that we do not have to reason things out again but we immediately know it. This is tacit knowledge, as opposed to explicit knowledge, which is "formal and systematic" (Nonaka and Takeuchi, 1995). Tacit knowledge, according to Nonaka and Takeuchi, is "deeply rooted in an individual's action and experience" (ibid., p. 8). It is intuitive and subjective whereas explicit knowledge is scientific and objective. Nonaka and Takeuchi borrowed the notion of tacit and explicit knowledge from philosopher Michael Polyani and have incorporated it into their theory of knowledge creation, which we will discuss later.

The Anatomy of Knowledge

Having positioned knowledge within a tetrad with data, information and wisdom let us examine in greater detail the nature of knowledge and its relation to the other members of the tetrad. Although knowledge is a term that we frequently use and make reference to, its exact characteristics are somewhat elusive because of the complexity of the phenomena itself. Knowledge results from the interplay of information and purpose; it arises when we extend our insight, or exercise our curiosity. Knowledge gives an additional level of meaning to information and provides it with utility. Information is a resource and knowledge the capability to exploit it.

Knowledge flows from and into many different directions—some organized, some chaotic, some arrived at by serendipity and some by the disciplined expansion of ideas. Knowledge can bring order out of chaos or it can become so convoluted that it generates disorder and chaos. There is a mystery about how knowledge emerges. Knowledge always seems so obvious and simple after it has been newly discovered and formulated and yet it takes so much effort and imagination to create and, sometimes, good luck as well.

Knowledge has many aspects and ranges of application from its strategic use to secure one's objectives to the creation of new knowledge either for its own sake or for its application to a practical problem. The utilization of knowledge to achieve one's objectives requires a different skill set than those required to create new knowledge or access existing knowledge; however, certain salient features pertain to all facets of knowledge processing whether they are pure and abstract or practical and concrete:

1. Knowledge is dynamic, constantly growing and changing as new data is collected, new experiences are incorporated and new juxtapositions of existing knowledge generate new insights.

2. Knowledge not only structures what we do, it also influences the way we gather new data, create information and discover still more knowledge.

3. Knowledge creates abundance in that it expands through sharing; it is self-generating or auto-poetic, feeding upon itself and multiplying. But like Shakespeare's description of Cleopatra in his play *Anthony and Cleopatra*, "She cloys not the appetite she feeds." Knowledge always creates an appetite and desire for more knowledge. The search for knowledge is never over—it is an ongoing, continuous process.

4. Knowledge is self-organizing.

5. New knowledge is not the work of a single individual but grows out of collaboration, sharing, dialogue and networking.

6. Knowledge arises out of trial and error, experimentation and an intimate interaction with data, information and one's experiences and self-reflection. Knowledge must always be tested because it can quickly become dated, especially in the current climate of rapid technological change.

7. Knowledge cannot be achieved by the passive reception of information. Knowledge must be seized and experienced so that it can be incorporated into one's world view or model of reality. (Robert Poupart—private communication)

8. Knowledge is also dangerous when it is used to exploit or take advantage of others or when one gets into trouble because one has too little knowledge but enough to create a problem. For example, we know how to harness nuclear energy to generate electricity, but do we know enough to safely dispose of the nuclear waste produced by this process?

Can Knowledge be Managed? The Need for a Collaborative Knowledge Management Strategy

As knowledge has become the principal source of wealth in the Knowledge Era, it is only prudent for an organization to develop a strategy for the development of its knowledge assets, as well as a plan for the sharing, dissemination and practical application of those knowledge assets. Surprisingly enough, not many organizations have embraced a KM strategy or if they have, only superficially. Many organizations confuse information for knowledge and what they deem to be a KM strategy is essentially a plan to improve the flow of information within their organization. A true KM strategy must include a plan of how to develop the knowledge that is needed to best use that information to achieve the organization's objectives. Not enough thought has been given to KM to date. Organizations have marketing strategies, communication strategies, information technology strategies—they even have waste management strategies—but most do not have a KM strategy.

Before discussing the nature of KM it is advisable to say a few words about terminology. Many people are critical of the term "knowledge management" because they believe that the term "management" carries with it the baggage of the Industrial Era and the outdated style of management of that period. We do not share this opinion. Language is a dynamic process and the meaning of the term "management," when coupled with knowledge, will have a completely different meaning than it has when it is used in conjunction with phrases like "industrial management," "management science" or even an Information Age term like "Management Information Systems."

Because the focus of knowledge management is on the management of the intangible assets of knowledge rather than on the management of hard assets, natural resources, technology, people or information, the meaning of management will take on a new nuance because of the context in which it is used. Knowledge management is a metaphor whose meaning is in dynamic flux. Consider the terms "computer literacy" or "media literacy," in which the meaning of the term "literacy" shifted from its literal (pardon the pun) association with literature to a more general meaning of having an understanding or ability to interpret and/or use text, computers or media. Just as management in the Industrial Era was different than in the Agricultural Age, and just as management in the Information Age was different than in the Industrial Era, so it will come to pass that management in the Knowledge Era will be different than it was in either the Information Age or the Industrial Era.

If we look at the dictionary definition of "manage" we learn that first of all the term manage derives from the Italian term "maneggiare" which means to handle, and hence there has been a considerable shift in the meaning of the term when it is used to describe the management of a business operation or an enterprise. Just to see the range of meanings and establish that the term does not have a unique meaning, here is a list of the meanings of the verb "to manage" from which the term "management" is derived (*The New Lexicon Webster's Dictionary*, 1988):

1. to handle, to manipulate,
2. to influence (someone) so that he does as one wishes,
3. to use economically and with forethought,
4. to succeed in accomplishing or handling, but with difficulty,
5. to be able to cope with a situation, and
6. to contrive to make one's budget suffice.

Of these six definitions probably the third is closest but in time, no doubt, a new dictionary definition will appear associated with the idea of KM. Coming up with a definition of KM that all practitioners of this discipline can agree upon may be even more difficult. Here is a set of definitions from a number of leading proponents of KM to complement the one we proposed above. Each in its own way helps us to form a better picture of KM:

KM means seeking out and building capabilities and aspirations of one another—Charles Savage

KM means creating value by leveraging intangible assets—Karl Erik Sveiby

KM means sustaining a collaborative advantage—Debra Amidon

KM means elevating organizational conductivity to improve our customer relationships—Charles Armstrong

KM means building the capability to create value—Hubert Saint-Onge

The reason that some people have difficulty with the term KM is that they sense a basic contradiction because knowledge is an open-ended process and traditional management is a closed system in which all the elements of an enterprise are controlled. Classical Industrial Era management implies the hierarchical control of a scarce or at least finite resource, such as money or capital; a natural resource, such as land, livestock, or a fossil fuel; technology, such as a machine or a whole industrial plant; or the time of a worker which represents a cost. Knowledge capital, a concept develop by Karl Erik Sveiby (see Chapter 3), on the other hand, is an open-ended abundant resource that creates more of itself. Knowledge capital is self-propagating, self-organizing, auto-poetic and autocatalytic. Capital has been traditionally hoarded, controlled, not shared and, hence, was always treated as a scarce resource. Capital and the means of production give power and the ability to control to those who possess it. Knowledge was commoditized and carefully controlled as a scarce resource during the Industrial Era. Trade secrets and patents became extensions of the power of the capitalists who had the resources to pay for the creation of knowledge or purchase its exclusive use from those who had already created it. Capitalists enjoyed a monopoly over wealth and the means to produce it. Capitalism paralleled the earlier manor system of the Middle Ages and the even earlier estate system of ancient Greece and Rome, in which landowners, through their ownership of the land, the means of production of that economic era, could exercise control over the peasants and enjoy the exclusive privileges of that system. It was only natural that the manor or estate system of the agricultural era became the model for the control of resources and the means of production in the Industrial Era.

The hierarchical system of top-down control that characterized the Agricultural and Industrial Eras was maintained in Information Age enterprises despite all the talk about the flattening of the organization, which was largely a myth. Mainframe computers allowed large corporations to once again control the means of production, namely the conversion of data into information. With the advent of microcomputers with a price tag considerably less than that of an automobile, anyone could duplicate the computing power of a large company. The end of the monopoly of computing spelled the end of the monopoly of knowledge. The last gasp of hierarchical control was the partial tam-ing of the microcomputer phenomena by MIS departments through the creation of LANs and WANs and the client-server architectures. The extra degree of freedom that microcomputing permitted laid the foundation for the next step in the evolution of the knowledge work-ers, however, through the advent of the Internet. Because the communication link between microcomputer users before the Internet could be controlled centrally, true liberation of the knowledge worker was not possible until the advent of the Internet.

With the Internet and its lack of a central control mechanism, the monopolies of computing, the MIS departments, are losing control over their clients. This explains the fierce opposition to the Internet that initially characterized most MIS departments. It also explains the continued resistance of many MIS groups to the Internet despite the overwhelming, rapid and unprecedented adoption of the technology by rank-and-file knowledge workers and the general public. Despite the fact that no communication medium has grown as fast or been adopted as quickly as the Internet in the entire history of human com-munications, those in control of most of today's large corporations are still wary of this technology and unwilling to fully support it financial-ly, despite its very modest costs. Almost all advocates and enthusiasts for the use of Internet technology in large organizations complain of underfunding and a lack of understanding of this phenomena. Part of this opposition is the traditional resistance to a new medium, but an equally important factor is that the people at the top realize they are losing control of their organization because this new medium stimu-lates cooperation across traditional lines of competition. Sometimes a company's confidential information leaks out of the organization through the Internet. Some people at the top only see this aspect of Net usage and the possible reduction of their competitive advantage in the marketplace. They do not see the increased productivity to their organization in particular and society in general that this new medium allows us to achieve through knowledge sharing.

The Need to Democratize Decision Making

A KM strategy must embrace all the members of an organization. The application of information to achieve a commercial enterprise's objec-tives can no longer be carried out by a small clique of senior managers, as had been the case in the Industrial Era when knowledge resided strictly with the owners of the enterprise and the inventors/engineers who developed products or services and designed production or resource extraction techniques. During this period, when information and events moved at a much slower pace, there was time for the owners and managers to absorb all of the information being generated in their commercial environment and then make the appropriate decision.

The time for centralized decision making is long past—knowledge and decision making must reside throughout the organization. Rather than assuming a posture of defense, as was the case in the Industrial Era, organizations must now be proactive. The pace has become so frenzied that decisions must be made on a just-in-time basis. All of the operations of the organization must also be in the just-in-time mode from just-in-time inventory to just-in-time training. The only possible way to operate on a just-in-time basis is to have distributed decision making throughout the organization. The time when a single expert could fix the problems that arose in an organization is long past—now due to the complexity of today's business environment, problems must be attacked by a collaborative team. Distributed decision making requires two factors, one technological and one organizational. The technological element is the use of an intranet to allow the rapid dissemination of information. The organizational element is the use of KM techniques so that knowledge can be accessed from anywhere within the organization on an as-needed basis.

The optimal way to develop such a KM strategy in a medium to large-size organization is to make use of an intranet that contains Web-enabled collaborative tools. The intranet, therefore, plays two roles: first, as a conduit for the rapid distribution of information and then as a tool to develop a KM strategy so that the knowledge is available to take advantage of the information. The intranet then becomes a knowledge network with specific tools, such as online learning courses, knowledge sharing facilities, a way to identify human resources within the organization, a casebase of projects and best practices, measurement tools, diagnostics tools, search engines, a help desk and a directory of coaches and mentors. We will describe such an intranet organized as a knowledge network in Chapter 8.

"Specifically, collaboration in product development (CPD) makes all process activities open so that team members can fully discuss, share documents, add components, vote and otherwise conduct a free exchange. In addition to this direct support for process, CPD can also be used to share knowledge, provide a well-defined recent running history, support lessons learned and more" (www.documentum.com, 2003, Ford Motor Co.).

The democratization of decision making and the delegation of authority throughout the organization is just a logical consequence of ready access to information that the Internet makes possible. Jack Welch, former CEO of GE, observed, "People within the company are going to have so much data on their hands that they will be able to challenge (a CEO's) decisions all the time. The pace of events is going to be so fast that people aren't going to wait for the next layer of approvals. There's going to have to be far more delegation. There's going to have to be far more participation. The leader must become an even more engaging coach, an even more engaging person" (Garten, 2001).

Lifelong Learning: Job Security in the Knowledge Era

One of the key elements of the KM approach is that all members of an enterprise must engage in life-long learning and the sharing of the knowledge that integrates with their role at work. Forty years ago, Marshall McLuhan described how the electrification of information reversed the fragmented patterns of work and learning characteristic of the Industrial Era and retrieved many of the holistic patterns of oral society in which learning and work were integrated. The Internet embodies the spirit of the integration that McLuhan identified. It literally integrates all forms of media by providing a global, networked digital medium that accepts any form of information that can be digitized, from text and visual images to audio and music. Information flows from one domain to another and by doing so breaks down the barriers between work and learning, entertainment and education, work and leisure, technology and culture, art and science. Computing and the Internet represent a new cultural milieu, a new form of economics, a new way to earn a living by learning a living, and a new way to live.

McLuhan (1964, p. 346) predicted that automation would end "jobs in the world of work." By the end of jobs, McLuhan did not mean that automation spelled the end of work but, rather a new way of organizing work. Instead of holding a job, he suggested, an individual would pursue a career and thereby assume a role in society. Consider the position of secretary, which has, due to the influence of information technology, evolved into the role of administrative assistant. Secretaries once took dictation, typed documents and served coffee. They worked from nine to five, at which time they put a cover on their typewriters, went home and forgot about work. Today's administrative assistants, on the other hand, are junior to middle managers. They make decisions, organize activities and anticipate problems rather than merely react to them. They stay late and work weekends if required. They are more immersed in their work than the secretary of yesteryear. They are more likely to learn more about their industry, take courses in their spare time to upgrade their skills and network socially with colleagues and associates in their field. Like many others in the work-force, they are not just earning a living by filling in time, they are pursuing a career and "learning" a living.

During the Industrial Era, it was common for an individual to work for the same company for an entire lifetime. Today, that is almost unheard of. An individual just entering the work-force will probably work for 10 or more organizations before retiring, if he or she retires at all. Moreover, the company that individuals work for might go through as many changes as their employees because of mergers, acquisitions, strategic alliances and restructurings. Between jobs, many of today's workers do not become unemployed; instead, they become a consultant or a casual worker. They move in and out of employment or from one company to another, from one project to another, or from one working group to another. The only thing that is constant is change.

One no longer works at a job; one lives a career. Individuals should like what they do because work is no longer a nine-to-five, Monday-to-Friday activity; it is an all-consuming way of life. Also, the nature of a career has changed. It is no longer a linear progression up a hierarchical ladder of increased authority and responsibility based on seniority. Organizations, particularly those in the private sector, are becoming like the Internet, where no one is in control anymore. Senior managers are increasingly frustrated by the fact that they are not always able to steer their organization in the direction they want. The reason for this is that today's organization, like the tribe or village in oral society, is becoming a self-organizing system. A system of command and control no longer works, but inspiration, motivation and leadership do. And that leadership and motivation do not necessarily have to come from the top but can originate from anywhere in the organization.

In an environment where change is pervasive—technological, economic, structural and organizational—there is no such thing as job security; the world is changing too rapidly. The only form of security is to have a set of skills that are up to date and in demand. This can only be achieved through lifelong learning, in which individuals are constantly honing and broadening their skills through reading, training courses, intensive study and working experience. The Internet is a useful ally for those who want to keep abreast because it facilitates regular monitoring of trends on a global scale and allows easy and instantaneous personal contact with those pursuing a similar career. The only defense against the rapid rate of change that characterizes our times is to try to anticipate the change that is about to take place and then set about to acquire the knowledge and skills that will be needed to cope with the new conditions, not only for today but for tomorrow and the day after, as well. In other words, one has to **"learn a living."**

Given the importance of lifelong learning, providing staff with the opportunity for continuous learning within the context of their work for the organization becomes an important factor in the recruitment and retention of employees. While we are on the topic of recruitment we should mention that hiring people with a collaborative spirit goes a long way towards creating a collaborative organization. Those charged with recruiting for their organization might want to consider administering an instrument like the Collaboration Quotient described in Chapter 7 to determine if the candidates seeking employment are oriented towards collaboration.

The reason that most employees leave their organization for another is not primarily for an increase in their salary but rather for an opportunity to advance their own personal career and to find new challenges. It is therefore paramount for an organization to be constantly challenging their staff by providing new learning opportunities. This benefits the organization in many ways, firstly by securing employee loyalty and secondly by having a better educated and better informed staff. Some companies such as American Airlines and Ford Motor Company have provided their employees with personal computers for home use and a free account with an Internet service provider so that they can learn at home.

Another important channel for life-long learning is the participation of staff in professional associations. Often times the employee will form stronger links with someone in their profession in a different organization than someone in their organization in a different profession. These extra-organizational links will actually strengthen the company, as the employee and hence his or her organization will benefit from what is learned from others following the same career path in a different organization, one that might even be a competitor.

And finally, in order for all staff to be continuous learners it is essential that they be given time during working hours for learning, for sharing thoughts and ideas with colleagues and for actual collaboration. If an employee's day is filled with too many functional activities there will be no time for the growth activities of learning, sharing and collaborating.

Online Learning: The Electronic Academy

One of the simplest ways for an organization to provide its employees with the opportunity for continuous learning is through providing them with access to the World Wide Web and to online, Internet-based learning modules. The interactivity of the Internet is a feature that contributes to its success as an environment for continuous learning. The Internet functions as an educational medium simply because its users are exchanging information with one another and interacting actively with that information by reading it and responding to it. The ability of the users of an online learning package to communicate with each other also makes it an ideal medium for collaborative learning. The Internet and associated intranets are very powerful KM tools that enjoy a number of advantages over CD-ROM-based multimedia for online learning—the principal advantages being the ease with which materials can be updated, the ease with which information can be distributed and the ease with which users can be networked to share their knowledge. The temporary advantage of CD-ROM-based media, of being able to deliver more information to a desktop, will soon disappear with the ever-increasing bandwidth of the Internet.

The Internet has certain pedagogical advantages in that the emphasis with the Net is on the interactivity of the user with the information provided, rather than the visual richness of the information. Educational television is an example of a medium that had all the bandwidth in the world to operate with but never succeeded as an educational medium because of its lack of interactivity. Visual richness does not guarantee learning, but interactivity does. The low-tech, "less is more" style of creating online courses and learning environments has the additional advantage of making use of a minimum amount of memory to permit rapid access and downloading of the course material.

Video conferencing is another example of a medium with a lot of band-width that does not have any particular advantage as a platform for learning or for collaborating because so much of the band width is taken up showing the faces of the conferees. Jon Wagner, an organizational development expert formerly with Hewlett-Packard, made the following observation: "I have seen more collaboration take place with Web-enabled collaborative tools such as NetMeeting or WebEx space, which makes use of an electronic white board than I have with video conferencing."

An advantage of online learning or a Web-enabled collaborative tool is that it takes place on the user's own desktop and hence is an extension of their workspace. It is easy for the user to make notes and copy pertinent sections on to their hard drive. It is also easy for networked users to share their learning experiences and to integrate the online learning courses into other knowledge sharing tools, such as a casebase forum, an idea pool or ordinary email. Online courses with two-way communication built in allow knowledge workers to interact with their program facilitator to permit coaching and mentoring as well as communication among staff to take advantage of collaborative learning and knowledge sharing. The Internet protocol facilitates the networking and sharing essential to the creation of a knowledge community and the emergence of a collaborative learning organization.

Another advantage of the Net is that it is an ideal medium for delivering and promoting individualized learning and/or individualized workplace productivity. Its ability to provide instant feedback without potentially embarrassing the user publicly makes it a very powerful educational tool in the hands of all employees. It provides knowledge workers with an information environment in which they can work in peace and at their own pace. The Internet enhances the individualization of learning by allowing the users to bookmark the Web sites that are most effective for them. It is also possible for them on certain select Web sites to create their own individual file folders so as to have continuity in their learning experience. Some Web sites do not have individual file folders but do keep track of each visitor and allow them to continue their learning experience from the point where they left off on their last visit. The Internet allows the delivery of online learning to staff so that they can study at their own leisure when they have the time and inclination or need to learn something new. The delivery of training in the classroom, instructor-led mode forces students to learn at a particular time not of their own choosing and to learn at a pace that works for the group as a whole. It is impossible to conduct classroom instruction at a pace that satisfies everyone. For some the pace is too fast and they fall behind, while for others it is painfully slow and they get bored and eventually disinterested.

Internet-based collaborative learning environments allow individual and group learning and they serve three functions:

1. They foster a spirit of knowledge sharing, collaboration and sensitivity to the needs of others, i.e., they add to their users' emotional intelligence or EQ of their users.

2. They help knowledge workers improve their technical skills, their strategic thinking abilities and their general intellectual competencies, i.e., they add to their users' IQ .

3. They facilitate learning and make the work environment more satisfying and interesting, i.e., they add to their users' level of motivation or MQ.

Creating a Knowledge Management Strategy

Developing a KM strategy involves four basic steps:

1. Dialogue, discuss, debate and define your objectives:
   • Know where you have been and what you valued—past experience,
   • Know what you know and know what you value—present situation, and
   • Define your future objectives consistent with your values.

2. Formulate a strategy:
   • Know how to get there, and
   • Know what are the milestones needed to achieve your objectives.

3. Devise the tactics:
   • Know what know-how and tools to use,
   • Know who to have on the team, and
   • Know how to achieve each milestone.

4. And then act:

- Know when to start,
- Know where to start,
- Know how to motivate yourself and your co-workers, and
- Know how to build a spirit of collaboration and cooperation.

What does it mean for an organization to have a KM strategy? If we think of a corporation as an individual, then a corporation's KM strategy may be likened to individuals' strategy to obtain an education and to apply their knowledge and learning to advance their career. If an individual's education consisted of nothing more than acquiring information (as was largely the case some 50 years ago) he or she would be woefully unprepared to deal with today's rapidly changing business environment. By the same token, if an organization's KM strategy focused solely on information flow, it would also be unable to deal with the challenges of doing business in the Knowledge Era.

Educational practices have, thankfully, changed so that there is less emphasis on gathering facts and information and more of an emphasis on the processing of information and the acquisition of the skills for self-study and continuous learning. This shift from rote learning to skill acquisition has been documented by a number of authors including Marshall McLuhan (1964) and Alvin Toffler (1970 and 1980), author of *Future Shock* and *The Third Wave*. It was also one of the themes in Bob Logan's (2000) book, *The Sixth Language: Learning a Living in the Internet Age*.

"The ostensible objective of an education system is the transmission of a body of knowledge, but equally important is the transmission of the methodologies and techniques for organizing information...the heart of an education program is not the information with which one becomes acquainted but the cognitive skills that are developed or acquired through understanding a body of knowledge" (Logan, 2000, pp. 229-30).

The Importance of Knowing What You Know and What You Do Not Know

The focus of KM is not only to organize what is known but also to understand and recognize what is not known. The following taxonomy of both our knowledge and ignorance of our knowledge and ignorance can be very useful for understanding how to manage our knowledge as well as our ignorance. Logic dictates that there are four possibilities concerning our knowledge and ignorance of our knowledge and ignorance. They are:

1. We know what we know,
2. We don't know what we know,
3. We know what we don't know, and
4. We don't know what we don't know.

Measurements and the collection of data allow one to know what one does know, to organize that knowledge and make it easily accessible. It allows an organization to know collectively what individuals know individually. Only by knowing or identifying what one knows through measurement can one determine what one does not know. Measurement activities make an organization think about what is knowledge, reducing the set of "don't know what we don't know." Measuring creates value. That which is taken for granted becomes important or significant if measured. By creating measures of collaboration we can encourage knowledge networking.

What Is a Collaborative Organization?

In this chapter we will answer the question—What is a collaborative organization and explore the historic roots of collaboration from hunting and gathering societies to today's Knowledge Era.

Commerce and Socialization

Most people assume that "competition" is the name of the game in business. Competition drives down prices, sharpens business planning, and insures that only the best stay in the market. Therefore, it should be a major surprise to most when we suggest that we need BOTH competition and collaboration, *and* that they are not contradictory.

A basic thesis of this book is the notion that collaboration is as essential as competition for an organization to manage its knowledge, align its functions and operate in a competitive and profitable manner in today's marketplace.

Most people are geared to an either/or approach and yet the paradox of business in the Knowledge Era is that both are absolutely essential and should occur at the same time. What is really hard to grasp is that they reinforce one another.

We are clearly in the midst of a major transition from the Information Age to the Knowledge Era. We can gain a perspective of what is happening today by looking at the way in which commerce, knowledge structures, competition and collaboration have co-evolved and cross-impacted each other in the past. We all know a lot about competition, but now we need to examine the historic role that collaboration and knowledge have played in the pursuit of commerce and likewise the way in which commerce has influenced the evolution of communications and information systems and hence learning and knowledge structures. We shall discover that collaboration is as much an ancient human tradition as competition and that it dates back to our hunting and gathering roots, but that it was disrupted first through large-scale agriculture and then by industrialization. The spirit of collaboration was kept alive through the science community, however, and has been on the rebound with the introduction of personal computers and especially with the use of the Internet by the business community and the general public.

Five Economic Eras

As competition is so well understood, we will for the purposes of our historical analysis focus on collaboration examining commerce from the perspective of the five economic eras listed below.

Five Economic Eras	
Name of Era	**Approximate starting date**
Hunting and Gathering	• primeval, from the dawn of human history
Agricultural	• approximately 8,000 BC
Industrial	• 1776—the year the Watt steam engine was invented and Adam Smith's ideas first appeared
Information	• 1946—the year of the first electronic computer, the ENIAC
Knowledge	• 1994—the year of the release of Netscape

By economic era we mean a historic period of time in which the commerce of the time is dominated by, but not exclusively limited to, one particular activity, whether that be hunting and gathering, farming, manufacturing or information processing. For example, in the Agricultural Age hunting and gathering still took place and the practice of farming required the manufacture of tools, as well as information and knowledge about plants, animals and the seasons of the year. The principal focus of the commercial activities of the Agricultural Age, however, was related to food production whether they were the service and manufacturing activities that support the growing of food or the trade and barter associated with agricultural commodities.

Agriculture survived into the Industrial Era, but it no longer dominated commerce; rather it supported manufacturing, the dominant form of commerce. After all, those engaged in manufacturing still had to eat to survive. Also, the way in which agriculture was practiced was deeply influenced by industrialization. The mechanization of the majority of farm work resulted in a dramatic reduction in the number of workers actually engaged in direct agricultural work. As well, the way in which farms were organized reflected the new industrial order. Large tracts of land were devoted to a single crop and animals were raised in feed lots rather than being allowed to range free.

In the same way that agriculture was mechanized during the Industrial Era, so it was that manufacturing became automated in the Information Age, resulting in a similar drastic reduction in employment in the manufacturing sector. Automation affects all aspects of hard goods manufacturing, including their distribution and support.

As we enter the Knowledge Era we should not expect that the Information Age will come to a sudden halt no more than we should expect agricultural and manufacturing activities to cease. What we can expect, however, is that knowledge creation and management, which is greatly dependent on collaboration, will increasingly influence the way in which all commercial activities are carried out, whether those activities are associated with agriculture, manufacturing, information processing or other areas of the service sector.

For more detailed information about the Five Economic Eras the reader is referred to Appendix 2 – Five Economic Eras: Further Considerations.

End of the Information Age

We have argued that the accelerated pace of the flow of information that interconnectivity has created requires a new approach to the management of knowledge and that these developments are ushering in a new economic era. The Information Age has come and gone. It only lasted 50 years, from 1946, when the first computer was built, to roughly 1996, the year that the Internet and the World Wide Web became an everyday fact for millions of users and Microsoft, after initially ignoring the phenomenon, finally embraced it with the release of its Web browser, Internet Explorer. The first years of the Information Age were exclusively devoted to the centralized processing of data into information by mainframe computers costing millions of dollars each and run exclusively by computer professionals. The mainframe era was followed by the introduction of minicomputers and dumb terminals that provided greater access to computing by nonprofessionals and a shift in emphasis from data processing to the internal flow of information within the organization. The introduction of microcomputers by IBM in 1983 had a tremendous democratizing effect in the workplace, which liberated many computer users from their dependence on their Information Systems department. While stand-alone microcomputing represented a step forward by dramatically increasing the number of users, it represented a step backward in terms of networking. It did not take long, however, to introduce software solutions that allowed microcomputers to talk to each other and to their organization's mainframe and minicomputers through local area and wide area networks. Electronic data interchange or EDI, on the other hand, allowed the exchange of financial and commercial information between organizations and represented the beginning of electronic commerce (e-commerce).

The Two Types of Information/Knowledge Workers

With computers we have learned how to transform data into information and then how to disseminate that information throughout an organization. Often an individual called a knowledge worker is really only an information worker. What we need are true knowledge workers who have the knowledge to make use of the information available so that the objectives of the organization or the enterprise can be realized. In the Information Age workers used their knowledge to process, disseminate, distribute and control data and information and were not true knowledge workers. **Our definition of a knowledge worker is someone who uses his or her knowledge to add value to the information so that it achieves the enterprise's objectives whether the enterprise is a business, an artistic activity or scientific research.**

Let us return for a moment to the initial impact of computing on organizations. Alvin Toffler pointed out that IT performs two opposing functions within the classical command-and-control hierarchical Industrial Era and/or Information Age organization:

1. IT supports the bureaucracy by making it easier for senior managers to control their organization, especially through large systems like mainframes, and

2. IT in the form of microcomputers, on the other hand, decentralizes computing power, and contributes to a flatter, more egalitarian and less bureaucratic organization.

MIS departments initially opposed the introduction of microcomputers, citing spurious reasons as to why they would not work. At the heart of their opposition was their fear that microcomputing would undermine their position of power in the organization. MIS was able to stage a counterrevolution through the establishment of client-server systems, one of the few innovations they openly embraced. Client-server systems have temporarily preserved the domination of organizations by MIS, but that is about to change once again with the shift in emphasis from information to knowledge. MIS departments will continue to play a central role in the activities of the organization, but their role will shift from decision makers to that of service providers. The Chief Information Officer (CIO) will give way to the Chief Knowledge Officer (CKO), who will be responsible for developing the organization's knowledge strategy and coordinating that with their company's IT strategy. And as we suggest later in the book, the CKO will morph into the Chief Collaboration Coordinator.

Alvin Toffler pointed out that the rise of profit centers in the '80s can be understood in terms of networking and the desire of senior managers to continue to control their departments, which, with the advent of microcomputers, were beginning to slip away. Profit centers in turn gave rise to "baby bureaucracies," similar to the larger organization to which they belonged. The next step that will involve KM will result in a new realignment in which profit centers will operate in a more coherent, collaborative and organic manner, pursuing objectives that reinforce each other's activities in an autocatalytic manner.

Two levels of organization will coexist in Knowledge Era enterprises: a bureaucratic one to control financial matters and to ensure security for shareholders and owners, and a flat self-organizing one to allow for the free flow of information, the sharing and co-creation of knowledge and for general all-around creativity. The coexistence of these two forms of organization will not be a source of conflict, but rather the tension between them will be a source of creativity just like the idea of competition and collaboration.

The resolution of the conflict between these two forms of organization parallels the relationship between chance and necessity, both of which are part of any nonlinear, dynamic, complex system. The behavior of today's organizations parallels the quantum mechanical duality of an electron, which is either a wave or a particle depending on the context in which it is encountered, i.e., hierarchical or democratic and competitive or collaborative. Knowledge Era enterprises will be a command-and-control or self-organizing organization, depending on the context.

The New Role of Knowledge in the Knowledge Era

In each economic age we surveyed, knowledge was used to create the tools and/or techniques that produced new wealth, but was not built into the commodities or products that were created. What makes today's relationship between knowledge and the economy different is the structural change in the relationship between knowledge and the products and services that businesses deliver to the public.

In the Industrial Era, knowledge was required to develop, manufacture and deliver a product or service, but there was a clear line between the knowledge and the product or service. Today that distinction is more difficult to make. Knowledge is now an integral part of the product (or service), its creation, its marketing and its support. In the Industrial Era the only knowledge workers were those who created the product through R&D and those who designed the manufacturing and distribution processes. Once the product and the processes for manufacturing and distribution had been designed, the remaining tasks in the organization could all be performed mechanically. A progressive company seeking greater productivity could therefore apply the scientific management theories of Frederick W. Taylor (1911) and make use of his time and motion studies. Taylor's original approach has undergone a number of transformations since its inception. The work of George Elton Mayo, the discoverer of the Hawthorne effect, revealed in the '30s that social factors, such as morale and team cohesiveness, could make important contributions to improving overall productivity as well. The work of Taylor and Mayo have been combined in many different ways since then. The Total Quality Management approach, for example, places more emphasis on the social factors, such as morale. The Business Process Reengineering approach, on the other hand, reverts back to Taylor's original idea of workflow in what might be characterized as extending time and motion studies to include the worker's computer organized within the framework of a client-server system.

No matter what new management approach has been developed, one basic paradigm has remained the same. Most workers in an organization are still treated as the units of a large machine or engine whose efficiency can be maximized by properly motivating each of the cogs in the overall mechanism to operate more efficiently by focusing on quality or excellence or designing the flow of work through them in a more logical way. The elimination of middle management in recent times flattened out the structure of organizations somewhat, but it did not change the fact that decisions are still made by a small elite at the top of the management chain. It did not change the fact that the only knowledge being harnessed for the well-being of the organization was that of the senior managers, with the exception of those involved in the R&D function. The elimination of middle management did not result in any structural change in the way in which personnel contributed their knowledge to the organization. It just allowed the senior managers of the organization to control their workers more directly and more efficiently by replacing middle managers with information technology systems. There is less bureaucracy, but the hierarchical command-and-control structure remains in place.

Computers were able to automate the mechanical processes of the Industrial Era because those processes were linear, fragmented and subject to centralized command and control. Replacing mechanization with automation permitted mass customization and increased efficiencies, but left the organizational structures of companies unchanged. The hierarchical structuring of companies for both decision making and knowledge input, which characterized the Industrial Era, has been retained in the Information Age by firms in the manufacturing sector, as well as those in the information sector. There are differences between these two sectors in that manufacturing deals with tangible resources, while the information sector deals with an intangible resource, namely information. Because of the centralization of information processing, at first with mainframes and later with client-server systems, the information sector still retains most of the organizational principles of the manufacturing sector. How else can one explain the well-known example of the former CEO of a major soft drink company, Pepsi-Cola, running a major microcomputer company, Apple. Yes, we live in the Information Age, where mechanization has been replaced by automation, but the real revolution, the knowledge revolution, has not quite hit. But it is on its way and the computer revolution was a necessary step in that evolution. The advent of the Internet and the World Wide Web, with its many possibilities of sharing information and knowledge, is paving the way for a new transformation.

The Internet and the Transition into the Knowledge Era

The Middle Ages, the Renaissance, the Enlightenment and the Industrial Revolution are terms that historians employ to identify an historic era, which suggest some defining characteristic of that era. These terms were coined long after the period that they describe was over. Those that lived during the Renaissance did not use this term to describe their own epoch. In more recent times, however, we have begun to use such terms to describe the times in which we are actively involved as a way of underscoring some phenomena that seems to define our time. For example, with the explosion of the first atomic bombs at the end of World War II, journalists wrote that we had entered the Atomic Age. Similarly with the development of jet airplanes there was talk of the Jet Age and with the advent of space travel, the Space Age.

Once the development and widespread use of computers and other forms of automation began to have a significant impact on business and commerce, journalists and business commentators began to speak about the Information Age or one of a number of alternatives including: the Age of Automation, the Computer Age, the Electronic Era, the Microelectronic Revolution and the Post-Industrial Era. We shall use the term Information Age because the defining characteristic of this economic era has been the increase and speedup of the flow of information through the use of information technology (IT), which is operated by a group traditionally known as Management Information Systems (MIS). The key word in these terms is information and it has been information that has been the focus of all analyses aimed at improving the efficiency or increasing the productivity of organizations during the Information Age. The most well-known example is Business Process Reengineering, discussed earlier, in which the focus of attention is the flow of information and work.

The principal thesis of this book is that information is no longer the defining characteristic of today's economy nor the most useful concept for understanding the massive restructuring through which we are presently passing. The defining characteristic of today's economy is "knowledge," which slowly is being acknowledged as the principal source of wealth. The interconnectivity that LANs and the Internet have made possible has created an environment in which knowledge will play a more fundamental role in business than information plays.

It is interesting that just at the point where we have reached the limits of our present methods of organization based on industrialization, automation and the computerization of information, the new medium of the Internet came into prominence. Perhaps it is not an accident, but rather the Internet flourished because this medium provided the kind of dialogue and integration that is required in today's business environment. Put differently, there is a need for new knowledge tools and the Internet (and intranets) arose in response to this need just as writing and mathematics came to the aid of agricultural-based economies 5,000 years ago, electromechanical computing machines arrived just in time for the U.S. 1890 census, and electronic computers came to the aid of the industrial economy 50 years ago.

The current transition from the Information Age to the Knowledge Era is part of a historic evolution in which new forms of knowledge and technology have emerged as needed—"Necessity is the mother of invention." Each epoch has given rise to new challenges that inspired innovation. The shortage of game led to agriculture. The technology necessary for agriculture led to mechanization and then to industrialization. The large numbers that had to be reckoned in the Industrial Era led to an information overload and to the need for computers and automation. The rapid rate of innovation that resulted gave a premium to knowledge and is leading to a full realization of the Knowledge Era.

The system of industrialization in which natural resources are converted into mass-produced manufactured goods thrives on innovation and new forms of knowledge. Industrialization coupled with the capitalist economic system based on the competitiveness of the marketplace puts a premium on developing cheaper and more efficient forms of production based on economies of scale. This competitiveness motivated new scientific and technological breakthroughs. With the development of the assembly line and the unprecedented large numbers that this system of manufacture entailed, the control of information became essential for success. A similar pressure to work with large numbers and complex data banks was also being felt in various fields of science and technology. The scientific motivation, combined with the financing of industry and government, led to the invention of computers and the advent of the Information Age.

Computing, with its rapid development, innovation and dissemination, has created an accelerated rate for the creation and obsolescence of knowledge so that the flow of information must take a backseat to an organization's strategy for the creation, sharing and implementation of knowledge if an organization wishes to remain competitive in today's world.

The turnover of knowledge is so rapid that organizations must rethink the relationship between their management of information and their development and cultivation of the knowledge required to use that information to achieve their objectives. In the less volatile Industrial Era and the early part of the Information Age, a company could leave the creation of knowledge to others and focus merely on the commercial exploitation of that knowledge in the marketplace. In that slow-moving environment, the relationship between knowledge and information was simple. The knowledge required to conduct business entailed a basic acquaintance with the appropriate information required to conduct one's business and the techniques required to manage that information. In today's business and technology environment that is not enough. One must not only be capable of dealing with today's information needs, but must be able to anticipate what information and knowledge will be required for tomorrow's tasks and know how to obtain that information and knowledge.

There is a parallel between the knowledge needs of business and those of pure science. Thomas Kuhn (1972), in *The Structure of Scientific Revolutions*, distinguished between two types of scientific activity, which he denoted as normal science and revolutionary science. In normal science the premises of science remain the same and the scientists extend the application of their knowledge to new domains and new situations. During a period of revolutionary science, on the other hand, the actual premises and paradigms for describing nature undergo fundamental change. The same kind of structure exists for the development of business knowledge. There is what we might call normal business knowledge, which permits an organization to conduct its day-to-day business in a static environment. Then there is revolutionary business knowledge that a firm must develop so that it can remain competitive tomorrow. Another parallel with science is the importance of community for knowledge sharing and creation, a theme we shall return to shortly.

With the advent of interconnectivity as represented by client-server environments, intranets and the Internet, a new paradigm is emerging where knowledge, rather than the control of the means of production, is regarded as the primary source of wealth. And perhaps even more radical is the notion that not all knowledge needs to be protected and secreted under a lock and key. A new attitude is emerging in which the free exchange of knowledge and information is seen as a benefit for both trading partners. We have arrived perhaps at the end of an era. The advent of the Knowledge Era represents the end of both the Industrial Era and the Information Age, a neo-industrial phenomena.

The transition from the Information Age to the Knowledge Era can be framed within Alvin Toffler's notion of waves of change of economic systems that he developed in his book *The Third Wave* (1980). He characterized the transition from hunting and gathering to agriculture as the first wave of change; the transition from agriculture to industrialization as the second wave; and the transition from the Industrial Era to the Information Age as the third wave. We view the transition that we are in the midst of where the focus shifts from information to knowledge as the fourth wave of change. (This section is inspired by a conversation one of us, Dr. Robert K. Logan, was fortunate enough to have with Alvin Toffler, but does not reflect Toffler's views. We are happy to credit him with whatever is of value here and accept sole responsibility for whatever misses the mark.)

In the Knowledge Era our concern with information will not suddenly disappear; that is impossible given the codependency of knowledge and information. It is just that information will no longer be the central focus of attention and the principal source of wealth. Rather, knowledge will become the primary source of wealth (Drucker, 1994), (Senge, 1990), (Savage, 1996), (Nonaka and Takeuchi, 1995) and (Logan, 2000) and the primary focus of attention. The dominance of MIS groups and the CIOs will wane, replaced by KM groups and the CKOs (Chief Knowledge Officers). This development will parallel the changes that took place during the transition from the Industrial

Era to the Information Age. Industrialization and manufacturing continued during the Information Age, but they were transformed by it. In a similar manner IS and MIS functions will continue to be important, but they will be transformed by knowledge structures, as will all forms and functions of commerce, education, politics and culture.

Knowledge Is Created by a Community

"Knowledge flows through communities, from
one generation to the next."
—*Takeuchi (2001)*

With the realization that knowledge is the key to success in the new Internet Era, organizations have been turning to KM initiatives as a way of dealing with the reality of the new economics, with varying degrees of success. One of the main themes of our book is that this success has been limited by a lack of collaboration, which in turn results from a lack of trust. The problem as we see it is that organizations lack a spirit of community, which is essential for trust, collaboration and the sharing and creation of knowledge. That knowledge creation is a product of community is a fact that is borne out throughout history. The notion that knowledge is the creation of solitary geniuses is a misguided myth. All of the breakthroughs in human knowledge have occurred within the context of a community of scholars or practitioners. While it is true that outstanding individuals are credited with certain discoveries, a study of the history of science and scholarship reveals that they were supported by a community of scientists and/or scholars.

In terms of philosophy the three greatest ancient Greek philosophers were linked in that Plato was a disciple of Socrates and Aristotle was a student in Plato's Academy. Discipline is about disciples and about disciplehood. Discipline is not about obedience or being trained by a trainer, but about learning with a mentor. One needs to challenge one's colleagues. The environment in which this interaction takes place is essential to the process. Knowledge transfer cannot take place in a command-and-control environment, which characterized Industrial Era schools and business. Knowledge arises out of interaction and interaction arises out of dialogue and collaboration.

As a final example outside of commerce, let us consider science, which is based on collaboration and competition. Almost all of the breakthroughs in science occurred within a community of scholars sharing their results and dialoguing with each other and at the same time competing with each other to see who would be the first to understand a phenomenon or solve a problem. Science was usually carried out within the context of a university, where freedom of expression and the freedom to do research are a respected tradition. The Internet, which was first populated by scientists and academics, is another environment in which the participants are free to pursue their interests, dialogue and collaborate. We shall return to this thought in Chapter 4 when we explore the nature of the Net in detail. But for the moment let us explore what collaboration means in the world of business.

Two Levels of Collaboration

The thesis of our book is that for an organization to be successful in the Knowledge Era, it must develop and implement a knowledge strategy, and for this to happen it must first become a collaborative organization. There are two levels of collaboration possible. One is the internal collaboration of all the stakeholders of an organization, which include management and staff. A second level of collaboration is for the company to engage in collaborative commerce, c-commerce for short, in which the organization collaborates with its customers, suppliers and business partners. Collaborative commerce can be defined as a business project in which two or more independent organizations have a common business goal and cannot accomplish that goal effectively and efficiently without the help of the other partner(s). One of the advantages of c-commerce, is that companies that have the potential to complement each other's competencies can do so without the messy business of engaging in a merger. In order for a company to successfully engage in c-commerce it must first achieve internal collaboration so we will first describe this form of collaboration before describing c-commerce.

An internally collaborative organization has the following properties:

1. There is a relatively free flow of information and communication at all levels and in all directions within the organization and between the organization and its customers and suppliers.

2. All staff have relatively free access to information within the organization and want to use it.

3. Staff are encouraged to acquire knowledge, and resources are committed to make this possible.

4. Knowledge is relatively freely shared within the organization.

5. The various units and working groups of the organization are not working at cross purposes to each other, but are in synch with each other with a common purpose.

6. There is a sense of community and hard-won trust within the organization and between the organization and its customers and suppliers.

7. There is a shared set of values.

8. There is a common goal or set of objectives that all members of the organization share.

9. There are overlapping networks that are interacting by sharing thoughts, ideas, experiences and knowledge.

10. Business units operate cross-functionally instead of being siloed barriers.

11. Managers, employees, customers and suppliers spend time learning about each other's activities, challenges and aspirations.

12. Diversity is welcomed.

C-commerce is basically the collaboration of organizations that work together on specific projects to achieve common goals. The 12 properties we used to describe internal collaboration of an organization must apply with equal validity between the collaborating organizations at least as far as the projects they embark on together are concerned. One cannot expect a total sharing of knowledge and information between the firms, as they may very well be competitors in commercial arenas other than the one in which they are collaborating. The importance of c-commerce cannot be overstated, as the following quote from the editors of *KM World* (1999) indicates: "Business collaboration will surpass competition and rivalry as the key tool for sustained business development....Knowledge managers need to expand opportunities for relevant, trans-enterprise interactions with partners, suppliers and most of all, customers."

The level of collaboration between organizations can vary depending on the nature of their interaction. At the most basic level the collaboration could be as simple as a supplier and a customer cooperating by using EDI to settle their accounts. At a slightly higher level would be e-procurement or electronically configured supply chains, which in the case of manufacturers increases their flexibility and reduces the inventories they have to carry. Software developers have created software solutions that facilitate supply chain management, and are used by a variety of organizations including ZF Meritor, a manufacturer of heavy-duty truck transmissions (KM World Editorial, 2001a), Michigan Gaming Control Board (Haimila, 2000), Pharmacia (KM World Editorial, 2001b), Mills Corp., a developer of retail and entertainment centers (KM World Editorial, 2001c), Tenneco Automotive Europe (KM World Editorial, 2001e) and Riello Group, an Italian heating supply company (KM World Editorial, 2002). In the case of the Riello Group, "the system provides employees...clients, installers and project designers, with an enterprise portal that gives them self-service access to product information and real-time collaboration capabilities" (ibid.). Another example is a project planned by Drug Trading Company Limited to make use of J.D. Edwards collaborative software in which customers and suppliers are linked "to share information about store sales. Suppliers will be able to keep store inventories at capacity without requiring individual replenishment orders" (www.jdedwards.com, 2002).

A more significant form of collaboration occurs when the supplier and customer collaborate in the design of a product or service (CPD—see Chapter 1) that depends in a critical manner on the ability of the supplier to help solve a problem for their customer's customer. And finally, the most intense form of collaboration occurs when two or more organizations form a partnership to offer products and/or services to the marketplace or to satisfy the needs of a third party.

In the next chapter we examine the way in which management thinkers, especially those concerned with KM and learning, have dealt with the idea of community and collaboration.

The Treatment of Collaboration in the Knowledge Management Literature

The Missing Link?

As we stated previously we believe that the success of KM has been limited because not enough attention was paid to collaboration. In this chapter we plan to review a number of management models, some of which explicitly incorporate KM for the way in which they deal with collaboration. This will not be a complete review of the management literature, but one that focuses on what we consider to be some of the key works of the past 10 years. We begin with two earlier models of management that do not deal with KM explicitly, namely Hammer's (1993) Business Process Reengineering approach and Senge's (1990) notion of a Learning Organization. We will then turn to the KM approaches of Sveiby (1997), Armstrong (2002), Nonaka and Takeuchi (1995), and Savage (1996). We will conclude this survey by looking at some very recent works that explicitly look at collaboration, namely Allee (2003), Amidon (2003), Beyerlein et al. (2003), Saint-Onge and Wallace (2003), Savage (1998), Skyrme (2001), Straus (2002) and Sveiby and Simons (2002).

Business Process Reengineering

Despite the many improvements of information technology during the Information Age and their expanded use in business, the computer's promise of a dramatic increase in productivity eluded the business community. Hammer and Champy (1993), who analyzed this problem, suggested that although computing sped up each individual business process, it was the flow of work from one group to another that was slowing down the overall process and preventing the optimization of efficiency. They believed that by redesigning and reorganizing workflows that had been inherited from the previous era of mechanization, new levels of efficiency could be realized through Business Process Reengineering (BPR).

"Reengineering is about reversing the Industrial Revolution. Reengineering rejects the assumptions inherent in Adam Smith's industrial paradigm—the division of labor, economies of scale, hierarchical control and all the other appurtenances of an early-stage developing economy. Reengineering is the search for new models of organizing work.... Task-oriented jobs in today's world of customers, competition and change are obsolete. Instead, companies must organize work around process" (ibid., pp. 27-28, 49).

The application of BPR and EDI, as well as the recent introduction of the Internet and the World Wide Web, contributed to the improved flow of information. Yet despite all of these improvements there still lingered structural problems that prevented the full realization of the initial promise of computing. Something was missing. **We believe what was missing and is still missing for most organizations is a viable knowledge management strategy and an environment of trust and collaboration.** A number of years after the release of his 1993 book and after BPR had been applied with some success in a number of companies, Michael Hammer acknowledged that his approach had had limited success because he had left the people out of the BPR equation. The BPR approach is fine as far as the efficient flow of information and work tasks go, but it still does not address the need for collaboration in today's organization. It treats the employees as though they were automatons whose job was merely to carry out the reengineered processes. There is not a sufficient opportunity for the workers to input what they have learned from their experience of doing their job. Mechanisms and forums must be created to allow the frontline workers to dialogue with each other and their managers so that they can discover together the best way to reengineer the processes with which they have first-hand experience.

Peter Senge and the Learning Organization

If knowledge is the source of wealth in the new economy, then careful attention must be paid to the learning process. Learning is not about acquiring a body of knowledge, but rather it is acquiring the methodologies and techniques for organizing information. The skill set for using information to obtain one's objectives is just as important for an organization as it is for an individual. Although many authors identified the importance of knowledge to the operation of an organization, Peter Senge (1990, pp. 3-14) was the first to recognize that just as an individual requires a learning strategy, the same is true of an organization. In his groundbreaking book *The Fifth Discipline* he introduced the notion of a "learning organization," which he defined as "an organization that is continually expanding its capacity to create its future." This entails for Senge not only "adaptive" or "survival" learning, but also "generative learning," i.e., learning that enhances the capacity to create. Senge maintains that in order to achieve this, an organization must pursue five disciplines, with a discipline defined as "a body of theory and technique that must be studied and mastered to be put into practice." The five disciplines Senge identified are:

1. Systems thinking, because the activities of an organization are a system of "interrelated action" and activities, which require that "the whole pattern of change" be discerned.

2. Personal mastery or the ability to "realize results that matter most deeply" to one, and which is achieved through a lifelong commitment to learning.

3. Mental models that are "deeply ingrained assumptions, generalizations or even pictures or images that influence how we understand the world and how we take action."

4. A shared vision that manages "to bind people together around a common identity and sense of destiny."

5. Team learning that occurs when "the intelligence of the team exceeds the intelligence of the individuals in the team" and requires dialogue. It also entails a team that learns to align its actions so as to produce a coherent result or effect.

The title of his book, *The Fifth Discipline*, derives from his belief that "systems thinking is the fifth discipline...that integrates the disciplines, fusing them into a coherent body of theory and practice."

Senge provides a number of insights that are useful to keep in mind when building a collaborative organization. One of the aspects of developing personal mastery, according to Senge, is "developing a more systemic worldview, learning how to reflect on tacit assumptions, expressing one's vision and listening to others' visions, and joint inquiry into different people's view of current reality" (ibid., p. 173). Another important point he makes is that collaboration requires a balance between advocacy and inquiry (ibid., p. 200). One must express one's position strongly, but not to the point of being closed to the possibility that someone else's position might be superior. Being open to inquiry allows one to question which position is truly superior. Another essential element to collaboration is what Senge terms "a shared vision," which in order to be effective must be built from the visions of the individuals that comprise the organization (ibid., p. 212). Of the five disciplines that Senge identifies, it is perhaps "team learning" that comes closest to collaboration. He describes "team learning" as "the process of aligning and developing the capacity of a team to create the results its members truly desire."

Senge whose book was published four years before the release of Netscape, developed his ideas on the importance of systems thinking before the use of the Internet in the business community. Our model of collaboration is based on using the Internet as both a medium of and a model for collaboration, yet we find many parallels between our thinking and that of Senge. Although Senge does not explicitly focus on collaboration, we feel his ideas support that notion and we certainly recommend him for further reading.

His notion that an organization must be looked at as a dynamic system supports the notion that the members of the organization must interact with each other in a collaborative manner. If this is not the case and the employees are merely carrying out the commands of their managers who are also controlling their actions, then such an organization is not a dynamic system, but rather a mechanical system more suited to the Mechanical Age (i.e., the Industrial Era) than to the Internet-configured Knowledge Era. The discipline of personal mastery will lead to collaboration if the skills that are mastered include listening, cooperating, assuming responsibility, being honest and respecting others. The continuous learning aspect of personal mastery is another key element that contributes to collaboration because the desire to learn and improve naturally leads to a desire to collaborate with one's employees so as to learn from them. The discipline of mental modeling and values sharing will also lead to collaboration as long as the stakeholders of the organization include collaboration in their mental model and shared vision of the organization. Team learning is the Senge discipline that becomes the medium through which collaboration can take place within an organization.

One of the advantages of a learning organization and one that collaborates is that it becomes self-sufficient. Rather than bringing in a new set of experts in the form of consultants each time specialized knowledge is required, organizations are attempting to generate the expertise they need from their own personnel by networking the knowledge that already exists internally or by acquiring the knowledge that is needed. In this way the knowledge that consultants bring to solve a problem does not leave when they are through with their assignment. Just as an individual whose education has been process oriented rather than exclusively information based can develop new skills quickly when and as needed, an organization with a learning and collaboration management strategy has the resiliency, agility and mental dexterity to generate the knowledge it requires on an "as needed" basis. This is just-in-time expertise.

Another resource for expertise is through the professional associations employees have with colleagues in other organizations, with whom they interact through professional societies or just socially. Jon Wagner (2002), with whom we (the authors) have formed an informal collaboration, reported how members of the Ontario branch of the OD Network share with the group the problems they encountered in their workday in their respective organizations. These problems were discussed by the group as a whole and solutions were sketched out that benefited all that participated, especially the member who brought up a real-life problem they were wrestling with in their organization.

Karl Erik Sveiby and the Concept of Knowledge Capital

An essential element in understanding the implementation of KM and the role of collaboration is the notion of knowledge capital, sometimes referred to as intellectual capital. This concept was first introduced by Karl Erik Sveiby as the intangible assets of an organization in the course of the KM work he carried out in Sweden in the mid '80s. He coined much of the terminology used today in the field of KM to describe intangible knowledge assets in his 1987 book *Managing Know-How* (Sveiby and Lloyd, 1987). He introduced the idea of knowledge capital (kunskapscapital) as the value of an organization's intangible knowledge assets. Sveiby identified three distinct types of knowledge assets, namely:

1. the knowledge possessed by the employees of the organization, popularly known as human capital,
2. the knowledge built into the structures and procedures of the organization, popularly known as structural capital, and
3. the external sources of knowledge possessed by suppliers and customers, popularly known as customer or external capital.

The term "employees" in the definition of human capital refers to all of the people that work for the organization. Although Sveiby initially called these three forms of knowledge capital—human capital, structural capital and customer capital—after working with these concepts for some time, he came to the conclusion that the term "capital" was not the best way to describe these intangible assets. He has subsequently dropped the term "knowledge capital" and in his 1997 book *The New Organizational Wealth* he uses the term "intangible knowledge assets" to describe knowledge capital and the terms "individual competence," "internal structure" and "external structure" for what he previously referred to as "human capital," "structural capital" and "customer capital," respectively. External structure, which roughly corresponds to customer capital consists of "brands, customer and supplier relations." Internal structure, which corresponds roughly to structural capital, consists of "the organization: management, legal structure, manual systems, attitudes, R&D, software." Finally, competence of the employees or individual competence, which corresponds roughly to human capital consists of "education, experience" (Sveiby, 1997, p. 186).

His original terminology of intangible assets in terms of human, structural and customer capital has stuck, however, and most workers in the field use these terms. Sveiby's term "knowledge capital," however, was transformed into "intellectual capital." "Although the concept of intellectual capital has been developing over the years, wide popular business interest was probably generated by a series of articles by Thomas Stewart in *Fortune* magazine" (Pogson, 1999). Subsequently, Leif Edvinsson sold Skandia, a life insurance company in Sweden, on the idea of implementing the notions in Stewart's article and became the company's Director of Intellectual Capital (Stewart, 1997, p. xv). Edvinsson might have picked up the term "intellectual capital" from

Stewart, but it should be noted that Karl Erik Sveiby was also employed at Skandia at this time and collaborated with Edvinsson. This is just one example of the many instances of the knowledge networking that took place within the KM movement itself.

The term "intellectual capital" is likely to be the normative term especially with the publication of two books on this theme by Edvinsson and Malone (1997) and Stewart (1997), both with the identical title, *Intellectual Capital*. Hubert Saint-Onge has also used the term "intellectual capital" in his early work, but now favors "knowledge capital." Charles Armstrong (2002), on the other hand uses the term "enterprise capital" in his model of KM.

The definition of capital found in *The New Lexicon Webster's Dictionary* (1988), which best describes capital in the phrase knowledge capital is "something stored up for future use," such as money or wealth, which when used to make an investment in an enterprise is referred to simply as "capital." Knowledge capital is therefore a form of wealth and has an intrinsic value. The metaphor carries with it the notion that "knowledge capital" is knowledge that has been stored for future use in such a way that it is easily accessible and it can be easily generalized to fit a new situation. The term knowledge capital gives rise to another image in terms of collaboration. It is sometimes the case with financial capital that a group of investors collaborate by pooling their capital to invest in a common enterprise. The analogy with knowledge capital is that individuals pool their knowledge resources or capital in a common intellectual enterprise and co-create new knowledge. As Shakespeare once noted, "Would not a rose by any other name smell as sweet?" Whether the term "knowledge capital," "intellectual capital," "enterprise capital" or "knowledge asset" is used is immaterial.

Although intellectual or knowledge capital as a creator of more wealth is a company's most valuable asset, it is not easy to measure because it is intangible. This is especially true of tacit knowledge, which, unlike explicit knowledge, is difficult to express or make visible. "Tacit knowledge is highly personal and hard to formalize, making it difficult to communicate or to share with others" (Nonaka and Takeuchi, 1995, p. 8). How does one manage an asset that is difficult to measure and in some cases even difficult to identify? The concept of knowledge capital has been formulated to deal with this challenge.

There are two operational ways of defining knowledge capital, one in terms of its effects on an organization in creating wealth and the other in terms of understanding the market value of an organization. We begin with the latter type of definition because it underscores the intangible aspect of knowledge assets or knowledge capital. A number of authors (Sveiby, 1997, p. 3; Stewart, 1997, p. 61; and Edvinsson and Malone, 1997, p. 4) have noted that there is a rather large discrepancy between the market value and the book value of many publicly traded companies, which accountants refer to as "goodwill," but which they identify as an intangible knowledge asset or knowledge capital.

A problem with defining knowledge capital as the difference between market value and book value is the difficulty in calibrating knowledge capital, an intangible, with cash and other tangible assets. Even converting the value of a physical asset into a cash value offers some problems. One formula is to reduce the original cost with some arbitrary depreciation factor to give an approximation of its worth. The true value of the physical asset to the company is still arbitrary because the liquidation of the asset does not always yield its book value. But these inaccuracies are small compared to that of valuing intangible assets.

A solution to the problem of placing a value on the intangible knowledge capital asset is to assign its value according to the following very simple formula, which works for a publicly traded company. The value of the knowledge capital is equal to its market value in terms of the price of its share, times the total number of shares, minus the book value of its tangible assets. "When a company is bought for more than its book value (the equity portion of its balance sheet), that premium usually consists of intellectual assets—anticipated revenues from patents, customer relationships, brand equity, etc., plus a premium for obtaining management control" (Stewart, 1997, p. 61). This number gives a rough measure of the knowledge capital, but it does not contain very much information. Also, the number fluctuates with the stock market. Currency fluctuations would result in fluctuations in the knowledge capital of a nation, which once again would be independent of its ability to create value. In fact when a country's currencies goes down, the market for its products and services increases because they cost less in the world market. These are some of the problems with assigning the value of knowledge capital as the difference between market value and book value.

The difference between a company's market value and its hard assets is perhaps more a reflection of the expectations the market places on the company's prospects for future performance and sales than of its knowledge capital, although some would argue that these are the same thing. We have trouble buying that argument because sometimes a fortunate market position has more to do with serendipity than the intrinsic value of an intellectual asset. For example, some organizations enjoy a monopoly position as a result of some accident of history or because they are a government agency and hence are ensured of a certain amount of sales independent of their intellectual capabilities or capital. The value to the public and the service they provide, however, does depend on their intellectual capital.

One of the reasons why it is difficult to develop a precise definition of knowledge capital is that there is no precise and definitive definition of knowledge upon which the definition of knowledge capital depends. The term for knowledge changes depending on the context in which it is used. A second difficulty with its definition is that knowledge capital is a metaphor and metaphors generally elude precise definitions. In fact, the power of a metaphor is in its ambiguity, which allows the user to make connections that might not otherwise be made. The power of the metaphor of knowledge capital is that it suggests that knowledge has monetary value and is susceptible to accounting practices. Knowledge capital, like all metaphors, has both service and disservice. Its disservice is that it suggests that knowledge is a commodity and not a process. Its value and service, however, is that it suggests that knowledge is an intangible asset with real monetary value and needs to be accounted for in valuing the net worth of a business.

Another critique that is made of the notion of knowledge capital is that it is a one-dimensional variable measured in the units of dollars. Some regard it merely as another variable for accountants to tally and perhaps impress their shareholders. They believe it falls short of providing a dynamic picture of the enterprise, arguing that it lacks the requisite variety to properly model knowledge capital or knowledge as the wealth-producing capacity or value of an enterprise. Ashby's Law of Requisite Variety reminds us that a model must replicate the complexity of a system it is modeling to be a useful tool for controlling or understanding that system.

In its defense we would argue that an approximate measure is better than no measure, and that the concept of knowledge capital has the potential of generating more sophisticated models because of the way in which it identifies an enterprise's three forms of knowledge capital, namely human, structural and customer capital. It also allows an understanding to develop of the relationship of the enterprise, with its customers whose needs it must satisfy and its suppliers whose goods and services are critical to its success. We believe that by understanding the dynamic relationship between these three forms of knowledge capital, one can develop a model of how knowledge creates wealth. A nonlinear dynamic linkage of the different forms of intellectual capital provides a more realistic model of an enterprise because of its additional variety.

Despite the difficulties of defining intangible assets and calibrating their worth or value against hard assets, one cannot ignore the idea of intangible assets. From Ashby's Law of Requisite Variety, which demands that a model have a level of complexity that matches the system it is modeling, we know that managing an organization strictly by the bottom line or the balance sheet will not work. We can take comfort in Gödel's Theorem, however, which states that no system is both logically consistent and complete. Without the notion of intangible assets the description of an organization is impossible.

Knowledge Capital—The Wealth Creator

In the previous section we critiqued the definition of knowledge capital as a one-dimensional number whose value is assigned as the dollar value of the difference between the market and book values of a company. Given the shortcomings of this definition we would prefer to define knowledge capital or knowledge assets in terms of its role in creating wealth. We would prefer to use the data on the difference between book and market values to reinforce the notion that intellectual assets are intangible and they create very tangible wealth that is valued by the money markets, which is what distinguishes intelligence or brain power from knowledge capital. As Stewart (1997, p. 67) explains, "Intelligence becomes an asset when some useful order is created out of free-floating brainpower—that is, when it is given a coherent form; when it is captured in a way that allows it to be described, shared and exploited; and when it can be deployed to do something that could not be done if it remained scattered around like so many coins in a gutter. Intellectual capital is packaged useful knowledge." Sveiby's definition of knowledge also incorporates this notion of action: "Knowledge is the capacity to act."

Another way to distinguish knowledge in general from intellectual capital is that knowledge becomes intellectual capital only if it can be used to create a competitive advantage in the marketplace. Underscoring the utility aspect of intellectual capital, David Klein and Laurence Prusak define it as "intellectual material that has been formalized, captured and leveraged to produce a higher-value asset" (quoted in Stewart, 1997, p. 67). Verna Allee (1997, p. 30) also links intellectual capital to the creation of value: "the value chain of enterprise is really a knowledge chain."

Let us turn then to operational definitions of intellectual capital by quoting Tom Stewart's definition of intellectual capital as "the intellectual material—knowledge, information, intellectual property, experience—that can be put to use to create wealth" (Stewart, 1997, p. x). Later in his book he expands on his definition by suggesting that intellectual capital is "a set of talents, capabilities, skills and ideas" (ibid., p. 55). Leif Edvinsson and Michael Malone, on the other hand, define intellectual capital as the sum of human capital and structural capital:

1. Human capital. The combined knowledge, skill, innovativeness, and ability of the company's individual employees to meet the task at hand. It also includes the company's values, culture, and philosophy. Human capital cannot be owned by the company.
2. Structural capital. The hardware, software, databases, organizational structure, patents, trademarks, and everything else of organizational capability that support those employees' productivity—in a word, everything left at the office when the employees go home. Structural capital also includes customer capital, the relationships developed with key customers. Unlike human capital, structural can be owned and thereby traded. (1997, p.11)

Edvinsson's definition has become the one that has been adopted by most practitioners who focus on the management of intellectual capital, with one small variation, namely that customer capital is disaggregated from structural capital and treated as a separate quantity. They divide intellectual capital into three distinct forms: human capital, structural capital and customer capital. Stewart also associates customer capital with customer relationships, but refines it by suggesting that it is "the shared learning between a company and its customers." He also includes brand equity as part of customer equity. Customer capital also includes customer relationships, loyalty and reach through the organization's different distribution channels. Sveiby expands the notion of customer capital by including the contribution of suppliers and therefore speaks of external capital.

One of the unfortunate properties of the human capital that sits in the heads of employees in the form of knowledge or experience is that it leaves the company when the employee leaves the company. An important part of the management of intellectual capital or knowledge is to convert this form of human capital into case studies to document the experiences and knowledge gained from past projects. By doing this the human capital is converted into structural capital and is preserved for future use independent of the actions or the whereabouts of the employees that originally generated this capital. By capturing experiences in terms of case studies, tacit knowledge becomes explicit and can therefore be easily transferred to other employees, thereby increasing the human capital of the organization. The effort required to produce case studies and then organize them should be regarded as an investment in human capital with a very favorable ROI.

Charles Armstrong and the Enterprise Capital Model

Given the current state of accounting methodology, tangible assets tend to receive the most managerial attention and a disproportionate amount of the resources available for investment. However, in the Knowledge Era, the intangible assets are the real source of strength and wealth for the organization. It is the intangible assets that uniquely distinguishes one enterprise from another in the marketplace. It is the accelerated accumulation and leveraging of intangible assets that represents the key challenge for knowledge economy companies. Charles Armstrong, along with Hubert Saint-Onge, have developed a dynamic model for the way in which the various components of knowledge capital interact with each other to produce wealth. In his Enterprise Capital (EC) model, Charles Armstrong describes the linkages between human, structural and customer capital. He describes the relationship of these three forms of capital by representing them as three overlapping circles in a Venn diagram reproduced here with his permission (See Figure 3.1). Here is his description of his model in his own words:

> The Enterprise is a community which extends beyond the company to a broader community made up of customers, vendors, suppliers, engineers, employees, etc. Everyone in this community can make a significant contribution to the value creation of the enterprise, which includes the financial capital of the organization, the tangible assets and the intangible assets.
>
> There are three sources of organizational knowledge, which are the intangible assets of the organization. These three sources are represented by the three intertwining circles in Figure 3.1, namely human capital, structural capital and customer capital. Human capital refers to the capabilities

of individual employees to provide solutions for customers. This requires a high level of initiative, learning agility and an investment in human resource development. Structural capital refers to the capabilities of the organization to meet market demands. It includes systems, products, culture, corporate strategy, market position, global reach and customer knowledge. Customer capital refers to the depth (penetration), breadth (coverage), attachment (loyalty) and profitability of the customer.

The area at which these three resources intersect produces the value creation resultant. Value creating relationships result from interactions among the three elements of enterprise capital—human, structural and customer capital. Relationships are an integral component to the creation of enterprise capital. The value creation resultant grows out the high-performance relationships between employees, customers and products and services that create wealth. When human, customer and structural capital are interacting effectively, value creation and financial performance of the enterprise grows.

1. Structural/human interaction: When employees put structural capital in the form of a database or a productivity tool to satisfy a customer's need, they create value for the organization.

2. Structural/customer interaction: The value of the enterprise capital increases, when structural capital, in the form of a training course, promotes customer learning and enables the customer to make better use of the enterprise's products or services. This is a good example of a "solution" orientation rather than a "product" orientation.

3. Human/customer interaction: Enterprise capital once again increases when employees work directly with customers to solve customers' problems or satisfy customers' needs. Success is assured when employees adopt a personal responsibility, customer-focus perspective and service orientation with a commitment to shared purpose with customers and suppliers. A failure to meet customers' needs and expectations is an opportunity to improve by correcting an internal preoccupation, filling a competency gap, learning to relate better to the customers or achieving greater strategic clarity. This is the opportunity to innovate with the customer.

In summary, organizations operate through the interaction of flows between human, structural and customer capital elements. It is important to note that our organizations also have untapped intangible resources that have not yet been called forth to create value. This is the organization's "value in waiting." The strategic and managerial challenge is to engage these capabilities to create value for customers. The effectiveness of this activity—the depth of engagement by people at the rock face between the elements—determines the amount of value created. (2002, private communication)

Figure 3.1: The Dynamics of Knowledge Capital

Value creation is driven by the interaction of the three key components of enterprise capital

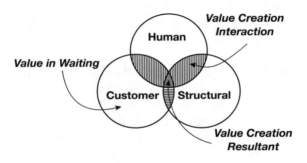

According to Charles Armstrong, KM occurs in the sweet spot where all three forms of knowledge capital overlap. The importance of Armstrong's contribution is his emphasis on the flow of knowledge from the three repositories of knowledge capital, namely the human capital in the heads of the employees of an organization and those of their business partners and allies, the customer capital stored in the heads of the customers and suppliers of the organization and the structural capital stored in the information and knowledge banks of the organization. This flow of knowledge requires the collaboration of the various stakeholders in the organization, aided by the knowledge structures that the organization has created through its data bases and procedures. One of the important distinctions to be made for knowledge sharing and collaboration is Nonaka and Takeuchi's distinction between tacit and explicit knowledge, which we have briefly mentioned but will study in more depth next.

A Model of Collaboration through the Exchange of Tacit Knowledge

Further insight into collaboration can be obtained by understanding the difference between tacit knowledge and explicit knowledge, a distinction originally made by the philosopher Michael Polyani, which Nonaka and Takeuchi (1995) have incorporated into a theory of organizational knowledge creation in their book *The Knowledge Creating Company*. One way to describe tacit knowledge is in terms of intuition. Tacit knowledge is personal, intuitive knowledge whereas explicit knowledge is the kind of knowledge that can be learned from a book. There is a vast difference between book learning and experience-based learning.

Intuition is defined in *Webster's New World Dictionary* as "the immediate knowing of something without the conscious use of reasoning." There are times when we know something to be true, but we do not know why or how we arrived at the understanding. One form of intuition arises because we know something so well and so thoroughly that we do not have to reason things out again, but we immediately know it. This is tacit knowledge, as opposed to explicit knowledge, which is "formal and systematic." Tacit knowledge, according to Nonaka and Takeuchi, is "deeply rooted in an individual's action and experience" (ibid., p. 8). It is intuitive and subjective, whereas explicit knowledge is scientific and objective.

They also use these two categories of knowledge to explain why Japanese companies differ from Western ones. They claim that Japanese firms make use of both tacit and explicit knowledge to become "knowledge creating companies" and hence are able to "create the dynamics of innovation," whereas Western firms traditionally dealt with explicit knowledge. Nonaka and Takeuchi suggest "that knowledge is created through the interaction between tacit and explicit knowledge." They also believe there is an important relationship between knowledge and belief. "Knowledge, unlike information, is about beliefs and commitment. Knowledge is a function of a particular stance, perspective or intention. Second, knowledge, unlike information, is about action. It is always knowledge 'to some end.' And, third, knowledge, unlike information, is about meaning. It is context specific and relational" (ibid., p. 58).

In their knowledge creation model, Nonaka and Takeuchi describe tacit knowledge as the knowledge of experience, whereas explicit knowledge is the knowledge of rationality. Tacit knowledge grows out of practice, is body centered and is subjective, whereas explicit knowledge arises from study, is of the mind and is objective. Tacit knowledge is arrived at all at once, whereas explicit knowledge is learned sequentially. Tacit knowledge is concrete and valid for a specific set of activities or experiences and can only be generalized if it is first converted into explicit knowledge. Explicit knowledge is abstract and hence more versatile because it can be generalized to new arenas of experience. Tacit knowledge is very reliable because it can never be forgotten, like riding a bicycle or swimming. Explicit knowledge is easily transferred, but also easily forgotten. It is only when explicit knowledge becomes tacit through use that it becomes reliable.

The contribution of Nonaka and Takeuchi is their ability to talk about the creation of knowledge in an organization through the conversion of tacit knowledge into explicit and back into tacit knowledge.

Nonaka and Takeuchi identify explicit knowledge as somehow peculiar to Western thinking, which they trace to either of two epistemological traditions, one based on rationality and the other on empiricism. The origin of tacit knowledge is not explained in their approach, but they claim that it is unique to Japanese firms and a source of their inspiration and success as knowledge creating firms. "Japanese companies, however, have a very different understanding of knowledge....They view knowledge as being primarily 'tacit'....The distinction between explicit knowledge and tacit knowledge is the key to understanding the difference between the Western approach to knowledge and the Japanese....It is precisely during the time this conversion takes place—from tacit to explicit and...back again into tacit—that organizational knowledge is created" (Nonaka and Takeuchi, pp. 8-9).

Charles Savage's Concept of Knowledging

The creation, acquisition or application of knowledge is a dynamic process and requires a dynamic medium for its transfer. The most effective medium for acquiring new knowledge is reflection on one's experiences either through self-reflection or dialogue with a co-worker who is willing to share their experiences and insights, i.e., their tacit knowledge.

Charles Savage has added a very important dimension to our understanding of the sharing of knowledge by introducing the verb "knowledging" to remind us that knowledge is more than just content, as in a body of knowledge, but rather the end product of the active process of knowledging. "Knowledge is not something that is possessed like a commodity....Known facts can be possessed, but the human process of knowledging is a much richer and more dynamic phenomenon....Knowledging is more than just 'knowing,' because it suggests an active and continual process of interrelating patterns" (Savage, p. 121).

Data Processing, Information Processing and Knowledge Processing

We shall use Savage's term "knowledging" and introduce one of our own, "knowledge processing," to describe those activities or processes associated with knowledge that includes sharing knowledge, learning new knowledge, co-creating or creating new knowledge, applying knowledge, managing knowledge, exploiting knowledge, mapping knowledge, classifying knowledge and organizing knowledge, all of which Savage sums up as "knowledging" or "the process of interrelating patterns." The term "knowledge processing," which we will use synonymously with knowledging, has been introduced because it explicitly carries with it the notion of processing and also because it parallels the terms of "data processing" and "information processing" and hence allows us to see more clearly the pattern and relationship of data, information and knowledge.

Data processing is the activity of structuring and patterning data to create information. Information processing consists of two basic forms of activity; one is the storing and retrieving of information for later use and the other is the transforming of information by structuring and organizing it whereby it becomes converted into knowledge in the sense of a commodity or something to be possessed by the knower. But as Savage points out, there is a higher level of processing, which he calls "knowledging" and which we term "knowledge processing" and which involves a systematic strategy for managing the organization's knowledge resources to optimize knowledge sharing and networking while creating the conditions to optimize the co-creation of new knowledge.

With each of the three stages of processing one can associate the following generations of computer technology: data processing and the mainframe; information processing, microcomputers and client server systems; and knowledge processing and the new media of the

Internet and the World Wide Web, or interconnectivity. The main-frames crunched data and spat out information for use by others. Microcomputers and networking allowed individual users to convert their own data into information and further refine that information through information processing, which was then made available to others through work group and departmental LANs or WANs. With the Internet, which entails global interconnectivity, powerful search engines, hypertext and hyperlinking we have an ideal medium for knowledge processing, sharing, networking and co-creation.

Table 3.1: Data, Information and Knowledge Processing

The Noun	The Verb	The Outcome	The Device
Data	Data processing	Information	Mainframe computers
Information	Information processing	Transformed information	Client-server systems and microcomputers
Knowledge	Knowledge processing	A business objective	Interconnectivity

Knowledging, Commerce and Science

Data processing, information processing and knowledge processing form an evolutionary chain of activities. Taken together they form a methodology, whereby basic perceptions and data are structured into information, refined into knowledge and transformed and systematized into "scientific" knowledge. "Knowledging" or "knowledge processing" is a research-based activity. It parallels for commercial activities what science does for natural phenomena. Science is the form of knowledge processing that is applied to nature, and KM is the form of knowledge processing that is applied to commerce. One does not ordinarily think of making the connection between the two. However, if one compares the scientific method, which is also a strategy for the systematic management of knowledge, one finds an interesting parallel between the study of nature by science and the conduct of business by knowledge.

The mission of science and business are different in that the focus of the former is strictly on knowledge and that of the latter on productivity and profit, but the systematic approach of the two forms of enterprise is quite similar. Those business firms, however, that have focused on knowledge first and not worried about immediate profits are actually faring much better in the Knowledge Era than those organizations who focused solely on profits, as has been the case with Netscape, which initially gave its product away for free.

Business may be regarded as nothing more than organized commerce and, hence, an organized form of knowledge, like science. Regarding business as a form of science is an excellent metaphor for Knowledge Era enterprises and one that we will use and develop throughout this book. The metaphors of KM and "business as a science" are more radical and useful notions than the metaphor of management science. Management science is more about the management of people than processes and, more often than not, posits a hierarchical command-and-control style of management in which it is assumed that the managers do the thinking and the employees execute their instructions.

The old style of hierarchical management science suffers from the fact that the information and experience upon which the managers at the top of the hierarchy base their decisions are always at arm's length from what is happening directly in the field where the customer interacts with the organization. Senior managers rely on information that has been filtered and gathered by their immediate subordinates. The knowledge that works its way up the hierarchical chain is invariably explicit so that the tacit knowledge of the frontline workers is not available to the decision makers. The senior managers must rely on their own experiences, which are far removed from those of their organization's customers.

Science and KM are parallel activities applied to different domains, namely nature and commerce, respectively. The dictionary definition of science is "organized knowledge," which we claim results from the further refining of knowledge by knowledge processing, in which knowledge is structured, patterned and organized into a scientific body of knowledge. But science is more than just a body of knowledge; it is an ongoing activity or process of constant searching, researching, observing, testing and experimenting.

Exploiting the metaphor of KM and knowledge processing as a form of science helps us to understand that in order to be successful, business activities must be pursued with the same systematic intensity as the sciences. This represents a major culture shift for the business community, where the focus has always been on the bottom line and turning a profit by manipulating and managing tangible assets. The business community is discovering that the key to success sometimes requires, instead of a focus on immediate profit, the development of the intangible assets of knowledge capital, which will insure the long-term viability and profitability of the enterprise.

A second reason for drawing a parallel between science and a KM-configured enterprise is because of science's ability to pool the efforts, experiences, knowledge and expertise of many different players working in different laboratories, institutes and universities all over the world to achieve a shared objective of understanding nature. If a business enterprise could be organized like a scientific community, then every member of the business enterprise would become a resource for gathering information and sharing tacit knowledge that could be pooled and refined into explicit knowledge that would benefit the whole organization. The central idea of KM is to make use of all the knowledge that resides in an organization, not just that of its senior managers. Science as an enterprise has no CEO; it is a completely democratic organization or community of scholars who share a common vision and whose mission is aligned.

Science is a great model for Knowledge Era enterprises and one beginning to be used under the rubric of a community of practice or interest. The science of KM is a more effective model than that of command-and-control hierarchical management science because of the rapid rate at which knowledge continues to grow and change. A hierarchical knowledge structure simply cannot respond quickly enough, whereas a KM-configured organization has the capacity for a quick response through the parallel processing of all the members of the organization.

Knowledge Communities in Science and in Business

In addition to being a process, a methodology and an organized body of knowledge, science is also a community, a knowledge community of experimentalists and theorists. Without a community to gather information, share ideas, test hypotheses and conduct experiments there could be no science. One of the central themes of the scientific method is objectivity, and without a community there can be no cohort of scientists to establish the objectivity of a result.

The idea of a knowledge community in the sciences is a natural one because scientists share a common goal of understanding the mysteries of nature and creating models that describe natural phenomena and permit reasonable predictions to be made. Scientists achieve their goals through collaboration, by sharing their results and their knowledge, for which they are rewarded with the recognition and esteem of their colleagues. Their standing in the community is augmented by their fellow scientists who acknowledge their publications, make use of their results and build upon them. Scientists compete with each other from time to time when they attempt to be the first to make a discovery, but the nature of their enterprise is such that there is an emphasis on cooperation rather than competition.

Business differs from science, however. While businesses share a common goal of earning profits, they regard each other as competitors, especially if they are in the same industry. But business, like science, is also a community activity. There are many advantages to business in forming a knowledge community that includes the company's employees, as well as their customers and suppliers. Customer loyalty and knowledge can be a valuable asset. The inclusion of customers is essential for developing and testing hypotheses in the marketplace, the final and only arbitrator of commercial success. Sometimes one's customers know what the marketplace wants and needs better than you and therefore they need to be listened to carefully. Also, one's suppliers are often in a better position to know what resources they have that can help you satisfy your objective and/or your customers' needs.

The need and desirability for a knowledge community of employees, customers and suppliers has been suggested and hinted at by a number of authors. Savage, in *Fifth Generation Management* (1996), suggests this can be done through knowledge networking, Senge, in *The Fifth Discipline* (1990), advocates the creation of a learning organization and Nonaka and Takeuchi, in *The Knowledge Creating Company* (1995), outline an elaborate process by which tacit knowledge is converted into explicit knowledge, which can then be shared throughout the organization and then converted back to tacit knowledge.

The creation of a knowledge community does not necessarily have to take place within the formal structure of an enterprise. Informal knowledge communities have begun to appear in the corporate world, where they are referred to as a community of practice (COP) or a community of interest. Siemens AG and Intel in 1997, together with a number of smaller firms and private consultants, created a COP called The Millennium Project to share their insights into the practice of KM in a series of face-to-face meetings and an online facilitated Web site (see www.gutenberg.com/~millennium). George Por created a community of practice by organizing the Knowledge Ecology Fair in 1998 (see www.co-i-l.com/kefair), which attracted participants from all over the world. His objective was to create an environment where people could work together naturally by taking advantage of the power of informal communication among peers and by harnessing their creativity and resourcefulness in solving problems as a way of meeting their commitments in their respective domains of work. The cooperation that is fostered in a COP cuts right across institutional or departmental boundaries. "A community of practice is a group of people who are informally bound to one another by exposure to a common class of problems" (Brook Manville, Director of KM at McKinsey & Co., 2003). Communities of practice can exist totally within an enterprise, cutting across departmental boundaries, or they can consist of individuals from different enterprises, some of whom may regard themselves as competitors. Their interest in the common problems and challenges they share transcends any possible conflicts due to the economic competitiveness of their respective organizations.

> Shell has created 13 communities of practice that encompass more than 10,000 users: three major communities for the sub-surface, wells and surface disciplines, and 10 smaller ones for the supporting cross-disciplines, such as finance; procurement; human resources; and health, safety and the environment. Based on a value review completed in 2000, Shell's Exploration and Production business realized benefits of at least $200 million per year through its knowledge sharing initiative. (Haimila, 2001a)

Recent Studies of Collaboration

We began thinking about collaboration approximately four years ago, but we were not alone. Other authors have been working on this concept as well, and have published books on the subject in the past couple of years. David Skyrme's (2001) book *Knowledge Networking* is an excellent guide to the IT aspect of collaboration and is one we commend to our readers who are interested in this aspect of collaboration. He also provides guidance on how to exploit human networks and innovate quickly with practical toolkits and checklists for building a knowledge organization.

David Straus' (2002) book *How to Make Collaboration Work* focuses on the team level as he builds on his previous team meeting book, offering five principles for creating more collaborative face-to-face meetings and offers practical advice for doing so. Each of these five principles he espouses is generally known as important for building good working teams, but they are not effectively nor consistently applied by most teams. His first principle is to involve all relevant stakeholders in the group decision-making processes that impact their work life. The second, which flows from the first, is to work at building consensus of all stakeholders, doing it diligently phase by phase. To facilitate project phase accord, Straus develops for his third principle a variation of conventional project management processes to ensure meeting participants are aligned and working in the same project phase. A related principle of group memory stresses the importance for collaboration that group meeting information is captured so it is current and accessible to all relevant stakeholders. A final principle designates use of a meeting facilitator to ensure a collaborative relationship process is used throughout a meeting so that the team leader is free to focus on content. This co-leadership approach is very valuable to use when teams are going through a culture change in group process.

Beyerlein et al. (2003), in their book *Beyond Teams: Building the Collaborative Organization*, give insightful prescriptives for becoming a collaborative organization with their 10 collaborative principles designed for application at the organizational level. They have based these principles on "the behaviors, values, and disciplines that once characterized effective teams" and translated and embedded them at the organizational level. The 10 principles they cite for collaboration include:

1. Focus collaboration on achieving business results.
2. Align organizational support systems to promote ownership.
3. Articulate and enforce "a few strict rules."
4. Exploit the rhythm of divergence and convergence.
5. Manage complex tradeoffs on a timely basis.
6. Create higher standards for discussion, dialogue, and information sharing.

7. Foster personal accountability.
8. Align authority, information, and decision making.
9. Treat collaboration as a disciplined process.
10. Design and promote flexible organizations.

   We are in basic agreement with these 10 principles, which in many ways parallel our thinking even though we arrive at our conclusions from a different starting point. We do differ with their interpretation of the first principle. We agree that it is always important to focus collaboration on business results, but we do not agree that collaboration for its own sake is without value. We believe that collaboration should be pursued as a goal in its own right even if there is not an immediate business advantage, because eventually an organization that adopts a collaborative mind-set will in the long run operate with greater coherence, alignment and unity of purpose and as a consequence will be more productive and more profitable. A company's profit is the difference between two very large numbers, namely revenues and costs. Any company that can embrace collaboration will operate more effectively and hence reduce its costs significantly, thereby increasing its profit. Also, by working collaboratively and co-creating knowledge the organization will create more opportunities for itself and thereby increase its revenues, which is another way to drive profitability. Our position is reinforced by the conclusions reached by analysts at Deloitte Research (Athey, 2002): "The benefits of effective collaboration spill throughout organizations and are often hard to attribute to specific functions, processes and initiatives. As a result, new metrics for evaluating performance in this virtual workplace are required." In Chapter 7 we will introduce the Collaboration Quotient, a metric we have developed for evaluating collaborative performance.

   In their book *Leveraging Communities of Practice for Strategic Advantage*, Hubert Saint-Onge and Debra Wallace (2003) focus on an extremely important collaborative mechanism, namely the community of practice. They describe the importance and interaction of both individual capabilities (attributes, competencies, mind-sets and values) and organizational capabilities (strategies, systems, structures, leadership and culture) to acquire and apply new knowledge in developing a knowledge-driven organization. Alignment of both individual and organizational capabilities creates the strategic capabilities for a knowledge strategy that successfully meets the demands of the knowledge economy. Their book describes the five core components of Clarica Life Insurance Company's Knowledge Capital Initiative:

1. Accelerate the generation of individual and organizational capabilities.
2. Develop a culture of self-initiative, shared ownership and collaboration.
3. Harness the power of the technology infrastructure.
4. Renew people management processes in support of building capability and a culture based on self-initiative.
5. Build a systematic and readily accessible knowledge architecture.

As their organizational development model, Saint-Onge and Wallace apply communities of practice in which individuals in a group make a collaborative effort to improve their practice. They postulate that successful COPs require a desire to collaborate, a commitment to learning and a passion to find a solution. Their book clearly demonstrates the core foundation of KM is a collaborative and uniquely human accomplishment.

Austin and Hesselbein (2002) have written a book that focuses on collaboration between nonprofit organizations and businesses.

In addition to the books we have reviewed above a number of our colleagues who have had a strong influence on our thinking have also published books and articles (and in one case a Web site) that we wish to mention. With their kind permission we have included excerpts from these works in Appendix 3 – Contributions from our Collaborative Partners on Collaboration. The list includes:

Verna Allee (2003): *The Future of Knowledge: Increasing Prosperity through Value Networks.*

Debra Amidon (2003): *The Innovation Superhighway: Harnessing Intellectual Capital for Sustainable Collaboration Advantage*

Karl Erik Sveiby and Roland Simons (2002): "Collaborative Climate and Effectiveness of Knowledge Work—an Empirical Study."

Charles Savage (1998): "The Value and Values of Collaborative Teaming: The Key to the Knowledge Economy."

KNOW Inc. (2003): *www.knowinc.com: A Source of Collaboration Tools*

The Five Collaborative Messages of the Internet, a Medium for and a Model of Collaboration

"I have a dream for the Web…and it has two parts. In the first part, the Web becomes a much more powerful means for collaboration between people.…In the second part of the dream, collaborations extend to computers."
—*Tim Berners-Lee, 1999, p. 157*

The Global Village and Nomadic Gatherers of Knowledge

In this chapter we wish to develop the hypothesis that the Internet serves as both a medium for and a model of collaboration and KM. The Internet is both the figure and the ground for knowledge networking: the ground in that its interconnectivity suggests the type of relationships necessary for knowledge networking, and the figure in the sense it is the ideal medium and platform for actually carrying out a program of knowledge networking and sharing. KM techniques are ideal for sharing explicit knowledge and information. When it comes to sharing tacit knowledge or co-creating new knowledge, however, collaborative techniques are absolutely necessary. Collaboration is the process where a group of people bring together their knowledge and insights to achieve a common goal they cannot achieve by themselves.

Their goal could be to co-create new knowledge or a new insight or perhaps to co-develop a new product or a new technique. The use of the Internet and the World Wide Web for KM and the sharing of explicit knowledge is a fairly straightforward proposition. While it requires careful planning and overcoming certain technical difficulties, it is easily doable. Collaboration, on the other hand, where new knowledge and insights are developed, is far more difficult and has both a technical and human or psychological dimension. We believe that because the Internet, without any managerial interference, has proven itself to be a natural environment for collaboration, there are important lessons to be learned about how collaboration can be encouraged in an organization.

In order to discover why the medium of the Internet and World Wide Web naturally stimulates collaboration we will make use of the work of Marshall McLuhan, who pioneered the study of media and whose insights into the effects of media on commerce, culture and education can teach us much about collaboration. Marshall McLuhan was an English professor at the University of Toronto who discovered that media are not passive conduits for carrying information or communicating ideas but rather they act as "living vortices of power creating hidden environments (and effects) that act abrasively and destructively on older forms of culture" (Innis, 1972, p. v, McLuhan's foreword). His insight applies to computing in general and the Internet and the World Wide Web in particular, and therefore gives rise to the need to reevaluate the patterns of commerce, learning and social interactions in the workplace in this, the Internet age.

McLuhan certainly demonstrated an uncanny ability to describe the landscape of cyberspace, a term we are certain he never heard. He once claimed that predicting the future was nothing more than paying close attention to and being a careful observer of what was happening in the present. What is remarkable about his achievement is that in 1964 when he wrote *Understanding Media*, workplace computing was in its infancy and restricted to mainframe computers in which jobs were run on a batch basis using punched-hole cards and card readers. His musings on computers filled 14 pages of the last chapter of his book and two pages in the introduction, yet as we will discover in this chapter, he seems to have covered the gamut of issues facing computing and collaboration in today's workplace when he suggested that with electricity and automation, human behavior would change. Nevertheless, his anticipation of the surfing of the Web, albeit obliquely, and his notion of the concept of a "Global Village," for which *Wired* magazine adopted him as their "patron saint," is nothing short of breathless as the following two quotes reveal.

> Men are suddenly nomadic gatherers of knowledge, nomadic as never before—but also involved in the total social process as never before; since with electricity we extend our central nervous system globally, instantly interrelating every human experience. (McLuhan, 1964, p. 358)

> If the Bell system wants to survive the competitive "war" of the eighties, it will emphasize diversity on a regional basis as its ultimate weapon. The private user, such as someone who utilizes special home or commercial information services, will be its prime target. The accumulation of large and sophisticated data bases in the late twentieth century will produce home/commercial high-speed information services utilized by the private user to obtain data for direct personal use. This tailored data will tend to give such a user an illusionary sense of a well-defined identity—assuming the information combination is not available in exactly the same pattern to someone else. That is the good news. The bad news is that all persons, whether or not they understand the processes of computerized high-speed data transmission, will lose their old private identities. For them, what knowledge there is will be available to all. So, in that sense, everybody will be nobody. Everyone will be involved in role-playing, including those few elitists who interpret and/or manage large-scale data patterns and thus control the functions of a speed-of-light society. The more quickly the rate of information exchange speeds up, the more likely we will all merge into a new corporate entity, devoid of true specialism which has been the hallmark of our old private identities. (McLuhan and Powers, 1981)

The reason that the Internet/Web promotes collaboration is that it was designed to do so. Said Tim Berners-Lee in 1999, "When I proposed the Web in 1989, the driving force I had in mind was communication through shared knowledge, and the driving 'market' for it was collaboration among people at work and at home. By building a hypertext Web, a group of people of whatever size could easily express themselves, quickly acquire and convey knowledge, overcome misunderstandings, and reduce duplication of effort. This would give people in a group a new power to build something together."

Another reason that the Internet promotes collaboration and will play a role in the reintegration of work and learning is that it replicates the patterns of oral society and creates what McLuhan termed the global village. Mary Cronin, describing the Internet user community, wrote:

> Global village has been applied to many different situations over the past few decades, some far afield from Marshall McLuhan's original concept of how computerized communication changes society. But it seems entirely appropriate that this phrase should become the description of choice for the Internet. The millions of people linked to the network not only have the common experience of using the same electronic tools and information resources regardless of location, they are also connected to each other in a new way, free to exchange ideas, solicit advice, consult, argue, without regard to national boundaries. (Cronin, 1994, p. 64)

The connectedness within modern day society due to electronic linkages, such as the World Wide Web, creates a need for greater collaboration between all of the members within the same organization, between customers and their suppliers and between organizations, even those that have considered themselves competitors. "Total interdependence is the starting fact....With electricity as energizer and synchronizer, all aspects of production, consumption, and organization become incidental to communications" (McLuhan, 1964, pp. 354, 359). The increased role of the customer in the design of products and services is a feature of the Internet-configured economy that McLuhan talked about almost 40 years ago: "The consumer becomes producer in the automation circuit....Marketing and consumption tend to become one with learning, enlightenment, and the intake of information" (1964, pp. 349-50). The notion of collaborative commerce or c-commerce is another aspect of today's economy that is facilitated by the Internet, which McLuhan talked about many years ago: "Naturally, when electric technology comes into play, the utmost variety and extent of operations in industry and society quickly assume a unified posture.... Many people have begun to look on the whole of society as a single unified machine for creating wealth" (1964, p. 348).

Is the Internet a Unique Language?

In the course of research into the use of computers for education one of the authors, Dr. Robert K. Logan (1995, 2000), recognized that computers are both a medium of communications and an information processing tool. This is a relatively obvious observation, one that applies to all forms of verbal language, namely speech, writing, mathematical notation, science, computing and the Internet. Logan showed that each of these forms of language actually comprise an individual unique language because they each possess their own unique semantics or vocabulary and their own unique syntax or grammar, which are the two core attributes with which linguists judge whether or not a system of communication is a human language (Paivio and Begg, 1981, p. 25). Logan also showed that speech, writing, mathematics, science, computing and the Internet form an evolutionary chain of languages (Logan, 2000).

Language is communications plus informatics. The justification for regarding each of these forms of communication and information processing as a language is that each becomes a tool that makes us think differently and gives rise to new forms of expression, and each has its own unique semantics and syntax. The vocabulary and grammar of written language, for example, is quite different than that of spoken language. And the same may be said of the languages of mathematics, science, computing and the Internet/Web. The syntax and semantics of the Net and the Web is quite different from all the other languages we have considered, including computing. The unique semantical elements of the sixth language, the Internet, are its Web pages, Web sites, intranets, extranets and portal sites. The unique syntactical element of the sixth language is the hypertext that makes it possible to link all of the Web sites and Web pages in cyberspace to form one huge global document. Another unique syntactical element is the Internet protocol, which allows all of the computers connected to the Internet to form one huge global network. McLuhan's prediction of a global village has been realized. Still another unique syntactical element of the Internet is the search engines, which increase access to knowledge and information and hence provide an extra level of communication that the other forms of verbal language cannot match. Search engines also facilitate people finding each other and hence contribute to the creation of a global knowledge community.

"The Medium Is the Message" and the Internet Is a Medium with Five Collaborative Messages

The Internet, the Web and associated intranets have already begun to revolutionize communications and the flow of information, but we are only at the beginning of the impact of this new digital medium. Its most lasting and telling effect will be the way in which it transforms collaboration and KM and gives rise to new forms of knowledge processing and new tools for the creation, sharing and application of knowledge or intellectual capital. In order to understand how it will transform knowledge transactions, it is essential that we understand the way in which the Internet creates new communication channels and changes the flow of information. In order to perform this analysis we are going to rely on the techniques and ideas of Marshall McLuhan and make use of one of his most famous one-liners, "The medium is the message."

A medium, independent of the content it mediates, has its own intrinsic effects on our perceptions, which are its unique message. "The message of any medium or technology is the change of scale or pace or pattern that it introduces into human affairs. The railway did not introduce movement or transportation or wheel or road into human society, but it accelerated and enlarged the scale of previous human functions, creating totally new kinds of cities and new kinds of work and leisure. This happened whether the railway functioned in a tropical or northern environment, and is quite independent of the freight or content of the railway medium" (McLuhan, 1964, p. 8). What McLuhan writes about the railroad applies with equal validity to the media of print, computers and now the Internet and the Web. "The medium is the message" because it is the "medium that shapes and controls the scale and form of human association and action" (McLuhan, 1964, p. 9). "The effects of a medium impose a new environment and set of sensibilities upon its users" (Logan, 2000, p. 18).

Every medium has a unique message independent of the content that it carries and our analysis has revealed that there are five unique messages of the Internet and the Web. We reached this conclusion on the basis of an extensive study of life insurance company Web sites we performed for LIMRA International, a Hartford-based think tank serving the life insurance industry (ibid., p. 286). If we can exploit these five collaborative messages, then we will be able to use this medium to its fullest capacity, instead of using it merely as an electronic billboard. A mistake that the users of a new medium frequently make is that instead of using the new medium to create new applications they only use it to marginally improve on an existing application of the older medium. For example, the printing press at first was used solely to make multiple copies of existing hand-written manuscripts before new genres were created that could take full advantage of its unique features.

Some media possess some of the five features of the Internet, such as the telephone, which makes two-way communication possible, but no other medium possesses all five collaborative messages of the Internet. To recap, the five collaborative messages are:

• The two-way flow of information,
• The ease of access to information enhanced by information design,
• Continuous learning,
• Alignment, and
• The creation of community.

Let us now examine how each of these five unique features of the Internet can be exploited to achieve our objectives of using the Internet as a collaboration and KM tool and medium.

The Two-Way Flow of Information

Many browsers of the Internet and creators of Web sites think of these media merely in terms of the one-way flow of information. They use the email feature as though it was a glorified fax facility that makes sending copies of the same message to multiple parties so much easier than a fax machine. There are even executives who have their administrative assistants read their email for them or print them out and deposit them like a telegram on their desk. They then dictate their response to their assistant, who posts it for them in their email account. This use of email loses the whole spirit of the two-way, back-and-forth flow of ideas that makes email such a dynamic and powerful tool for knowledge sharing, networking and co-creating. One of the unique aspects of the two-way communication that the Internet makes possible is the speed with which the communication takes place. Although this was true of the telephone, what makes the Internet unique is the fact that written messages can be transmitted at the speed of light. Space and time both disappear with the Internet, and the world, as McLuhan said, truly shrinks to the dimension of a global village.

A sub-optimal use of the Internet is non-interactive Web sites, which merely transmit data or information without providing their visitors with any opportunity to feed back information or to act upon the information they have encountered. Many creators of Web sites fool themselves into believing that they have created an interactive Web site merely because they have created some engaging graphic designs that momentarily catch the eye and duplicate a visual effect of a video medium like television or a CD-ROM. The only interactivity that counts from the perspective of a meaningful exchange of knowledge or ideas is one in which people are communicating or dialoguing back and forth with each other. To use a Web site merely to transmit a message without encouraging visitors to feed back information and communicate is to fail to properly exploit this new medium. First, one loses the opportunity to engage one's visitors and maintain their interest. The visitor to a Web site is actually looking for interaction—otherwise they would be using some other noninteractive medium. A noninteractive site will ultimately fail to engage the interest of the visitors for very many visits. Second, one loses the opportunity to promote dialogue, which is the very foundation of knowledge sharing and the creation of community. Without a channel for two-way interaction, the visitor becomes a passive consumer of information instead of a potential collaborator who might be able to provide valuable feedback.

Also, dialogue is a necessary condition for the creation of new knowledge, as one learns about the experiences of others that parallel their own experiences. One learns by sharing and comparing experiences with others who share similar interests and concerns. Knowledge never has been created in isolation but historically by communities and schools of thought where individuals are in communication and dialogue with each other, as we pointed out in Chapter 2 in the section entitled Knowledge Is Created by a Community. The myth that knowledge is created by a solitary thinker working alone in a library or a laboratory is exactly that, a myth. Alexander the Great, who brought Greek culture to the world, was a student of Aristotle, who was a student of Plato, who was a student of Socrates. Pythagorean societies, Plato's Academy, Aristotle's Lyceum, the great libraries at Alexandria and Permagon, the religious monasteries of Asia and Europe, Jewish Talmudic institutions and the European universities of the Middle Ages are all examples of knowledge communities that thrived on dialogue and the sharing of experiences. In a knowledge community the thoughts, ideas, concepts, information and knowledge of many different people are working together to create a synthesis and hence new forms of knowledge that are more powerful than the production of any single individual. Now, with the Internet, that dialogue does not have to be limited to those who are living within a local geographic proximity to each other. It can happen on a day-to-day basis by members of a worldwide community because of the two-way communication capacity of the Internet.

An interesting example of this is illustrated by the way that Otis Elevator Co. is making use of Vignette technology to set up Web-enabled two-way communication with its customers across the globe. It operates 51 distinct sites in 26 different languages, which provide "online account management, customer communications and various other customer services...[including] e-Direct which allows customers to create specifications for new elevators, place orders, and track projects and e-Service where customers can monitor their own company's elevator operations" (www.vignette.com, 2003). As a result of this facility Otis is assured the loyalty of its customers.

The Ease of Access to Information Is Enhanced by Information Design

The ease of access to information and the speed with which it is transmitted are some of the chief advantages of the Internet for delivering training, promoting dialogue and sharing knowledge. The hypertext of the World Wide Web allows one to provide information and lessons at different levels of depth and detail that users can access in the order that makes the most sense for them and that best accommodates their individual learning styles. Hypertext and search engines also allow the pooling of information and explicit knowledge within the extended organization, which includes the organization's personnel as well as their customers and suppliers. The trick, however, is to present information—explicit knowledge, ideas, proposals or lessonware—in a format that makes it easily accessible, attractive and engaging so as to avoid information glut. This requires an understanding of the techniques of information design. Interestingly enough, it is not flashy designs that make for a successful exchange of information and ideas, but rather a carefully thought out presentation of information in easily digestible chunks. Flashy presentations or "eye candy" catch the eye initially, but in the long run people tire of them. In the end, people are seeking information and intellectual engagement in the use of a knowledge network and this focus should never be sacrificed for the sake of flash. There is nothing wrong with attractive design and amusing graphics, but they should always enhance learning and dialogue, not compete with it or waste time.

Apropos of not wasting time, the three cardinal rules for information design on the Internet are:

1. Users do not like to wait,
2. They do not like to scroll, and
3. They do not like to read.

We live in an era of rapid change, when the speed of response and the speed to market are critical for success. "Satisfaction must be delivered faster than fast. The Internet has compressed, almost eliminated, the time available to please customers. Providing optimal and just-sufficient information to people is critical to capturing the fleeting moment-of-opportunity" (KM World Editorial, 1999). Remaining competitive will require just-in-time responses to rapidly changing conditions. It is often difficult for organizations to bring together a team face-to-face to meet a challenge that is time sensitive. This is where a properly organized intranet can be invaluable. Internet technology closes gaps in both space and time.

Making an investment in making information readily available to all members of an organization has a number of positive effects, as was borne out by the experience of Sinclair Knight Merz, one of Australia's leading global professional services consulting firms. They made use of Open Text's Livelink to create what they called the "Worldwide information-Sharing Environment (WiSE), an infrastructure designed to improve the global management of documents and communication." The system contributed to making Sinclair Knight Merz a collaborative organization, as Peter Nevin, one of its managers, concluded: "Our business is a combination of knowledge and people, and we aim to deliver world-leading skills through local operations. Livelink has freed both up to ensure that wherever project teams are located, they have the support and experience of any and all their colleagues across the world. In short, Livelink has transformed us into a true collaborative enterprise" (www.opentext.com, 2003).

Another example of the link between ease of access to information and collaboration comes from Ford Motor Co. which prides itself on its history of making use of IT and a company-wide intranet.

> Today Ford's Intranet is used daily by 15,000 people from 800 facilities and 150 manufacturing plants worldwide. It contains over 1,000 Websites and upwards of one million documents. The Ford team is now working to create a collaborative work environment that uses the universal accessibility of the Web to bring together the resources and the people required to enhance its competitiveness in global markets. Today the eRoom solution is the cornerstone for Ford's extended enterprise collaboration. (www.documentum.com, 2003)

The importance of information design so that knowledge workers are comfortable within the information environment in which they work is underscored by the experience at Hill & Knowlton with their collaborative knowledge network:

> Because HK.net is accessible via a Web browser, an email client, or a file folder system, it allows each user to work in the manner he or she is most accustomed to working, requiring no change in procedure for account teams who are used to handling information in specific patterns. Similarly, because HK.net is Web-based, employees and clients can exchange information and publish email messages, presentations and documents with no administrative intervention or technical support. Instead, teams can instantly create online spaces for collaboration and manage the organization of saved information within the system. Consequently, HK.net has been able to avoid the traditional pitfalls of technology investments that consume time and money to implement and then remain unused because they require massive changes in employee habits and company practices. Instead, HK.net has gained widespread popularity and now serves as a vital asset in acquiring new business. HK.net is currently accessed by over 1,700 employees and clients. (Graham interview, 2003)

Continuous Learning

The Internet is a natural medium for continuous learning because of its two-way communication and its ease of access to information. Students can take a course or share knowledge at their convenience at work or at home. They can review or revisit material whenever they want or need to. Instructors, coaches and mentors can be made available via email. If an enterprise creates a knowledge network stocked with learning and dialoguing tools, motivated employees will use it to increase their store of knowledge. It is therefore essential in creating such a facility to provide users with hard information and access to explicit knowledge so that they can learn about new ideas, upgrade their skills and add to the human capital of the organization.

The Internet promotes continuous learning because it is so easily accessible and hence users can pursue educational activities at any place and any time whenever they have free time and are in the mood for learning something new. They do not have to conform to a schedule not of their own making, as is the case with classroom learning. They can pursue an almost unlimited number of topics depending on their interests and their needs. The Net and the Web have the following features that make learning more attractive, entertaining and effective:

1. Many graphical interfaces,
2. Interactivity in which the user can experience instant feedback, reinforcing a learning experience,
3. Two-way communication that enables users to dialogue with other students, subject experts, coaches and mentors,
4. The ability to quickly research a topic of interest and pursue multiple paths to one's goals,
5. The ability to work at one's own pace in an environment of one's own making, and
6. The choice of different learning environments to find a format compatible with one's learning style.

The Internet has great appeal for the post-TV generation. Surfing the Net is not a substitute for the learning that takes place through reading, doing or dialoguing face to face, but it is another channel that can provide a true learning environment because of its interactivity and two-way communication possibilities, especially when making use of a Web-enabled collaborative tool like WebEx or NetMeeting. By combining graphics and text the World Wide Web appeals to those users who have grown up with television, which dramatically reduced their attention span as compared to the pre-TV generations. This insight explains why users do not like to wait, read or scroll.

In addition to accessing information and explicit knowledge, there is another dimension to continuous learning that involves the sharing of tacit knowledge among the members of a knowledge network connected by an intranet. To achieve this goal it is important to provide members of the community with access to each other so that they can find each other and identify their common interests. Having made contact, the members of the putative knowledge community must have the appropriate communication and knowledge-sharing tools so that they can learn and co-create new knowledge together. This will provide a value-added resource to an organization's work and learning environment and an increase in its structural capital that allows co-workers not located in the same place to collaborate. The knowledge network can also be extended to include both suppliers and customers. Adding suppliers to the knowledge network will increase structural capital by integrating their knowledge into the organization, while adding customers to the knowledge network will increase the organization's customer capital. Continuous learning is good for business because it builds all three elements of intellectual capital: human capital through the individual's personal development, structural capital by sharing tacit knowledge within the organization and customer capital by including customers in the organization's knowledge network.

Turner Construction Company, based in Dallas with US $6.3 billion in sales in 2001 and 45 offices across the U.S., has invested heavily in continuous learning because of the important role it plays in the success of the company. Using Open Text software, it built a collaborative knowledge network providing users with many online training courses and other sources of information. "Personnel trends indicate that it is critical for the workforce of the present and future to develop broader and deeper skills through a continuous education process. Through Turner University (www.turneruniversity.com), individuals have the opportunity to take online courses that can enhance job performance and personal goals, adding value to both their company and clients. At the same time, Turner is adding significant worth to its clients and strengthening relationships with its partners," said Thomas C. Leppert, Chairman and CEO of Turner. "Turner is taking a leadership role in our industry to be the first to develop an online university with construction-related educational courses," said James I. Mitnick, Senior Vice President and creator of the TKN concept. "Through Turner Knowledge Network (TKN), Turner can reach tens of thousands of individuals with consistent content on a just-in-time basis, 24/7, anywhere in the world. Our goals for Turner Knowledge Network extend well into the future to become the 'go to' place for construction learning in the United States. We will continue to work cooperatively with our partners to shape TKN's evolution as the number one online resource in the construction industry" (Turner, news release, 2003).

Online training courses are successfully competing with classroom training. Web-enabled learning systems, such as Centra's Symposium, are able to combine the convenience of online training with the collaborative interactions of classroom training. Armstrong Building Products Operations (BPO) used Symposium to train all its sales representatives throughout the U.S. in a format whereby the users could learn by doing. "Symposium's application sharing capabilities allow us to host the sales automation application on a PC at headquarters and simultaneously walk all participants through the new features of the product. If an individual does not understand something, we give them control of the application so they can actually input data or work through a process. It is incredibly effective," said BPO's Dennis Armstrong. "BPO wanted to retain the traditional collaboration between leader and participants, believing interactivity is an important part of the learning experience. Symposium meets that need, keeping participants engaged by enabling them to talk to the session leader, asking questions and receiving immediate answers. Participants can raise their hands, answer yes or no, and give feedback in real time. Leaders can track individual participants to ensure they understand the material and are keeping pace with other participants" (www.centra.com, 2003). Collaborative learning is a useful tool in building a collaborative organization and should be exploited whenever possible.

Alignment

The Internet, through the World Wide Web, provides a medium or platform for the integration and alignment of an organization's business processes. Enterprise Resource Planning (ERP) software solutions also promote alignment because they allow a customer to order an entire business solution from an organization without having to deal with individual business units. In those cases where ERP failed, the failure was due to the lack of a collaborative spirit among the different business units in the organization.

Before the existence of personal computers and the Internet, the various processes that constituted one's business activities could be easily divided into compartmentalized activities, which could be addressed one at a time. This is the basis of the specialization that was so successfully used during the Industrial Era. This way of doing things is slowly changing as a result of computers and the Internet, which integrates so many of today's business functions. An intranet configured as a knowledge network also permits the integration of the knowledge and learning activities of all the staff of an organization. It makes knowledge and information resources available to everyone and allows the organization to align and integrate its knowledge creation activities, which in turn leads to synergy.

Once a knowledge network is in place and functioning internally, the next logical step is to open a component of the network to the enterprise's partners, namely, its suppliers and customers. Aligning one's interest and knowledge activities with one's partners makes good business sense.

The Internet provides an organization with the potential for total connectivity with all of its customers and suppliers and, hence, permits the integration of a number of its key activities, including marketing, advertising, sales, order fulfillment, distribution, customer support, market research, market feedback and product research and design. For these activities to work well together, they must be coordinated and aligned so that they are working together within a strategy to achieve the overall goals or objectives of the organization. The alignment team must therefore consist of experts in marketing, communications and information technology.

This approach is similar to the one that Charles Savage advocates in his book *Fifth Generation Management* (1996, pp. 92, 132): "The word customer may no longer be appropriate; perhaps we could use the word 'co-creators' because we will be creating our futures together....Working 'with' (as opposed to 'for') requires a cultural change, a change in which trust and openness are essential and we discover and build upon one another's capabilities."

When considering alignment we must keep in mind that alignment requires integration but goes beyond mere integration. Business Process Reengineering (BPR) was a technique that integrated business processes in such a way so as to maximize the efficiencies of computing by insuring an integrated flow of information and work. Alignment takes the process of integration represented by BPR a step further. BPR redesigns business processes so as to achieve a continuous flow of information without wasting time between handoffs from one working group to another. Alignment takes those reengineered processes and aligns them so that the processes are all working to achieve the same overall goal of the organization, eliminating situations where profits centers, by pursuing their narrow goals, are working at cross purposes to each other. Alignment is to the Internet and connectivity what BPR is to computing.

Microcomputers allowed working groups or profit centers within an organization to pursue their own information-processing strategies to fulfill the tactical objectives of their particular division. These subdivisions often found themselves in conflict with each other and with their MIS department. MIS departments lost control of the information-processing activity within their organization and the organization as a whole lost a certain degree of coherency or alignment. With client/server systems and BPR, MIS departments were able to seize control of the computing agenda, but this did not bring working groups back into alignment.

The computing climate is once again undergoing volatile change because of the rapidity with which the Internet and the World Wide

Web are penetrating the business world. The connectivity of the Internet is poised once again to reconfigure the information and communication functions of the organization and hence reconfigure business processes so that they are more aligned. Each time a new information technology emerges, a period of chaos and rapid change occurs in which new applications and methodologies are discovered that are often in conflict with the previous way of doing things. From this chaos a new level of order emerges, as has been pointed out by Prigogene and Stengers in *Order Out of Chaos* (1984).

At first the older patterns are repeated using the new technology, or as Marshall McLuhan long ago pointed out, the content of a new medium is always some older medium. The first marketing uses of the Internet were traditional advertising techniques in which the content of television and print ads were repurposed for Web sites. The true leverage of Internet technology and the increased connectivity it provides will not happen until this new medium is fully digested, understood and integrated into and aligned with the traditional objectives of the organization. The organization and its technology form a nonlinear dynamic system so that as the Internet begins to penetrate the corporate psyche, the new capabilities of the Internet manifest themselves and the objectives or goals of the organization will begin to change.

The ability of the Net and the Web to facilitate global communications linking the organization with its customers is also ideal for setting up internal communications links within an organization so as to align the activities of the organization's staff. Intranets can be used to create knowledge networks or collaborative learning environments in which the tools and resources for knowledge sharing and co-creation are only a mouse click away. In Chapter 1 we showed the effectiveness of Collaboration in Product Development (CPD), in which a Web-enabled collaborative environment brings together a team with a diverse background and aligns their project. In the case of Ford's CPD, eRoom brought together "product engineers, program managers, systems integrators, purchasing agents, and others from both the development firm and its suppliers" (www.documentum.com, 2003).

Once again we remind readers that in order to be effective these intranet-based systems must complement face-to-face interactions where people get to know each other personally. Merely by creating such an environment the members of an organization will become better informed of each other's activities and a certain degree of alignment will automatically fall into place. This process of creating a collaborative learning environment can be enhanced by individuals within the organization creating their own home pages and those of their working group. This will contribute to the coherency of the organization's outside communications and the alignment of its operations and activities. It allows an organization to share its knowledge more readily. In Chapter 6 we will fully explore in detail the ways to build a collaborative learning environment.

The Creation of Community

Perhaps the most important of all the features of the Internet is the way in which it creates community. It does so through the exploitation of the other four messages of the Internet, namely two-way communication (which makes people feel involved), ease of access to information through information design (which makes people feel that their needs are being looked after), continuous learning (which makes people feel that their minds are engaged and respected) and alignment (which integrates the needs of an organization with all of its stakeholders, including its customers and its suppliers). An intranet-based knowledge network, by being available 24 hours a day, seven days a week, is always there for members of the enterprise's community, supporting their information needs and providing an environment for learning, knowledge creation and sharing and the development of new ideas, products, services and approaches to doing business. It also embraces the new notion that the competition of the past is being replaced by "co-opetition," which is a blend of cooperation and competition, and is characteristic of the new way of doing business. Competitors are not just external, they are also internal. There is frequent competition among business units within an organization. This is the first place to begin building co-opetition.

We want to offer a few little caveats to our thesis that the Internet is a technology that naturally creates community. First, the Internet does not automatically create community. Careful thought and planning must go into creating a community on the Net. Secondly, once created, a community does not go into automatic pilot, but rather it must be sustained by creating ongoing activities or else it loses its original impetus or steam. Thirdly, building or sustaining a community with Internet technology, without a certain amount of face-to-face meetings, is extremely difficult. We have found that the most effective use of the Internet as a community building tool is when it is used to sustain a community of practice or interest that has had a chance to meet face to face and bond with each other.

How Do the Five Messages of the Internet Facilitate Collaboration?

Before exploring the ways in which the Internet can contribute to collaboration, it is important that we recognize that Internet technology is merely an enabler and that there is a lot more to KM and collaborative learning than net-based communications. Collaboration and KM is about people working together in a very intimate way, and that requires a lot of face-to-face interaction. What Internet technology can do is help channel and guide those interactions so that they are more productive. Internet technology can be used to bring together the right people and to identify the different skills and experiences required for a particular project, i.e., to find the right people to collaborate with. Internet technology can be used to bring cohesiveness and alignment to the knowledging activities of an enterprise or a community, but it cannot be a substitute for the intellectual development of the individual members of the team using the traditional media of oral dialoguing and conferencing face to face, such as in working lunches, war rooms, seminars; the use of the telephone and fax; the study and reading of written texts; the preparation of written reports and texts; as well as good old-fashioned solitary reflection and thinking. The Internet is only one ingredient in the collaboration and KM equation, but it can play an important role as the glue that keeps an intricate web of co-workers and co-creators linked to each other, although it is no substitute for face-to-face interaction. "It is not enough to just be able to connect and access. You need to interact synchronously. Some think internetworking and automation may eliminate the need for person-to-person interaction. This is wrong and dangerous" (KM World Editorial, 1999). "Though today's technology vendors promise that virtual meetings are as effective as those conducted in person, many experts disagree. To be most effective, participants in virtual communities need occasional opportunities to meet face to face. Face time facilitates communication, but more importantly it allows members to shape deeper knowledge and build mutual trust. There is ample evidence that collaborative efforts are less effective without some face-to-face encounters" (Athey, 2002, p. 20).

With this understanding of the enabling role of the Internet, let us examine its five unique messages, (1) the two-way flow of information; (2) information design and the ease of access to information; (3) continuous learning; (4) alignment; and (5) community and how they can contribute to collaboration and KM.

1. There are a number of ways in which the two-way flow of information that characterizes Internet technology can contribute to KM activities. These include:

   • Knowledge sharing,

   • Mentoring and coaching to facilitate learning,

   • Dialoguing, whereby new knowledge is created,

   • Identifying, defining and refining shared values,

   • Identifying, defining and refining shared goals and objectives,

   • Creating project teams,

   • Obtaining just-in-time help and assistance, and

   • Creating and maintaining a casebase and best practices log.

2. Information design and the ease of access to information with Internet technology contributes to collaboration and KM because:

   • Knowledge is the strategic use of information to achieve a goal or an objective and hence information is the raw material of KM,

   • Good information design facilitates the learning process and the acquisition of knowledge,

   • Presenting or displaying information and explicit knowledge in easily digested chunks makes them easier to manage,

   • Hyperlinking and the use of search engines makes information and explicit knowledge easier to manage,

   • Just-in-time and real-time information and explicit knowledge is essential for KM in today's rapidly changing environment, and

   • Information is essential for finding collaboration partners.

3. By serving as a medium for continuous learning, Internet technology facilitates knowledge sharing by:

   • Providing learning materials on each user's workstation,

- Allowing easy access to a virtually unlimited supply of information,
- Allowing for interactivity with information and explicit knowledge,
- Providing two-way communication and hence dialogue with co-workers, customers and suppliers to achieve organizational objectives and goals, and
- Finding people to collaborate with for learning, sharing experiences and knowledge, co-creating new knowledge, implementing projects and coordinating activities by pooling knowledge.

4. Internet technology aligns and integrates the learning and working environments of the organization as a whole and for each of the individual members of the organization because:
   - An intranet allows for collaboration through the pooling and alignment of knowledge within an organization so that individuals can build on each other's knowledge to create new knowledge structures,
   - An intranet can be used to align personnel that might not ordinarily come into contact with each other. This allows them to align their activities, pool their tacit knowledge and easily form working groups for special projects. The careful organization and design of information about people, such as their competencies, experiences, aspirations and values, is essential to achieve these objectives. It is not only what you know but who you know that is essential for collaboration and KM, and
   - Ultimately an intranet allows for the alignment of all of the knowledge within an organization with its objectives and goals.

5. Internet technology facilitates the creation of community by:
   - Facilitating dialogue by taking advantage of two-way communication,
   - Providing additional channels for the sharing of ideas, knowledge and information,
   - Facilitating the creation of COPs and knowledge networks, especially among participants who might not enjoy geographic proximity, and

- Creating an environment and spirit so that individuals will want to collaborate and share knowledge.

Of the five messages of the Internet, the most powerful for stimulating collaboration is community, and certainly there can be no collaboration of any value without a strong sense of community. "Some may be tempted to view community as one of those squishy words that rarely shows up at the top of a CEO's agenda. But research and experience suggest that collaborative efforts without a strong basis in social cohesion and a sense of community fall short in creating value" (Athey, 2002, p. 10).

As a result of the effects of the five collaborative messages of the Internet, the way in which Web documents are created is often collaborative because of the very nature of the medium. David Weinberger (1999b) points out that documents traditionally "(1) are by an individual, (2) take a position on some topic (and) (3) are published when done." But as Weinberger points out, documents on Web sites are the opposite of this. They are started by a single author "but the site's value comes from the interactive content from many contributors."

The Correspondence between the Five Collaborative Messages of the Internet and Savage's Five Principles of Knowledge Networking

In a chapter entitled Knowledge Networking in his book *Fifth Generation Management* Charles Savage identifies five principles that characterize the Knowledge Era and parallel the five collaborative messages of the Internet.

The parallel of our five collaborative messages of the Internet and Savage's five principles, which we will demonstrate below, confirms for us that the Internet is the appropriate model and medium for collaboration and KM. Savage suggests "that there are five conceptual principles of the early Knowledge Era: (1) peer-to-peer knowledge networking, (2) the integrative process, (3) work as dialogue, (4) human time and timing, and (5) virtual enterprising and dynamic teaming" (Savage, 1996, p. 199). We have found the following correspondence between his five principles of the knowledge era and the five collaborative message of the Internet:

Savage's Five Principles	Five Collaborative Messages of the Internet
1. peer-to-peer knowledge networking	1. two-way communication
2. the integrative process	2. alignment
3. work as dialogue	3. continuous learning
4. human timing and time	4. ease of access to information through information design
5. virtual enterprising and dynamic teaming	5. community

1. Peer-to-Peer Knowledge Networking and the Equivalence of Two-Way Communication

"Peer-to-peer knowledge networking has three aspects: technology, information, and people. The technology of peer-to-peer networking allows each mode to communicate directly with every other node, without having to filter through a hierarchical arrangement" (ibid.). What Savage is describing is the two-way communication capacity of the Internet, which when combined with the other features of the Internet, such as community building and alignment, can result in the type of peer-to-peer knowledge networking that Savage describes.

2. The Integrative Process and the Equivalence of Alignment

These two categories are virtually identical; they only differ in their formulation. Alignment is also a key concept for Savage, who speaks of the need to align the organization's knowledge and vision with the customer's needs or anticipations: "The alignment process is critical for management…to see and respond quickly to customer signals" (ibid., p. 227).

3. Work as Dialogue and the Equivalence of Continuous Learning

"Work then involves processes and products.….We grow as we are able to master a process and see the results of the effort embodied in the product.…Our mastery of the process and the resulting product inspire us to want to use our skills, vision, and knowledge to bring out variations on the product by varying our techniques. This is really a self-dialogue, combining vision and knowledge in a dialogue with ourselves and others. When we are engaged in a process that is creative, innovative, or experimental, what we are learning becomes available for future efforts" (ibid., pp. 207-10). For Savage, work or mastering a process is a continuous learning process and a form of self-dialogue.

Savage wrote that "Feedback from the process is important in order to improve it; feedback from the use of the product will add knowledge and vision as the next version is developed and produced" (ibid.). The Internet is the perfect tool for collecting feedback for products and building knowledge and a vision to improve them. And this process can be greatly enhanced through the use of the Internet.

4. Human Timing and Time and the Equivalence of Ease of Access to Information through Information Design

In our description of the ease of access to information through information design, above, we emphasized the importance of just-in-time information to remain competitive in a time of rapidly changing conditions. Savage also stresses the importance of timing: "Timing is even more critical today in terms of time-to-market, windows of opportunity, and cycle time" (ibid., p. 215).

Information design in cyberspace is the sensitivity to the timing of the delivery of information to the reader or user. What is so powerful about hypertext is that readers or users can order the timing of when they access information as their interests dictate and hence they can create alternative futures depending on their needs.

There is also the need of the firm to organize its legacy information, including its history, so that it is readily available to its personnel on an as-needed basis. Savage makes this point in his discussion of human time and timing: "Notice how little thought is given to our company's legacy, the knowledge that is distributed among file drawers, in hundreds of different databases, and in the hands and eyes of our professionals. It is the legacy that is really the key asset of the enterprise....We must continually arrange and rearrange its significant patterns to use it" (ibid., pp. 221-22). In other words, Savage is suggesting that effort must be made to make information easily accessible through information design.

5. *Virtual Enterprising and Dynamic Teaming and the Equivalence of Community*

Virtual enterprising and dynamic teaming require the existence of community, as pointed out by Savage (ibid., pp. 232-33): "Virtual enterprising treats groups of activities as projects, with teams working in an iterative and parallel manner to form a collage of teams....Working together, on a peer-to-peer basis...these dynamic teams are the crafts-teams of the enterprise. They embody work as dialogue, using human time and a strong sense of market timing."

A community that has channels of communication available, like an intranet for the exchange and sharing of experiences, will often begin to self-organize and create opportunities for virtual enterprising and platforms for dynamic teaming if it can find a common goal or task. "Research studies indicate that geographically dispersed teams can often work as effectively as co-located teams, if not more so. A dispersed group must communicate more explicitly, requiring clarity of thought, whereas co-located groups often tend to communicate haphazardly. Dispersed groups also periodically find ways to communicate face to face" (ibid., p. 231).

Clearly, the five conceptual principles formulated by Savage to characterize the Knowledge Era parallel the five collaborative messages of the Internet, which characterize the unique way in which this medium shapes the interactions of its users. This is not to suggest that the use of Internet technology will automatically lead to Knowledge Era forms of commerce involving virtual enterprising and dynamic teaming, but the Internet is certainly an important tool in leading the way to this new form of commerce. The parallel between Savage's observations of Knowledge Era business activities and our independent observations of the effects and impacts of the Internet support the main thesis of this book—that interconnectivity of Internet technology and KM form an autocatalytic system of mutual support.

The Five Collaborative Messages of the Internet and Senge's Fifth Discipline Approach

As with Savage's model there is an overlap of Senge's approach and the five collaborative messages of the Internet, although the correspondence is not quite as direct. We remind the reader that Senge proposed that it takes five disciplines to create a learning organization, namely systems thinking, personal mastery, mental models, building shared vision and team learning. There is a fairly direct connection of personal mastery and team learning with continuous learning. Both systems thinking and team learning contribute to alignment and vice versa. There is a similar connection between community and alignment, on the one hand, and building a shared vision and mental models, on the other hand. Community and alignment contribute to building a shared vision and mental models and, vice versa, a shared vision and mental models contribute to building community and alignment. Finally two-way communication and the ease of access to information are necessary tools for building a shared vision and mental models.

By comparing our five collaborative messages of the Internet model with those of Senge and Savage we are not suggesting that one model is any better than another. They are basically independent mappings of the collaboration space by three different approaches with slightly different emphases. Senge focuses on the creation of a learning organization through the use of systems theory, while Savage focuses on KM through the use of dynamic teaming. Our approach makes use of the Internet both as a medium for and a model of collaboration. The three approaches, Senge's, Savage's and our own, are akin to three different coordinates systems and as such they each provide different insights into the challenge of developing collaboration and, hence, each is useful in its own way. Having made these comparisons we now proceed to elaborate on our model of a collaborative organization.

The Logan-Stokes Model of Collaboration

We believe there are seven basic organizational building blocks from which one can construct a successful collaborative organization, because a successful organization is essentially a group of individuals who work together with:

1. The same **vision**,
2. A **leadership** they respect,
3. A level of **trust**,
4. Common **goals**,
5. **Strategies** for achieving those goals,

6. A set of **tactical objectives** needed to carry out their strategy, and who

7. Take **action and implement** their goals, strategies and tactical objectives to guide their day-to-day operations.

The five collaborative messages of the Internet as applied to an organization, namely two-way communication, ease of access to information, continuous learning, alignment and community are critical for developing these seven organizational building blocks. For an organization to be collaborative, people who make up the organization must form a community with a shared vision and an ability to trust and respect each other and the leadership of the organization. By a shared vision we mean an image of the kind of future that the members of the organization want to create, guided by their values and fueled by their knowledge. Leadership based on community and two-way communication not only emanates from the senior executives but is diffused throughout the organization by managers and employees who are trusted, empowered and motivated. In an economic environment where change is so rapid, the vision and the goals of the organization must be continually updated, which requires continuous learning to keep up with the needs and demands of the organization's customers.

In order to create an atmosphere of trust there must be a sense of community within the organization in which there is two-way communication and easy access to information. To create a sense of community, on the other hand, there must be both trust and a shared vision. Also, in order to have all the members of the organization motivated and ready to embrace the plan of action, there must be an alignment of the individual goals of the employees and their managers and the goals of the organization as a whole. Alignment is also necessary for the coordination required to carry out the organization's strategies for achieving its goals. Once a strategy is in place, tactical objectives must be formulated that will require the ease of access to information and two-way communication. Finally, the implementation of the action plan based on these tactical objectives will require all five collaborative messages: a sense of community to motivate people to collaborate and work together, continuous learning to have the skills to carry out one's assignment, alignment, the ease of access to information and the two-way communication to ensure the coordination of the individual actions required to implement the action plan to realize the tactical objectives, the strategy, the goals and the vision of the organization. In short, each of the five collaborative messages of the Internet contribute in varying degrees to the realization of the seven basic organizational building blocks that make for a successful collaborative organization.

Our model of collaboration within an organization is based on the notion that the Internet/Web has demonstrated its natural capacity for collaboration, and therefore the five characteristics that we have identified as the five collaborative messages of the Internet will naturally promote collaboration. As such, we use them as our model or metaphor for collaboration within an organization. They are the ideals that a collaborative organization must strive for because together they help the organization to formulate its vision, provide leadership, achieve trust, identify its goals, devise its strategy and tactical objectives and deploy and implement its action plan.

Although all five collaborative messages of the Internet contribute to the strengthening of the seven organizational building blocks of which a successful collaborative organization is composed, some of the messages are more strongly correlated with the building blocks than others. Table 4.1 describes these correlations and summarizes the discussion in the above paragraphs.

Table 4.1: Correlation of Seven Building Blocks with Five Messages

1. Vision	requires	• community, continuous learning
2. Leadership	requires	• community, continuous learning, two-way communication
3. Trust	requires	• community, ease of access to information
4. Goals	require	• continuous learning
5. Strategies	require	• alignment, ease of access to information
6. Tactical Objectives	require	• alignment, ease of access to information, two-way communication
7. Action and Implementation	require	• continuous learning, alignment, ease of access to information, two-way communication, community

The relationship of the seven organizational building blocks of a successful collaborative organization and the five collaborative messages of the Internet is not a simple causal one, as a cursory reading of Table 4.1 above might indicate. The relationship is reflexive and iterative in that the seven building blocks require the five collaborative messages, as indicated above, and the five collaborative messages depend on all seven of the building blocks, but the strongest correlations are as listed in Table 4.2.

Table 4.2: Correlation of Five Messages with Seven Building Blocks

1. Two-way flow of information	through	a strategy, an action plan
2. Ease of access to information	through	a strategy, an action plan
3. Continuous learning	through	a shared vision, common goals
4. Alignment	through	a shared vision, trust, common goals, leadership
5. Creation of community	through	a shared vision, trust, common goals, leadership

The reason that the five collaborative messages of the Internet and the seven building blocks of a successful collaborative organization are so intertwined and their relationship is nonlinear is that a collaborative organization is a complex adaptive system. Although the main thesis of our book, as incorporated in our title, is an organization must "collaborate to compete," it is also true that collaboration makes an organization adaptive and, hence, ensures that it can sustain itself. In today's networked global economy, being competitive, sustainable and adaptive are all synonymous. All organizations are complex, nonlinear systems, but it is only those organizations that achieve a certain level of collaboration that become adaptive, particularly in an environment that is rapidly changing.

When we suggest that collaboration can be facilitated by the five collaborative messages of the Internet, we are not suggesting that the Internet is the only, or even the primary, channel of communication for collaboration and KM. Rather we are suggesting that the communications and interactions that take place within the organization should always embrace or mimic the five collaborative messages of the Internet as principles that promote and facilitate collaboration. As to what is the most appropriate medium for collaboration, there is no one particular medium that stands out above all the rest. Rather, every possible medium that facilitates two-way communication, ease of access to information, continuous learning, alignment and community should be used, and therefore includes face-to-face meetings in groups or between individuals, telephone conversations, video conferences, email, listservs, Web sites, intranets, Web-enabled collaborative technology, snail mail, white papers, journals, magazines and e-zines. We will have more to say in Chapter 6 as to what information technology and media should be deployed to maximize collaboration.

In addition to the correlation we have suggested between the five collaborative messages of the Internet and the seven organizational basic building blocks of which a successful collaborative organization is composed, we would also like to include in our model of collaborative knowledge management the notion of knowledge capital that we discussed in Chapter 2. We remind the reader that knowledge capital consists of three basic components, namely human capital, structural capital and customer capital, which are dynamically linked. We believe that these different forms of capital and their interactions with each other are useful because they help us understand how to make connections for the purpose of collaboration between the traditionally siloed areas of marketing, sales, production, R&D, finance, personnel, administration and operations. The division of knowledge capital into its basic components creates a model that can be used to facilitate the conversion of one form of knowledge capital into another, as well as coherently building new forms of knowledge by combining and aligning the basic components of knowledge capital. New knowledge is generated by the two-way flow of information between the three forms of knowledge capital.

Where human and structural capital overlap, two transformations take place:

1. Human capital in the form of tacit knowledge is transformed into structural capital through codification, and
2. Structural capital is transformed into human capital by catalyzing and framing new forms of tacit knowledge.

Where human and customer capital overlap, two more transformations take place:

1. Human capital is transformed into customer capital as employees inform or teach customers about the advantages of their products and/or services, and
2. Customer capital is transformed into human capital by customers informing or teaching employees ways to improve their products and/or services to better serve their needs.

Where structural and customer capital overlap, two more transformations take place:

1. Structural capital catalyzes and facilitates the customers interaction with the organization to generate customer capital, and
2. Customer capital is transformed into structural capital through the customer's feedback to the organization.

The Role of Values in Developing a Model of Collaborative Knowledge Management

In developing our model of collaborative knowledge management our focus to this point has been primarily on knowledge with some discussion of the need for trust and community. What has been missing from our discussion has been talk of the role of values, which is a critical factor that must be included. As we have pointed out, the failure of KM to have had a greater impact is due to the fact that the human side of the equation has not been properly taken into account. What has been missing, in our opinion, is the consideration of values. To discuss this aspect of collaborative knowledge management we must first understand the relationship between knowledge and values. The best place to start this discussion is by revisiting the difference between tacit and explicit knowledge.

Explicit knowledge, which is easily formulated, is objective, analytic and values free. Tacit knowledge, which is subjective and experientially based, tends to carry implicitly within itself the values of the person or organization possessing the tacit knowledge. As Nonaka and Takeuchi explain, new knowledge is created by the interaction of these two forms of knowledge. During a discussion of this point at a workshop on KM in May 1996, hosted at the CIBC Leadership Centre, and organized by Hubert Saint-Onge and facilitated by Charles Savage, the question arose as to how these two seemingly opposite forms of knowledge could be brought together. Having earlier in our discussions been asked to consider different topological forms when considering alternative forms of organizational development, one of us (Dr. Robert K. Logan) suggested that tacit and explicit knowledge could be thought of as lying on the opposite sides of a Möbius strip. One can create a Möbius strip by taking a strip of paper and twisting it and then connecting its two ends. If one runs a finger along the surface, one will soon discover that there is a continuous path to the opposite side of the strip from where one started. The relationship between tacit and explicit knowledge is similar to the relationship between knowledge and values, as explicit knowledge is objective and tacit knowledge is personal and value laden. The Möbius strip provides an interesting model of these two relationships. It is the twist in the strip that creates this unique topology that unites the two opposite surfaces into one continuous one. It is the same in collaborative knowledge management. What is required is a twist that links knowledge and values, as well as the tacit and the explicit.

Karl Erik Sveiby has developed an interesting understanding of the relationship of wisdom and knowledge, on the one hand, and information and data, on the other, which provides another insight into the relationship of knowledge and values. Sveiby's approach is based on the dichotomy between tacit and explicit knowledge. For Sveiby, wisdom and knowledge are tacit and difficult to represent and transfer. They can only be achieved through experience. Information and data, on the other hand, are explicit, easily represented, stored, transferred, processed and reprocessed. It takes wisdom and knowledge to write a book or an article and to choose a subject and an audience that are aligned. It takes knowledge to order the information one has gathered and to write intelligently with insight about the subject. In the end, however, what is created—the book itself—is nothing more than information and an assemblage of data. Readers, by virtue of their tacit knowledge and experiences, can use that information and data to create their own knowledge and perhaps add to their store of wisdom, but this happens only as a result of the interaction of their knowledge and wisdom with the data and information contained in the book or article. This insight is at the root of Marshall McLuhan's famous one-liner: "the user is the content."

The Value Web

We conclude the chapter by introducing the idea of the organization value web: collaboration encourages group cohesiveness, which encourages loyalty and retention, which encourages excellence and passion. The end result is the successful collaborative organization that maximizes the intelligence and innovation of its entire human resource population to best meet the challenges in today's and tomorrow's global competitive business world. An example of this is provided by Hill & Knowlton and their use of their collaborative knowledge network, HK.net.

> Our collaborative enterprise application, HK.net, helps our senior managers work with people's professional development within the firm. If you think of professional services firms and how you "care and feed" these invaluable consultants, you find that your best people want to be able to work on the exciting projects to test themselves, to increase their understanding of certain interesting issues. With HK.net the world literally opens up to them as we can give them the opportunity to work on exciting projects beyond their local practice or even the country that they are from. This engenders much more of a sense of commitment to the firm and that definitely helps our senior management team protect, what is truly our competitive differentiator, our people. (Graham, interview, 2003)

CHAPTER FIVE

Three Psychological Dimensions of Collaboration

Cognition, Emotional Intelligence and Motivation

In this chapter we examine the psychological aspects of collaboration. We begin by examining the relationship between competition and collaboration, which we show are not necessarily diametrically opposed to each other. We then describe the three psychological dimensions of collaboration, namely cognition, emotional intelligence and motivation. We conclude the chapter with a discussion of the relationship of collaboration, consensus, cooperation and teamwork and show that collaboration and consensus represent a higher level and more intimate interaction than cooperation and teamwork.

Individual and Organizational Conflict, Competition, Cooperation and Collaboration

We can look at two different orientations or work styles with respect to achieving objectives:

1. A task orientation in which the focus is on the immediate and direct achievement of short-term objectives, and

2. A relationship orientation where the primary focus is to build relationships with colleagues, customers and suppliers, with an eye to achieving long-term objectives.

At one extreme, people with high task orientation would strive to achieve their goals without much thought to its impact on their relationships with others. At the other extreme, individuals who put a very high premium on developing long-term relationships might do so at the sacrifice of achieving their short-term goals and objectives.

The ideal collaborative behavior that is desired is one in which tasks and objectives are achieved not by sacrificing relationships but rather by building productive relationships that will serve one's long-term interests. Individuals act collaboratively not just for the sake of building relationships; but rather because they can better achieve their objectives with the cooperation of their colleagues who find themselves in a similar position.

The 1974 work of Kenneth Thomas and Ralph Kilmann, the *Thomas-Kilmann Conflict Mode Instrument*, which focused on conflict management, can also teach us about collaboration. They developed an instrument based on the two dimensions of assertiveness and cooperativeness, which identifies five different types of behavioral working relationships, as displayed below.

Table 5.1: Five Types of Behavioral Working Relationships

Assertiveness	Cooperativeness	Behavioral Working Relationship
1. Low	Low	Avoiding
2. High	Low	Competing
3. Medium	Medium	Compromising
4. Low	High	Accommodating
5. High	High	Collaborating

Thomas and Kilmann (ibid.) pointed out that all the behavior modes could be useful in certain situations and each represents a different set of social interaction skills. They stated the positive benefits of each behavior mode and the negative downsides when a behavior mode was used inappropriately in a situation. They also found that an individual tended to rely more heavily on certain ways of dealing with co-workers and clients because of previous experience or personal temperament.

This matrix serves as a useful starting point for examining collaborative behavior in knowledge-based organizations. Each behavior mode can be considered an appropriate individual tactical response for a given situation. Given our focus is on collaboration as an organizational strategy, we learn that to achieve this, personnel should be encouraged to be both assertive and cooperative. Assertiveness can be encouraged by empowering personnel to take decisions and initiatives without direct managerial supervision, while cooperation can be encouraged through community-building processes.

Competition and collaboration are often thought of as opposites. One either competes or collaborates but how can one do both? The resolution of this apparent paradox is quite simple. At either the organizational level or the individual level, in order to be a partner worthy of collaboration, one must be competitive, i.e., as good as one's putative collaborative partners. Therefore, our first axiom is:

"Organizations and Individuals Must Be Competitive to Collaborate!"

But organizations and individuals cannot survive in isolation. Given the complexity of today's business climate one must collaborate to be competitive. An organization or an individual that works alone without collaborating faces the danger of quickly becoming isolated because of the rapid rate at which things change in the world of business because of the explosive nature of technological innovation. It is only through collaboration one can stay abreast. Therefore, our second axiom is:

"Organizations and Individuals Must Collaborate to Compete!"

The concept of collaboration transforms from a tactical procedure to a strategic imperative. Collaboration becomes much more than a particular outcome to negotiate toward, or one of the better of different alternatives in a team environment. It becomes a key corporate strategy for achieving sustainable world-class standing in the global knowledge economy.

An organization collaborates through its individual members. Collaboration is about human relationships. Notwithstanding the impressive collaboration technology that exists today and even with advances that will continue into the future, the collaborative creation of knowledge wealth and the willingness to share it are individual human acts. For collaboration to succeed, individuals need to be trusting and trustworthy. However, trust is not enough. Robert Axlerod, in his book

The Evolution of Cooperation (1984), demonstrates that other human qualities are essential for cooperation to succeed in the long term, especially if the other partner is not always in a cooperative mood and acts selfishly at times, as is often the case in the real world. The two most important qualities are standing up for one's rights so that a relationship does not become exploitative, and at the same time being able to forgive a transgression so as to reestablish cooperative behavior. Not surprisingly, collaboration turns out to be a complex psychological phenomenon. To understand how individuals become better collaborating partners, we now examine the psychological environment in business that supports collaboration and the important cognitive, emotional and motivational competencies that individuals must develop.

The Three Psychological Dimensions of Collaboration

Collaboration is a complex activity that involves three basic components, all three of which are necessary but not sufficient by themselves. Effective collaborators must possess the cognitive skills, the technical skills and the ability to communicate to be able to contribute to the collaboration process. They must have the emotional intelligence or social skills to be able to work with others and adapt to personalities and personal quirks different than their own. And finally they must be motivated to make the extra effort and take the care that collaboration requires. We have, therefore, grouped the skills and attitudes for developing an effective collaborative organization into three competency components, which we refer to as cognitive skills, emotional intelligence and motivation, which we measure by IQ, EQ and MQ respectively. We use the term IQ, derived from "intelligence quotient," in the metaphorical sense as a measure of analytic business skills and not as the measure of general intelligence used by educators to determine the learning capabilities of a student. In a similar fashion, EQ (emotional intelligence quotient) and MQ (motivational quotient) are also metaphorical measures, respectively, of business-related emotional intelligence and motivation. IQ is usually thought of as a static quantity that is a measure of brain capacity independent of the experiences of the individual. In our case we believe that IQ, EQ and MQ can improve as a result of education, training and experience. We use these terms as measures of competence rather than as potentiality. In Chapter 7 we will create a measure of the ability of individuals and organization to enter into collaborative relationships in terms of what we will define as the Collaboration Quotient (CQ), which will depend on IQ, EQ and MQ.

1. **IQ** measures the cognitive skills associated with business activities and includes strategic analytical thinking, creative thinking, problem-solving ability, decision-making skills, an ability to communicate and technical skills for making use of IT.

2. **EQ** measures the level of emotional intelligence associated with business activities and includes an inward-focusing component, namely emotional behavior awareness and self-management, and an outward-focusing component, namely social relationship building and maintaining skills, with a particular focus on trust building.

3. **MQ** measures the level of motivation associated with business activities and includes self-motivation and the development of social motivation to actively engage others and work with them collaboratively.

Successful collaborators must be well balanced and possess all three of these skill sets. If someone is motivated and has the cognitive skills to contribute but is unable to work with others, their contribution to the organization will be minimal. If they are not motivated, no matter how capable they are socially and intellectually, they will not contribute very much. And finally, no matter how socially skilled and motivated an individual might be, they must be able to bring new ideas to the table and therefore their technical and cognitive skills are essential for collaboration. It therefore follows that a successful collaborator is a well-rounded individual who is smart, affable and enthusiastic. We now turn to a description of the three sets of qualities required for collaboration: intellectual competencies, emotional intelligence and motivation.

Intellectual Competencies or Cognitive Skills

The intellectual competencies that can contribute to collaboration include analytic, communications and learning skills, as well as such specific skills as the ability to formulate goals, devise strategies and develop tactical objectives. Intellectual competency includes the ability to remain informed of the latest developments in one's field and hence the ability to pursue continuous learning.

The analytic skills include the data processing, information processing and knowledge processing skills that we discussed in detail in Chapter 3. They include the ability to process, organize, store and share data and/or information and ability to use information to achieve one's objectives.

In addition to these skills, which basically entail explicit knowledge skills and can be taught and improved upon, there are some intellectual abilities, such as creative thinking in the formulation of a vision for one's work, one's working group and one's organization and decision-making skills. These two types of skills are acquired through experience and/or the exchange of tacit knowledge with those who possess these skills.

Emotional Intelligence and Emotions in Business

The use of the terms "emotions" or "emotional" within a business environment have been avoided until most recently, with the exception of within advertising and marketing departments. Within management, reason and rationality have prevailed; emotions were to be avoided as antithetical to the analytical business-reasoning process. The prevalent view was that an individual's psychological states were not only personal but irrelevant to the workplace. In fact, in the past, even to admit to personal stress at work was an indication of one's inability to successfully deal with their business environment and was considered a career impediment. It is not surprising that individuals were reluctant to talk about their emotions lest it be misconstrued with negative consequences for their career. Emotions were viewed strictly as problematic and not essential for the organization's good or success. Even expressions of positive emotion could be considered suspect. Not only were negative emotions suppressed, but even positive caring emotions were discouraged.

Against this background of the misunderstanding of emotions in business in the previous hierarchical command-and-control era, we find the increasing acceptance today of emotional competencies in the workplace as essential for building collaboration. This acceptance is due, in part, to the rise of the knowledge society, where individual knowledge workers gained more control over their own lives than previous industrial workers had. Another factor was the use of personality assessment instruments by major executive search firms and the increasing widespread use of self-report personality-style inventories.

These created a positive environment that allowed for the acceptance of the idea of emotional intelligence.

Personality Styles in Business

Psychological research in the area of personality has had an increasing influence within the business organization as human resource professionals applied research on how personality variables influenced how individuals approached their work, established and maintained relationships and made decisions. General acceptance of personality styles in business came from two different tracks: 1) executive search firms that used psychological assessment in recruiting, and 2) management workshops that included self-assessment tools or inventories.

Executive Recruitment

The value of understanding individual personality strengths and developmental areas through the assistance of personality assessment inventories has been especially important in choosing business leaders and senior executives. Executive search firms have long valued the importance of choosing not only the most intelligent candidate with a strategic business sense and proven experience, but one who also possessed the necessary personality traits and leadership competencies to operate effectively within an organization's culture. It was, and is, accepted knowledge that personality plays a critical role in the cultural fit of an incoming senior executive into a new organization. Consideration of personality traits takes on even greater importance when an executive is being chosen to change the direction or culture of the organization.

Personality Self-Assessment

Today in business, there are many different types of self-scoring personality assessment inventories. They range from general personality instruments that assist workshop participants to better understand their interpersonal behaviors so they can increase their managerial effectiveness, to specific behavioral assessment instruments to improve negotiating skills, conflict-resolution skills and many others. These self-scoring assessments focus on common behaviors that fall within a

range of acceptable business conduct. Their intent is to provide sufficient personal awareness information so that individuals can learn
about their particular style in dealing with business-relevant interpersonal situations and plan ways for self-improvement.

An exemplar is the Myers-Briggs Type Inventory (MBTI) that
popularized the usage of self-scoring personality assessment within a
business setting. It created the widespread business acceptance of the
importance of human personality traits on organizational and business
practices. The MBTI can be considered the prototype of personality
inventories used in business, having spawned numerous derivative
assessment instruments. The acceptance of personality assessment created opportunities for individuals to look more openly at their
interpersonal behaviors in business. They could take a proactive
approach to building their interpersonal social competencies to work
more effectively with their business associates and, in the process,
enhance their career development. The growing acceptance of the
Myers-Briggs Type Inventory and related personality assessment
instruments used by consultants led to more psychological openness in
business. This prepared the business community for the introduction
and growing importance of emotional intelligence.

Emotional Intelligence in Business

A brief survey of how emotional intelligence (EI) came to be accepted
in the business community increases our awareness of how it can be
used for increasing trust, building better social interactions and
enhancing collaborative relationships. Howard Gardner (1983) wrote
about the theory of multiple types of intelligences in his book *Frames
of Mind: The Theory of Multiple Intelligences*, in which, among others, he
introduced the concept of personal intelligence. The importance of
"other" intelligences to predict success was initially championed by
Gardner within the broader arena of educational reform. An important
construct of these "new" intelligences was that one could learn to
improve one's relationships, creativity and other skills in both one's personal and business life, unlike the concept of the traditional IQ.

Expanding the concept of intelligence to include non-intellectual
competencies set the stage for the acceptance of emotional intelligence,
first in the academic and then in the business world. Emotional intelligence as a term was first postulated in 1990 by Peter Salovey of Yale
University and John Mayer of the University of New Hampshire.

They defined emotional intelligence simply as the intelligent use of your emotions, in which you intentionally make your emotions work for you to help guide your behavior to achieve the results you want. Becoming more emotionally intelligent was based on four building blocks, these being the ability to:

- Accurately perceive and appraise emotion,

- Access feelings when required to facilitate understanding of oneself and others,

- Understand emotions and the knowledge one can obtain, and

- Regulate emotions to promote one's emotional and intellectual development.

This concept of emotional intelligence provided a structural framework for a more comprehensive view of emotions, not as unconscious uncontrollable forces that overwhelm us at the most inopportune times, but as trainable competencies that individuals could learn to be more successful at in their personal and professional lives. The specific emotional intelligence stages for awareness and understanding that were postulated made it more feasible to learn how to become more emotionally intelligent.

Mayer and Salovey next published an article entitled "The Intelligence of Emotional Intelligence"(1993). It was fast becoming evident that their research had struck a resonant chord in the professional field. Two books based on their idea of emotional intelligence appeared shortly thereafter, namely Daniel Goleman's *Emotional Intelligence* (1995) and Hendrie Weisinger's *Emotional Intelligence at Work: The Untapped Edge for Success* (1998).

Another researcher, Reuven Bar-On had been working in the field of emotional and social competencies since the early '80s and his first assessment tool, the Emotional Quotient Inventory (EQ-i) was published in 1997. Based on his research, he divided emotionally and socially intelligent behavior into five dimensions:

1. **Intrapersonal**—how well we understand and can express ourselves: the competencies of emotional self-awareness, assertiveness, independence, self-regard and self-actualization,

2. **Interpersonal**—how well we understand others and can relate to them: the competencies of empathy, social responsibility and interpersonal relationships,

3. **Adaptability**—how well we cope with and adapt to change: the competencies of problem solving, reality testing and flexibility,

4. **Stress management**—how well we can deal with stress: the competencies of stress tolerance and impulse control, and

5. **General mood**—how motivated we are to deal with daily life: the competencies of happiness and optimism.

The acceptance of emotional intelligence within the business community was further confirmed with the success of Goleman's second book on emotional intelligence entitled *Working with Emotional Intelligence* (1998). Increasing numbers of researchers found that emotional intelligence played an important role in professional success. It is our premise that the reason that emotional intelligence has attracted so much attention is that its importance increased in the networked, knowledge-based economy that has characterized commerce since the introduction of personal computing and, in particular, the Internet.

Warren Bennis argued, in his foreword to *The Emotionally Intelligent Workplace*, edited by Cherniss and Goleman (2001), that emotional intelligence was the most important overall indicator for professional success, outstripping both technical skills and traditional IQ. He found that the higher the position within the organization, the more important the factor of emotional intelligence. He also suggested that the realization of organizational change required an increase in the emotional competencies of all the members of the organization, not just the executives and the managers.

In the same collection of essays, in an article entitled "An EI-Based Theory of Performance," Goleman (2001) presented a refinement of his earlier model of emotional intelligence in which he identified 20 distinct competencies grouped into the following four domains:

1. Self-awareness,
2. Self-management,
3. Social awareness, and
4. Relationship management.

In *The Handbook of Emotional Intelligence*, edited by Bar-On and Parker (2000), several noted authors [Saarni (1999 & 2000); Mayer, Salovey and Caruso (2000)] reflect on the different conceptual definitions given to emotional intelligence and emotional competencies. They describe the mix of motivational, emotional and cognitive components, which has been included under the rubric of emotional intelligence and competency, and conclude there is no one definitive approach to emotional intelligence. Some researchers believe emotional intelligence should be viewed as personality traits important for success in life, while others consider emotional intelligence as a set of important mental abilities for processing emotional information. In his foreword, Goleman comments that this rich diversity of theoretical perspectives is a positive sign of healthy ferment and growth. He suggests that the field's maturation has led to sound measures for assessing emotional intelligence.

For our part our approach is a commonsense one that focuses on the practical application of emotional intelligence, which we believe is critical for effective performance in the workplace through the creation of productive relationships. Our goal is to show how individuals and organizations can learn to work better together through collaborative relationships to achieve greater results. We therefore focus on those emotional competencies that are the most significant for promoting and sustaining collaboration, as listed below.

Emotional Quotient Competencies

The emotional competencies that we are concerned with include the following:

Intrapersonal Competencies

Self-awareness: Maintains awareness of internal emotional states and has the ability to differentiate between emotional states; awareness of emotional strengths and gaps,

Self-management: Employs effective personal strategies to lessen or eliminate acting out of disruptive emotional states,

Self-confidence: Develops and maintains a strong and realistic sense of one's capabilities and value to others,

Adaptability: Can adjust emotions, thoughts and behaviors to new dynamic situations; tolerant of different ideas and perspectives,

Stress management: Achieves and maintains an internal equilibrium and calmness within a changing environment,

Responsibility: Keeps commitments to others within agreed-upon parameters on a consistent basis, and

Trustworthy: Knows one's own values, principles and feelings and acts consistently in accordance with them; acts ethically, fairly and reliably in relationships with others.

Interpersonal Competencies

Empathy: Sensitivity to and concern about others' emotional states; ability to see one's own behavior from the other person's perspective,

Effective communication: Actively listens in genuine dialogue and presents ideas clearly and persuasively,

Social awareness: Understands group relationship issues and interpersonal dynamics between team members and among organizational stakeholders,

Relationship development: Fosters constructive networking relationships within diverse internal and external organization groups,

Leadership: Takes on a leadership role and responsibilities for benefit of the group or organization, and

Collaborative teamwork: Actively builds dynamic teams of diverse individuals to collaborate in creating new solutions to achieve goals.

Motivational Attitudes

Having positive motivational attitudes is a critical success factor for effective collaboration. Even if individuals have the intellectual and emotional intelligence competencies for successful collaboration they will never achieve it unless they are fully motivated. There are so many natural barriers to collaboration that only a motivated worker can achieve it. We all know individuals who are very intelligent, extremely sociable and empathic and who accomplish little. They do not respond to opportunities. They may start projects, but they never see them through to completion. They may handle their current job well enough, but they are not interested in taking on bigger challenges with increased responsibilities. Although they have the potential to make a positive contribution to a collaborative team, they just are not interested in getting involved. They are the classic underachievers. Although some emotional intelligence theorists such as Bar-On (2002), Mayer and Salovey (1993), Goleman (1995, 1998, 2001) and Saarni

(1999, 2000) have included motivation under the rubric of emotional intelligence, we believe that it is better to consider motivation separately as an emotional attitude and not a competency for practical operational reasons. One cannot teach motivation, one can only inspire it or perhaps stimulate it by providing employees with challenges, a topic we will return to shortly.

The motivational categories used by the emotional intelligence community are consistent with the traditional theories of psychologists like Maslow. Maslow places motivation within his framework of the well-known hierarchy of needs as the need for belongingness, interpersonal relationships and community, as well as the need for self-esteem, self-regard and self-actualization so as to fulfill one's potentialities. David McClelland's achievement motivation is identified directly as achievement drive or as assertiveness. Douglas McGregor's Theory "Y" motivation factor is based on the premise that individuals want to learn, and is currently expressed in an initiative competency, and the motivation factor of wanting challenging work to grow through is included in the self-actualization competency.

Chris Argyris defines two motivational systems of values as bureaucratic/pyramidal versus humanistic/democratic, which are supported by his theory that a healthy individual continues to grow from immaturity and dependence to maturity and independence. In an organization that exhibits a humanistic/democratic value culture, human relationships are motivated by values of authentic trusting relationships, alignment and commitment, and psychological success. In a bureaucratic/pyramidal value culture, human relationships are motivated by clearly defined direction, authority and control emphasizing rational behavior and achievement. Our position is that collaboration is best motivated within a humanistic/democratic value culture.

Motivational Goals

There are a number of different activities that can help individuals become more aware of their personal values and life purpose that are key motivators. We list here selected general motivational attitudes that form the foundation for successful and sustainable collaboration and are worthy of being supported by the organization through a system of incentives and recognition and reinforced through communication.

Self-Motivation (Intrapersonal)

- **Passion:** A prime intrinsic motivator for individuals who feel strongly about a vision and proactively direct their physical, mental and emotional energy to achieve that vision,
- **Self-actualization:** The ongoing dynamic process to realize one's full potential to create a meaningful life in both personal and professional realms,
- **Achievement:** Sets personal goals and objectives based on internal and/or external standards and measures progress against these standards,
- **Assertiveness:** Expresses one's own feelings and principles to others and stands up for one's own personal rights without becoming aggressive,
- **Initiative:** Self-starts relevant actions to exploit opportunities to achieve goals and objectives and finds innovative ways around barriers,
- **Optimism:** Maintains a positive and constructive outlook for the future and the realization of one's vision, and
- **Persistence:** Maintains a singular focus on goals even when faced with resistance.

Interpersonal Motivation

- **Commitment:** Aligns personal goals with the goals of the organization and team and devotes full energies to fulfill one's obligations,
- **Cooperativeness:** Shares information and knowledge with others in working towards mutual goals and builds the relationship in the process,
- **Compassion:** Acts consciously of others' needs, combined with a genuine desire to assist them, and
- **Social responsibility:** Acts as a constructive member for the good of the group or the organization without requiring immediate personal benefit.

Inspiring, Stimulating and Rewarding Motivation

While emotional intelligence competencies can be learned and practiced to improve one's collaborative interpersonal skills, motivational competency is not such a set of learned skills but a set of attitudes. Motivation has another dimension of psychological depth and commitment to core personal values that goes beyond simply applying more skillful behaviors to a situation or relationship. A lack of motivation is different than a lack of self-confidence in one's knowledge or skill level, which can be directly improved. Motivation is a question of passion and personal purpose in life—something that cannot be directly taught in a training class. However, motivation is not always a strictly personal matter as it can be stimulated by a shared vision, by shared values or by a sense of community to which one is committed.

There is a practical operational reason why we distinguish motivation from emotional intelligence in our consideration of collaboration. The strategies to increase motivation are different than the strategies to increase either IQ or EQ through effective training programs and/or one-on-one coaching. Individuals do not necessarily respond positively to a direct appeal to increase their motivation. External reinforcement programs have been used with some degree of success in an attempt to motivate individuals to increase their performance and productivity and to act in a more collaborative manner. These include financial reward programs, such as commission payouts, performance bonuses, profit sharing and stock options, as well as high-profile recognition programs such as annual president's club for high achievers and other special contests involving sought-after perks, such as travel vacations. These incentives have for the most part been restricted to account executives or salespersons.

However, this approach can sometimes lead to unfortunate consequences from a collaborative organizational point of view, because some individuals, even some teams, become excessively competitive within their own company and weaken community and create misalignments. Such incentives unwisely formulated may benefit certain individuals, but do not benefit the organization as a whole in either the short term or long term. They can, in fact, wreak havoc within an organization, even to the point of bankruptcy, as has happened with some formally stellar major U.S. companies. External financial motivators may work well enough when company and stock market are in a growth mode, but become major motivational problems when company stock is not doing well or when the market is declining.

We are not postulating that financial incentives are inherently wrong; they have been and will continue to be a potent factor as extrinsic motivators. The caveat is, however, that as extrinsic motivators, rewards and punishments have limited usefulness for building a collaborative organization since a transactional work culture is reinforced with no long-term influence for developing self-initiated behaviors. When the external reward conditions change, individuals' behavior change. When the external reward system stops reinforcing specific behaviors, individuals stop those behaviors. This extrinsic motivation mind-set does not support self-leaders who take personal initiative—essential for building a collaborative organization.

In addition, the philosophy of these external financial reinforcers comes out of an industrial era mind-set where individuals, and even teams, were pitted against each other in the same company to achieve the highest sales goals. This brought results in an era when output was concrete and measurable and performance could be tied to achievements over baseline. Yet even in this environment, studies demonstrated that while money was certainly important, it was not at the top of the list of what motivated individuals to come to work every day. Herzberg's two-factor Motivation-Maintenance theory places financial compensation in the category of work maintenance satisfiers or dissatisfiers along with working conditions and company policies. Both motivation and maintenance factors are essential for optimal individual motivation. Financial compensation is a critical satisfier or dissatisfier, inadequate compensation is a dissatisfier and inhibitor of optimal motivation, and fair compensation is a maintenance satisfier and support for optimal motivation.

Intrinsic motivators, which are internal and subjective, are the key motivational forces for self-directed learners and self-leaders essential for a collaborative knowledge organization. Individuals who align their passionate interests with the organization's compelling vision create their own challenging work. All other intrinsic motivators flow from this key true motivator, such as achievement drive, self-growth and actualization, advancement with increased responsibility and recognition for accomplishments. One of the uses of a knowledge network that we propose in the Chapter 8 is a personal Web page for each individual member of the organization, where his or her business achievements and acquisition of skills can be publicly recognized.

In developing a successful collaborative organization strategy, individual motivation becomes an even more critical component to get right. Our definition of a collaborative organization goal is one in which individuals willingly participate to co-create and share knowledge within the organization.

A continuous learning culture supports each individual's growth to maturity and independence through realizing their career vision and aspirations. A noble and compelling vision is the greatest organizational element to help individuals understand and align their passionate motivation, but there are no guarantees that passion will take root and flourish in everyone. That comes from the individual's own questioning and searching in the depth of self. Intrinsic motivation comes from a higher order level of belief and purpose in life than skills and behaviors. A supportive culture of encouragement to realize one's inner vision promotes individuals to align with the organization's vision to achieve common objectives. Internal motivation and external motivators combine synergistically.

Culture Change and Stimulating Motivation through Communication

Communication can play an important role in inspiring and motivating employees, particularly in a time of organizational change. Here is an example from the implementation of a collaborative knowledge network system at Turner Construction as related by Jim Mitnick, the creator of the system.

> The real issue within a lot of companies, and I don't think that ours is much different, is really the change management that you have to go through to implement a new collaboration process that utilizes technology. We're really made up of lots of engineers, and engineers like to do things the same way. So when it comes to changing, there is a big divide between those that are really new out of school called generation X and the long-term, experienced employees. The 30s and under—they get it big time and they want more and more—technology drives a lot of the things that they do, whereas the more mature or experienced employees just don't feel comfortable with this, the latest Internet technology. So the change that has to take place deals with "reverse" mentoring, the younger "troops" mentoring the more seasoned, experienced "troops." It involves an awful lot of communication to everybody, a lot of hand-holding when necessary. They are relearning.
>
> I have said a thousand times within our company that what we are really trying to do is make knowledge networking as simple as turning on the faucet or turning on the light switch— it just works all the time. And we are trying to weave the Turner Knowledge Network into their daily lives so

that it's just normal. Whether they are going to their email, or they are going to do some collaboration where they're scheduling a virtual meeting or they are trying to find a document through the search engines, or the way it's tied into our Web-based training—it's just normal—this is the way we do business.

And how you get people to do that is everything from the big-stick rule where you kind of have to whack some people and drag them kicking and screaming to participate. And then you have those who absolutely think it's the best thing in the world. I have people every day telling me "I can't believe that we really got this thing built for our staff—it's unbelievable!" And yet that individual six months ago could have been the one who couldn't really figure it out. But then all of a sudden the light went on. I guess the moral of the story is to communicate it over and over again, time after time, until finally everybody begins to see what's really going on. But you still are never going to get everybody. There are some who just say, "Look, I'm just not interested. I'm going to finish up my career and I'm going to do it the way I have always been doing it." Choices will eventually have to be made in those cases. (Interview, 2003)

The problems Mitnick faced to motivate his employees to use the Turner Knowledge Network arose with a number of Turner's customers as well. Organizational change affects all aspects of a company's operations.

Our customers are an interesting group because we have very sophisticated customers and we have very unsophisticated customers. Let me give you some examples. Those that really understand what we are doing recognize we're really forcing them, literally by contract, to improve their skills and knowledge, once they go through the various Web-based courses that we're delivering to them. They may initially go in kicking and screaming, but at the end of the day, the surveys and the results that we get indicate to us very clearly that this was absolutely the right thing to do. They recognize the value of these courses and the access to information and knowledge whenever they want it is extremely valuable to them.

But there is always going to be another group, and we have those, that technology doesn't work for. So that's the frustration. You have those that don't have any problem and they just see the tremendous value, and you have those that really struggle to get through it because the technology isn't there yet. We think it's there, but it's not there for all of our customers and suppliers. That's one of the biggest frustrations that we still have. I think if you look forward to maybe two to three years from now—I think a lot of this will go away. (Ibid.)

Collaboration, Consensus, Cooperation, Teamwork and Trust

We believe that trust is the most important factor for creating collaborative relationships. Trust is created as each person gains increased confidence in the collaborative partner's ability and desire to deliver on what he or she commits to. In the past trust was based on loyalty to one's organization. However, because of downsizing, mergers and acquisitions over the past two decades, the concept of loyalty to one's organization has diminished or even disappeared. It is also the case that in a knowledge-based economy one often feels a stronger bond to members of one's profession in other organizations compared with co-workers in one's own organization who work in other fields.

Today, one of the first and most significant challenges facing organizations that want to become more collaborative is establishing greater trust between individuals working within the organization. There are no simple "off-the-shelf" solutions. Each organization must first accurately assess the level of trust within its own culture and then develop an appropriate strategy to build trust and collaboration internally within the organization and externally with customers and suppliers. Building trust takes sustained commitment and perseverance.

Trust and collaboration support each other. As trust increases between individuals, they become more willing to share and collaborate in working together. As individuals collaborate in working together to create new knowledge, they become more trusting of each other. The same process of collaboration and trust building occurs between organizations. Trust and collaboration involve a complex interaction of both emotional competencies and motivational attitudes, as well as cognitive skills.

To better explain how the collaborative organization differs from the command-and-control one, we will contrast the new approach of collaboration and consensus that we are advocating with the older industrial paradigm of teamwork and cooperation. This is not a question of either/or but rather a classic example of both/and. We are not advocating that cooperation and teamwork be replaced by collaboration and consensus but rather that collaboration and consensus should enhance teamwork and cooperation and make them more effective.

Collaboration was not a concept that had much validity in a closed-structured management-employee hierarchy. Even though over recent years an important shift involved building teamwork among individuals working together on projects, information flow could still be essentially controlled. Teams still received only the information they needed to perform their task. Information flowed more freely within the team structure, but teams were still operating within a hierarchical information structure. Some may feel that calling a team collaborative is simply an issue of semantics, using a different name for a well-organized team that is working efficiently. Our position, however, is that collaboration is first and foremost an enterprise-wide strategic imperative for building a vibrant culture of knowledge co-creation and sharing. The distinction of collaboration as a strategic imperative, contrasted to a tactical objective, is the same rationale for distinguishing collaboration from teamwork. A team is usually task oriented and breaks up once their objective has been reached. A collaborative community, on the other hand, builds a long-term relationship built on learning together and sharing knowledge.

Because of the speed and worldwide access of knowledge that the Internet provides, the scope of who can access this vast knowledge database has vastly increased. This fact alone has changed forever the ability of an organization to control the information it deems appropriate to each level of the organizational hierarchy. Prior to the Internet this information control could be restricted relatively easily to specified groups of individuals. Individuals within an organization could know only what those in higher positions wanted or allowed them to know. It is our position that with the Internet this is no longer possible and organizations must move from teamwork to collaboration.

Sometimes there is a lack of understanding over the distinction between teamwork and collaborative teams. Collaboration is a higher level, more encompassing concept that can include the cooperation of different working groups within an organization or the cooperation of distinct businesses who may or may not be competitors. For example, one wouldn't use the term "teamwork" but rather "collaboration" to describe two companies working together on a common goal. Even common teams within each organization would be collaborating together with the teams from the other organization. This strategic connotation is an essential reason for using collaboration as our conceptual vehicle in this book.

Teamwork usually involves a common team objective that all team members are working to achieve, each member contributing their part to the team and subordinating their goals to the team goals. Collaboration can include this concept of teamwork as a subset, but it is also more expansive in that collaborating members, individuals and organizations can have different goals and objectives, unequal in scale, scope and timing, but still collaborate effectively together to help each member reach his or her unique goals. This potential disparity in goals and objectives requires a greater fundamental level of trust among all coalition members.

Collaboration also describes individuals working together to achieve common and individual goals that are more strategic in nature. Collaboration can encompass different business units internally or different external business stakeholders having different visions and strategies working together to achieve their common and unique goals. Even competing business organizations can collaborate together to achieve mutually beneficial strategic goals. Collaboration also entails the co-creation of new knowledge or the joint formulation of objectives, whereas teamwork is usually limited to implementing actions plans that have been formulated elsewhere.

Consensus Building

In the Industrial Era employees did not expect nor were they expected to have any input into the work that they did since that was solely the manager's job to determine. However, in the Knowledge Era the relationship between knowledge workers and their managers has changed. Knowledge workers expect to have more control over their work and want to be more involved in the decision-making processes concerning the work they do. Consensus in decision making involves input from all team members and collaboration among them. When there is consensus among all the players, everyone becomes more committed to achieving the results mutually agreed to. It is our position that in the knowledge economy, without some form of consensus, individuals will feel taken for granted or patronized, and one will not even be able to obtain effective cooperation.

One of the great powers of teams that collaborate successfully is their ability to integrate perspectives from diverse team members with different expertise and professional backgrounds. These collaborative teams are able to minimize personal conflict and maintain focus on the task of generating and evaluating competing ideas and problem solutions. In fact, one of the signs of a well-functioning collaborative team is its ability to encourage dissent and seriously debate contrary ideas to expand the potential solutions environment for breakthrough results. Team members trust each other, so they can be vulnerable with untried innovative ideas. They trust each other to be assertive in presenting their ideas with passion but not aggressive in attacking those who disagree. Heated debates over ideas are not just tolerated, they are demanded of all members. Passive group-think conformity is eschewed. Ultimately, out of this crucible of dynamic creative tension, a forged consensus of innovative solution is achieved. A group harmony in commitment to the team's findings and course of action is attained.

Based on this dynamic team atmosphere of trust, respect and acceptance of diversity, collaborative teams can successfully integrate supplier and/or customer partners as valued team members. These extended teams can successfully expand their problem-solving universe to include the relevant needs, goals and objectives of their collaborating customers or suppliers to arrive at more comprehensive and innovative outcomes that make all participating strategic partners more competitive.

As an example of where an atmosphere of trust and respect and a tolerance of diversity is essential for the successful execution of a collaborative project, we turn to a description of collaboration in product development (CPD) at Ford, making use of Documentum's eRoom.

> CPD may demand some alternative behavior on the part of the engineering staff. In cases where individual contributors dominate, the move to collaboration may be slow. In cases where team-based design and development is prevalent, collaboration may be more accepted and embraced. Collaboration requires openness and sharing of ideas. It requires less fearful contributions and commenting. It provides an avenue for discussion, for sharing and for team growth outside of traditional meetings. Product development engineers tightly locked on personal control of information, for whatever reason, may be difficult to move into collaboration without some incentives. On the other hand, for product development engineers disillusioned with too many meetings, it provides a means to stay connected without the need for "boring" meetings. (www.documentum.com, 2003)

The Collaborative Team Process

Teams that collaborate successfully consistently work within a structured problem-solving or critical thinking format so that all team members are working in the same problem-solving phase at the same time. There are a number of approaches to problem solving and they all postulate the same generally six accepted creative and critical thinking skill phases [VanGundy (1992), De Bono (1985) and Straus (2002)]. All team members must be personally knowledgeable and proficient in all six creative problem-solving stages, as their creative and evaluative cognitive skills (i.e., divergent and convergent thinking) and contributions are essential at each stage of the process. The six stages are:

1. **Problem identification.** Determine if there is a problem and from a list of potential problem areas develop a priority list to choose which problem the team will tackle,

2. **Fact finding.** Expand the knowledge base to increase understanding of all the facts and facets of the chosen problem area,

3. **Problem definition.** Define the most productive problem definition possible, including problem scope,

4. **Idea generation.** Generate many ideas and possible problem solutions to the defined problem,

5. **Solution finding.** Evaluate solution ideas against criteria established by team to arrive at most acceptable solutions, and

6. **Acceptance or decision making.** Gain agreement on what solution to choose and commitment to implement successfully.

Many teams make the mistake of focusing on consensus building only at the final stage of decision making, and have skipped over some or all of the first five stages. But if there isn't consensus starting at stage one of what the problem is, there certainly won't be consensus at stage six of what to do about it! Consensus building must take place at each and every stage to arrive at a final consensus of commitment to action. All team members must consistently work together at the same time within each stage so that they are literally in phase in their efforts. Much miscommunication and frustration in group processes occurs when team members are not coordinated in their efforts and unknowingly work on different phases of the problem-solving process simultaneously. In this chaos some team members may be wanting to decide on what problem solution should be chosen, others are in the stage of generating more alternative ideas to consider and some team members may still be engaged in extensive fact-finding! It is no wonder that it may seem arriving at any type of consensus would be a minor miracle in this all-too-common situation.

Having covered the psychological dimensions of collaboration, we are ready to consider the practical steps in building the collaborative organization, which will be the focus of our next chapter.

CHAPTER SIX

Practical Steps in Building the Collaborative Organization

In Chapter 4 we outlined our model for building the collaborative organization in terms of what we call the seven building blocks, which consist of:

• Vision,

• Leadership,

• Trust,

• Goals,

• Strategies,

• Tactical objectives, and

• Action and implementation.

These seven building blocks are themselves enriched by and supported by the five collaborative messages of the Internet. Making use of the seven building blocks and the five messages we plan, in this chapter, to describe the practical steps that need to be taken to build the collaborative organization. The seven building blocks provide a framework within which building the collaborative organization can take place, as these activities are the basic elements of a successful organization. The five messages, on the other hand, describe the manner in which these activities should be carried out, namely through two-way communication, ease of access to information, continuous learning, alignment and community. As we have argued before, these properties of the Internet have contributed to it operating as a natural collaborative medium without any managerial or executive input. If these principles are used in carrying out the activities as encompassed in the seven building blocks, then a spirit of collaboration is sure to infuse the operations of the organization as a whole. The Internet is not just a tool that can be used for collaboration; it is also a model for collaboration.

Before returning to a discussion of the five messages, we will first describe how the spirit of collaboration can be made part of all the activities of the organization, from the formulation of its vision, its goals, its strategies, its tactical objectives and its action plans to its exercise of leadership and its creation of trust. As an organization is a nonlinear dynamic system, one cannot talk about vision without bringing in trust, leadership, goals, etc. Each of the seven building blocks we have defined depend on each other in a nonlinear manner and although we are forced to introduce them one at a time, we will move back and forth between them as we develop our recommendations for the practical steps needed to build a collaborative organization. Our choice of these seven activities as a way of describing an organization was heuristic, as was the choice in the order in which we present them. They represent merely one coordinate system to describe an organization, but we believe the one that makes the most sense from the standpoint of discussing collaboration. We begin with the seven building blocks and then describe how the use of the principles incorporated in the five messages of the Internet support these building blocks of a collaborative organization. We will also bring in some of the notions of psychology in business and emotional intelligence that we discussed in the last chapter.

The Seven Building Blocks

1. Vision

A compelling vision inspires collaboration, especially if collaboration is made an explicit part of the organization's vision. The more inspiring and engaging the organization's vision, the more its members dedicate themselves to realize that vision. A vision will capture the imagination of and motivate the members of the organization if it is aligned with their personal vision, which is why it is important that there should be input from all members of the community in developing the organization's vision. If an organization's vision is arrived at only by the senior leaders without any collaborative input and then transmitted through the organization by fiat, there is the risk of individual misalignments, conflict and a diminution of motivation. An informed, well-focused and involved community supports the organization's vision when it has had the opportunity to discuss and present its collective views in support of the vision. The positive effects of collaboration through active dialogue, consultation and feedback can be very powerful even if the final decision is arrived at by a smaller group of senior leaders.

Passion for a vision that one internalizes is an intrinsic motivator. While passion, commitment and motivation cannot be directly mandated or taught, creating a vision that inspires and a challenging environment that enhances motivation is essential to the success of an organization. Working to achieve an exhilarating vision worthy of personal dedication and sacrifice is a critical factor for inspiring collaboration. A powerful vision creates passionate individuals who closely align their personal goals with the organization's goals. Great causes and great visions motivate individuals to put aside their own self-interests, individual differences and personal conflicts to work together for the common good.

However, while a compelling vision can arouse great passion in individuals, it is not automatic. Many of us have known great projects that have failed because key individuals essential for its success have not bought into the vision. Issues surrounding involvement, participation, commitment and even consensus must be appropriately addressed with all key individuals to foster a passionate commitment to the vision that is shared by all members of the community. This is why the collaborative participation of developing the vision is so important. The greater the opportunities individuals have to contribute their ideas and feelings to the organization's vision based on what motivates them and impacts positively on their working environment, the more they will be aligned and committed to working toward its attainment. One of the additional benefits of soliciting input into the formulation or modification of the vision is that it creates an important opportunity for collaborative dialogue.

Having made the point that collaborative input increases motivation, the question arises as to how a community can have input into the organization's vision. A vision is often thought of as that of a single individual or a very small group of individuals. However, if one looks at the history of those who started the computer revolution, one learns that visionaries like Bill Gates and Steve Jobs were actually part of a tight-knit community of "computer geeks" who shared a common vision, and that these visionaries became the founders of their respective organizations because of the leadership role they played within their community.

The value of multiple inputs into vision formulation is that the senior executives who finally formulate the actual vision of the organization are learning from the first-hand experience of their employees and managers, many of whom are in direct contact with customers and suppliers and, hence, are in better touch with market realities. This process of gathering input from throughout the organization fosters respect of and acknowledges the valued contribution of all its members. When individual members feel confident to offer their insights and suggestions, they will feel a greater ownership in all the activities of the organization, from formulating goals, strategies and tactical objectives to implementing action plans.

Unless one is dealing with a start-up company, most vision exercises are a question of modifying an existing vision. A major change in organization vision is always a dramatic process, as certain individuals support the current status quo vision and others support the new vision. In such dramatic times the conditions leading to the change need to be clearly communicated to all members of the organization so that they can collaboratively participate in the vision-modifying process. Time spent in collaborative discussions of changes best enables individuals to positively realign themselves with the emerging new vision and become its enthusiastic, motivated supporters. The vision alignment process is especially critical when an organization makes dramatic changes to its vision and direction in response to rapidly changing conditions in their marketplace or the economic environment.

Ion Global Australia, an e-business consulting firm, has helped many of its clients to recognize the need for change and to create vision and direction for the organization by engaging a broad spectrum of the organization's staff. "Ion consultants use SiteScape Forum to combine input from the frontline experience with structural thinking...customers can readily see the need for organizational changes, contribute to the process, and see the logic behind any changes, all in one easily accessible site" (www.sitescape.com, 2003). A new vision for the organization is achieved collaboratively with the help of Ion's facilitation.

Another example of large-scale collaborative change is the pioneering work of Dannemiller Tyson Associates. Dannemiller organizes one- to two-day workshops with up to 300 people at a time in a single room to work through a change process for its customers. Its success illustrates the notion that the collaborative development of an organization's vision is both feasible and desirable. The profit from such an exercise is not just the new organizational vision that emerges but the understanding that each participant has of the problems faced by the other members of their organization. The large-scale collaborative development of a new vision is superior to the one in which the vision is created by a few people at the top of the organization because the organization not only emerges with a new vision but it has a better understanding of itself.

The two examples we cited from Ion Global and Dannemiller Tyson involved collaborative input into creating a new vision, which is a highly desirable path. There are instances, however, where the vision can come from one or two individuals at the top who are able to communicate that vision to their organization's members and obtain their "buy in," as was the case at Turner Construction. The vision of creating a collaborative knowledge network started at the top with their CEO and chairman Tom Leppert, who tasked senior vice president Jim Mitnick with its implementation. It was the strength of this vision and the detailed way in which it was laid out and communicated to the organization that made for a successful cultural change and the implementation of the Turner Knowledge Network.

> The real key to what we're doing is having very strong commitment from the top and having the right vision. And this wasn't done in a vacuum by any means. We laid out a very detailed program that we wanted to do up front. And I think that some of the things that we're doing are fairly unusual and a lot of other companies haven't done it for whatever reason. We're just relentless in terms of the commitment and the support from the top that's trying to drive the change in business—which is absolutely necessary.
>
> And there's a thousand reasons why we're doing this. But bottom line it's intended to make us better builders, increase our skills and competencies, add value to our customers, train our subcontractor base so that they're not just better but they're the best. And that in turn equates to added value to us as their customer and added value to our owners that we do business with every day, whether it's an owner-architect, or whatever. Anyhow the bottom line is pretty simple, we're trying to basically teach risk avoidance, how to manage things better, how to be better business people, and become more profitable at the end of the day. It just makes a lot of sense. (Mitnick, interview, 2003)

Aligning Personal Visions with the Organization's Vision

A collaborative organization in a knowledge economy is built on self-motivated, self-managed individuals. The most direct way to ensure that individuals are aligned with the corporate vision is to ensure that they are clear about their own personal vision that motivates their lives. Without this understanding, they cannot willingly align themselves and commit to the organization's vision. In the knowledge economy a collaborative organization is the best model to support people's continued learning development to develop their emotional, cognitive and intellectual competencies in becoming more valued collaborative partners. This continuous learning process better aligns them to the organization's collaborative culture as a key motivating force.

Individuals collaborate because they realize they cannot achieve a shared vision by themselves. Collaborating with others makes it possible to realize their personal dreams. In Maslow's hierarchy of motivation, a powerful vision works at the level of self-actualization. For example, the defense of one's country has been one of the most powerful "organizational" visions that has led individuals to put their country's needs over their own personal needs. In peacetime great visions like NASA's goal of putting a person on the moon and then creating an outer space station have inspired individuals to work collaboratively to achieve extraordinary goals never thought possible. Nonprofit organizations also work with compelling visions for social change. In the U.S. the Peace Corps has brought individuals from many diverse disciplines together to work collaboratively to grapple with seemingly intractable social issues and challenges around the globe. Businesses with great visions have motivated people to work together collaboratively to create innovative products and services that have changed the world. In the high-tech field examples include Netscape, Hewlett-Packard and Apple.

Understanding the critical importance of becoming more collaborative for achieving the organization's vision is essential for creating the focus and motivation to successfully initiate the enterprise-wide cultural change and to persevere to its successful implementation. It is also important that collaboration itself becomes part of the organization's vision. In order to motivate such a transformation, certain questions must be addressed. The most fundamental question is:

• What is it about achieving the organization's core vision that demands it become more collaborative to increase its success?

Other questions that one might wish to consider are the following:

- Are the more traditional management-employee attitudes and relationships inappropriate to meet the organizational demands in an expanding knowledge economy?

- Is internal competition within the organization hampering the ability of internal divisions to work together successfully?

- Is the traditional hierarchical culture of the organization preventing it from attracting or retaining the type and quality of knowledge workers that are essential for the organization's success and growth?

- Are customers demanding that the organization become more coherent in meeting their needs?

- Are the organization's current human resource assets being used so inefficiently that it is causing a loss of market share?

- Are there new opportunities beyond the current capabilities of the organization that it can take advantage of by working with others?

- Have new competitors entered the market that require collaboration with other organizations to maintain the organization's market position?

- Has the organization developed new products or services that cannot be brought to market alone?

- Has an external threat developed within the organization's sector, such as a regulatory issue, that requires the organization to collaborate with other organizations, even competitors?

2. Leadership

Because collaboration does not occur naturally in the competitive environment of the business world, leadership is needed to build a collaborative organization. That leadership cannot be autocratic and it must emanate from all levels within the organization, i.e., leadership in a collaborative organization is the responsibility of every member of the community. That having been said, it is still critical that senior executives set an example by directing the affairs of the organization collaboratively by inviting input from and dialoguing with all quarters and all levels within the company. The nature of leadership to build the collaborative organization is quite different than the traditional form of leadership in a hierarchical organization in that knowledge is inclusive, leadership is pervasive, communication channels are open, relationships are built on trust, and leaders must be involved in IT and Internet issues. Let us expand on these points:

KNOWLEDGE IS INCLUSIVE

The leadership style in a collaborative organization is quite different than the traditional style that was characteristic of a command-and-control organization. Executives in a hierarchical organization control knowledge through an exclusion process, since knowledge is perceived as the means to power within the organization. Information is carefully portioned out to subordinates so that the higher level individual still maintains control over the integration of knowledge. Individuals are given only the information that they need to have in order to do their immediate job. In a collaborative organization knowledge is viewed as an empowering force that increases in value by inclusion, involving many individuals in the organization. Individuals throughout the organization should be able to access all information relevant to their needs. A limited number of proprietary secrets or privileged personal information files are, of course, still maintained in the strict privacy that they require.

Ford Motor Co. makes an effort to share knowledge and create a collaborative environment with the idea of creating its future leaders. "Newly appointed managers around the company are trained in the techniques and philosophies of the new economy as they work on highly strategic projects and initiatives. Many Leadership Development Center programs rely on the eRoom solution to facilitate global project collaboration and accelerate technology acceptance among Ford's future leaders" (www.documentum.com, 2003). By combining the development of leadership and collaborative skills at the same time, Ford is insuring that its future leadership will embrace the collaboration paradigm.

LEADERSHIP IS PERVASIVE

In a hierarchical organization, position and title determine an individual's leadership level. Subordinates at lower levels are expected to defer to someone higher in the organization, regardless of their knowledge about the issue at hand. Leadership is determined by hierarchical rank.

In a collaborative organization, leadership is pervasive and dependent on an individual's expert knowledge for providing guidance and direction to the group. Leadership can be assumed by different collaborating members as individuals willingly take authority and responsibility commensurate with their knowledge and contributions.

COMMUNICATION CHANNELS ARE OPEN

In a hierarchical organization communication is strictly controlled with individuals only communicating upward through their direct manager. Although an individual can speak to their peers, an attempt to "go over" the manager to speak to someone higher is considered insubordinate. The same communication restraints are placed on all lower ranking employees as well; they can only communicate up through their supervisor. In a collaborative organization, communication networks are more open. Multilevel communication is not only possible but actively encouraged. Since open flow of information is vital to a collaborative organization, Internet-enabled communication is established for ease of information access and two-way communication throughout the entire collaborative network.

RELATIONSHIPS ARE BUILT ON TRUST

In a hierarchical organization, relationships are built around the authority and power that come from the individual's position in the hierarchy. Relationships have a political component based on power; political savvy becomes a major competency for success. In a collaborative organization, relationships are built on aligned goals and objectives and the individual's commitment to both the task and the relationship. Individuals work together with respect and commitment to each other within a trusting community.

LEADERS MUST BE INVOLVED IN IT AND INTERNET ISSUES

One cannot expect individual members of a firm, however, to spontaneously optimize the organization's use of the Internet by pursuing their own particular interests willy-nilly. Leadership must come from a broadly based group of managers with experience in both marketing and information technology. Responsibility cannot be relegated to an MIS department that is unable to develop a strategic direction for sales, marketing and customer support. As Harvard business professor Michael Porter (1985) points out, senior managers and owners of a company cannot seriously fulfill their managerial responsibilities without becoming directly involved in the management of the information technology in their organization. An organization's champion of technology who is not in the position of the decision maker is well advised to find a way to get members of senior management to sit down in front of a computer and discover for themselves the power of the Internet. Once they use it and explore its possibilities, senior managers will discover what a powerful tool it is. A modest investment in time and training is required to become familiar with the Net, but it is well worth it, as any regular user will attest.

How Does Everyone Become a Leader?

One of the paradoxes of building a collaborative organization is that the leader of the organization must inspire his employees to follow his lead without becoming followers but leaders in their own right. Louis Gerstner, in his book *Who Says Elephants Can't Dance?: Inside IBM's Historic Turnaround*, described the tremendous effort it took him as head of IBM to encourage his people to work together collaboratively so that one of the world's greatest companies could regain its creative edge.

> In the end, my deepest culture-change goal was to induce IBMers to believe in themselves again—to believe that they had the ability to determine their own fate and that they already knew what they needed to know. It was to shake them out of their depressed stupor, remind them of who they were—you're *IBM*, damn it!—and get them to think and act collaboratively, as hungry, curious self-starters. (2002, p. 188)

Gerstner described with great irony and wit the paradox of trying to promote collaboration through dynamic leadership when he wrote "at the same time I was working to get employees...to follow me there, I needed to get them to stop being followers" (ibid.).

A continuous collaborative learning environment actively promotes programs that upgrade leadership skills for all its members regardless of their level or position within the organization. In a collaborative knowledge organization, all individuals must become not just self-managers but, more importantly, self-leaders as well. As self-leaders they take the initiative in defining and solving challenges and problems within their sphere of responsibility. Leadership training is not just for individuals once they receive the designation of manager, as was the case in the traditional hierarchical model.

Leadership programs build up creative and critical thinking competencies. Individuals learn how to develop more creative ideas through divergent thinking skills and how to evaluate these original ideas so that the most innovative ones are implemented. As more individuals develop these skills, self-confidence grows and collaborative decisions are more easily and effectively made.

As self-confidence grows in their decision-making skills, individuals become more willing to accept responsibility for their decisions and act in a leadership role. The organization grows through this increase of self-leaders who are now competent to meet their team's challenges head on. This proactive right-in-time, right-at-point leadership frees the next levels of management to deal with higher order issues. Managers are not spending scarce time having to resolve issues that have been delegated up to them by insecure staff.

How Does the Leader Lead in Order to Make Followers into Leaders?

Senior leaders must lead as collaborative role models in the transition to a collaborative culture. In this fundamental culture change, not only senior managers will be waiting to see whether senior leaders "walk their talk" about collaboration; every manager and staff member will also wait to be assured this change is real. The vision to a collaborative organization must be clearly and continuously communicated throughout all levels of the organization by senior leadership. This is not a one-time communication kickoff event, it is an ongoing process lived daily. Positive collaborative actions exemplified by senior leadership at every opportunity give confidence to others to assume a leadership role.

Senior Executives Must Empower and Teach Everyone to Be Ready to Take a Leadership Role

Senior leaders must create attractive and supportive leadership growth opportunities in the organization. However, because of the organization's previous culture, managers and staff may be initially unwilling to become personally vulnerable by making decisions when they might be wrong. In this case, managers and staff first need to develop self-awareness of their strengths and development needs so they can enhance their emotional and cognitive competencies for leadership and good decision making through continuous learning.

Appropriate workshops combined with online training programs must be readily accessible for developing the supporting emotional and motivational competencies, such as leadership itself, self-confidence, initiative, relationship development, communications and other competencies relevant to a specific individual. Collaborative culture changes of this magnitude do not just happen over time, they require a well-planned and implemented human resource continuous learning strategy.

Individuals grow more self-confident in their leadership skills as they are supported by the organization through positive leadership experiences and constructive feedback. As individuals build increased levels of trust with each other, they become more motivated to take on appropriate leadership roles.

Managers play a pivotal role in this self-leadership growth within the organization. As managers themselves become more confident self-leaders, they more willingly expand leadership opportunities for those reporting to them. They do this through delegation of appropriately challenging tasks in a supportive environment and one-on-one constructive coaching to ensure their direct reports' successes.

LEADERSHIP MUST COME FROM MOST QUALIFIED, NOT JUST BY TITLE

A collaborative organization is the best structure for leadership based on meritocracy. A command-and-control organization is hampered by its own rigid hierarchical structure where marginally competent, even incompetent, individuals can be misplaced in higher positions of power and authority. In these situations, leadership revolves around power struggles as these individuals fight to maintain their positions. A strong hierarchical organization further promotes political infighting and unhealthy competition as many individuals vie for the few managerial positions available since the winner "takes all." In this internal competitive leadership environment there is one winner for the title, but many more excellent individuals become the "losers" and may leave the organization for better opportunities elsewhere.

In a collaborative organization, leadership is not based on the artificial power of an arbitrary title. It is leadership based on depth of experience, innovative problem-solving skills, effective decision-making skills and the ability to bring together and motivate diverse groups of individuals to work together to achieve a common vision and goals. Collaborative leadership is earned, not won. In a collaborative organization where trust and respect for individuals is strong, leadership is more easily relinquished to someone more competent in a particular field or discipline when the team goals and objectives demand it.

Even in the most collaborative organization there is, of course, a stable hierarchical reporting structure to ensure consistency and stability. It would be chaos indeed if you had to figure out who you were reporting to each day. But this hierarchy has more to do with administrative and managerial functions, which must be stable and robust, such as project coordination, hiring or assignment of staff and project and performance reviews, to name a few. However, even in these functions, a collaborative culture ensures that there is much more collegial input and even shared decision making in all these functions.

COMMAND AND COLLABORATE

We have argued that the best kind of leadership in a collaborative organization is one that is diffused throughout the organization and is not of the command-and-control type. This is somewhat an idealistic position, especially when an organization is making a transition from a command-and-control organization to a collaborative one. The following case study illustrates that sometimes, in order to get collaboration going in an organization, it has to be mandated from the top in what we call the "command-and-collaborate" mode. We thank Jim Mitnick, senior vice president at Turner Construction, for relating to us his experience of introducing a collaborative knowledge network, TKN, to his organization.

> Every one of our projects as of January 1st (2003) is using 100% online collaboration through our project management systems. That in itself is a significant change of culture. To make that work, it had to be mandated— "You will do this by January 1st, there are no options." And when you put it that way to your staff, they go, "OK. We're engineers. We follow the book. You say we do it, we figure out the way to do it." So I don't think that's been a real difficult challenge. I think using the tools and getting everything out of them and really understanding the transfer of knowledge, that's the challenge. So one of the things we have done is develop online training that teaches how to do project collaboration. That's even better, because now we're getting a double whammy; we're teaching people how to teach themselves.

This all started when our brand new chairman at that time, Tom Lep-pert, came to me one day and said, "I'd like to pull you out of operations and put you in charge of a project." At that time I was involved in running seven or eight of our business units and all I had done my whole career is build buildings. I wasn't a computer guy by any means, I wasn't a full-time trainer, and I knew nothing about Web-based training. But all Tom said to me, as a real visionary, was "I want you to go away and figure out how we can train a thousand new engineers a year across our entire company and have it consistent." That's all he said. I went away, I read a lot, went everywhere I could possibly go. I went back to Tom and our then-presi-dent, and made a presentation to them about the development of what we call the Knowledge Network that integrated document management with KM with learning, self-learning and instructor-led training, that would map skills and competencies to our performance evaluations and would have proficiencies and skills and skills gaps and learning maps and learn-ing plans and all these things you read about.

And at the end of the presentation, after a lot of dialogue, he turned to me and said, "Here's a million bucks, get me a pilot program in 120 days." There's a guy who has got some guts. He just pulled a number, he had no idea whether this thing was a hundred thousand, or a million. Here's a million bucks, develop a program. So we developed a program, we integrated everything in literally 120 days. That was the pilot, it proved what worked and didn't work. What we proved was our infrastructure would not support it. It took us a year from that point, and we changed our entire infrastructure (by making use of Open Text software). We modified our infrastructure to make sure we could support the TKN internally, make sure we could support it externally through the Internet and dial-up con-nections. We piloted it in three of our business units and then, based upon the feedback we have gotten since then, we have been developing different additional content and improving it literally on a daily basis.

So the leadership came really from our chairman. It doesn't go any higher than that. Basically this was not done by committee, he just said, "Do it now." Somebody says to me to do something and I'll figure it out, I'll use my best judgment and I'll get it done. And that's what we did. We're not part of HR, it's not like there was a huge committee that you had to go and get a 100% consensus. It was just do it. But some big companies will do it like that.

And there's a lesson I learned from one of our chairmen years ago. He basically said to me, and I've used it as an example over the years, "Look, the worse thing you can do is never make a decision. If the decision you just made was wrong, fix that decision until you finally get it right." And that's been our philosophy with the development of our knowledge network. We made our best judgment, we knew that some of the stuff wasn't going to work, we fixed it. And then we kept going on and we hopefully keep making it better and better over the years. (Mitnick, interview, 2003)

Although the implementation of the TKN was mandated from the top, the reason that it was successful was that the leader of the project did his homework and collaborated with others to learn how to put together a collaborative system that would work.

One of the things we did up front was we went out and created TKN champions. We identified key people in every one of our business units around the United States and brought them in and trained them. They went out and they basically really pushed this information down through the food chain, throughout the company. I have never seen a group as excited as this group was. These were young men and women that might be with us anywhere from four to five years and up to 20 years. They knew the company well enough, they were in leadership positions, they felt comfortable in standing up and making presentations. People in the regional offices respected them; they were very sharp individuals. They have taken the TKN, which they said is terrific, and they're promoting it. I don't have to promote, all I do is share what's going on. I became the "Tom Leppert" of TKN. I provided the vision and the leadership to them. They then took it and they made it work throughout the entire enterprise. (ibid.)

3. Trust and Loyalty

Trust and loyalty are perhaps the most important ingredient's for building a collaborative organization because collaboration is a value-creating relationship that demands trust, loyalty and respect. Trust and collaboration are mutually self-supporting. They form an autocatalytic set in that trust catalyzes collaboration and collaboration catalyzes trust. Trust and collaboration, on the other hand, create loyalty—loyalty to one's co-workers and loyalty to the organization. As trust and loyalty increase between individuals, they become more willing to share and collaborate when working together. As individuals collaborate in working together in creating new knowledge, they become more trusting of each other as exemplified by the following two excerpts from two different case studies.

Through Livelink's shared technological infrastructure, Northrop Grumman Integrated Systems is creating networks that build trust among its employees. Advancing collaboration as the online medium to transform business areas into product teams and communities of practice across geographical and cultural boundaries provides a documented process for innovation that is transferable and can be reprocessed for future initiative to reduce reinvention and rework. (www.opentext.com, 2003)

While trust has always been an important anchor to any CEO, its value is heightened today. Employees work in flexible teams with fewer guidelines than they once had; companies are more dependent on outsourcing and partnerships, and virtual organizations are becoming increasingly the norm; executing deals requires a high level of cooperation among employees resident in different countries, and every great company is in a continuous state of organizational change. The ethos of trust—between leaders and their colleagues and employees and among workers themselves—is the glue that holds everything together in the new economy. (Garten, 2001, p. 124)

Just as important as developing trust within an organization is developing a level of trust with one's customers. An example of trust building through collaboration is the way in which Hill & Knowlton archives its interactions with its customers and shares that information with them when there is a turnover in staff.

We have had instances where our client has had turnover and we were able to give the new person, or team, a chance to catch up on everything that was done by pointing them to a discussion archive or email messages where budgets and previous plans were discussed. This has helped us to show our client's senior management that we are keeping this collaborative knowledge base as a shared resource for the benefit of both our companies. It demonstrates that we are very intent that new people who join on our side and their side are kept up to date with what's happening. For the customers where we have had these instances of turnover or renewal, that's when that trust relationship gets more deeply embedded. (Graham, interview, 2003)

The iterative process between trust and collaboration can start with small steps and quickly build to consequential trusting and collaborative relationships. It is therefore imperative that the core values of trust and respect are communicated and supported throughout an organization that values collaboration.

There is no trust "formula," except to do the right thing consistently. Telling the truth, keeping commitments and accepting responsibility are examples of the visible behaviors that leaders and managers need to model to support these core values. There is no one simple answer to increasing trust, but whatever is done must be genuine. Trust must be lived and be the consistent basis of action, not just something that is preached about. Trust is something that is built slowly over time but can be destroyed in an instant by an insensitive act.

An effective collaboration process creates new knowledge by bringing together specialists with diverse backgrounds and experiences who, more often than not, have different personality styles to boot. This can be very positive when it results in diverse opinions and perspectives that lead to new breakthroughs, but it can just as easily give rise to a negative atmosphere of personal conflict and mistrust. This is where emotional intelligence becomes a critical competency so that the collaborating partners are aware of their emotional responses and are able to manage them in a positive manner so as to be able to work together and communicate with each other productively. Education programs in effective communication and the acceptance of diversity are an important way to build trust and increase the emotional intelligence of the organization's personnel.

It is important that an organization keep all its commitments to its members, even outperforming its members' expectations whenever possible. As we pointed out earlier, the merger and acquisitions craze of the last two decades led to downsizing, rightsizing and dehiring processes in order to optimize the economies of scale that motivated a number of mergers. Because it happened within a command-and-control culture, employees had no say in the matter; managers were ordered to cut payroll to reduce overhead. It was no surprise that the individuals who were dehired no longer had faith or trust in the company that laid them off or in the next company that hired them. For those individuals who still retained their jobs there was a critical unintended consequence: They also lost their faith and trust. They quickly realized that they could lose their jobs in the next round of cutbacks. Trust and loyalty has shifted as a consequence of the downsizing culture that afflicted the business world in recent times and it has shifted to the employee's personal career and in many cases to colleagues in their profession. Rather than a focus on the well-being of one's employer, today's workers are concerned with making contacts and building up their job skills in preparation for their next career move.

It would be unrealistic for us to suggest that a collaborative company cannot lay off workers if the survival of the organization is at stake. If information is freely shared, as we have suggested, then employees will understand the need for cost cutting when it is absolutely required. With appropriate information, employees can collaborate to provide and implement cost-cutting solutions necessary for the financial health of the company. What we consider a bad business practice from the standpoint of building a collaborative organization is downsizing strictly for the sake of increasing profits. If the organization expects loyalty from its employees, it must reciprocate by showing loyalty to its staff.

One of the serious challenges in creating a collaborative organization that must be overcome is the general climate of mistrust that has been created by those senior executives who placed their personal fortunes ahead of their corporate responsibilities and were responsible for their companies going bankrupt, leaving thousands of employees and shareholders seriously affected. Complete openness on the part of senior management is the only way to restore that level of trust required for the employees of large corporate organizations to collaborate with each other and the senior levels of their organization.

What Are the Concrete Steps that Senior Executives and Managers Can Take to Increase Trust and Openness in Their Organization?

Senior executives' demonstration of trust is the most important strategic step to promote trust in the transition to a more collaborative organization. But it is not a single event, but an ongoing process that is lived through action.

Senior leadership must strongly believe in the importance of becoming a collaborative organization and building the foundation of trust necessary for its success. They must publicly promote trust as a personal core value and the organization's core value. It is essential that an enterprise-wide collaborative process for redefining or augmenting the organization's vision and core values of trust and respect involves all the organization's members. Led by senior leadership, this collaborative process itself is key for building an omnipresent trusting atmosphere. Building a trusting culture takes time and effort and senior leaders need to be indefatigable in promoting a collaborative vision built on trust within the organization itself and with its suppliers and customers.

Increased sharing of appropriate organizational knowledge with all members demonstrates an increased level of trust throughout all levels of the organization. Increased knowledge begins to break down the artificial barriers of mistrust between management and employees as they begin building trust to collaboratively work together to build a better organization. This does not mean that all information is indiscriminately made public; trade secrets, company negotiations, privileged personnel files and other sensitive financial information still are held in appropriate confidence. But most organizations find that much more can be communicated than is currently being communicated.

Senior executives must also publicly demonstrate their trust in others through actions, starting with the managers who report to them. How is this trust manifested by senior leaders? By appropriately delegating to others the responsibility and accountability for significant challenges critical to the organization, as well as the necessary resources and tools for successful goal completion. At the same time these managers are demonstrating their trustworthiness by successfully meeting these challenges, they are placing their trust in those reporting to them through a similar delegation process. Trust-building activities cascade down throughout the entire organization.

However, it should not be construed that this trust through delegation is given lightly. It must be earned. As self-leaders, all individuals in a collaborative organization have the personal responsibility to demonstrate their trustworthiness by being fully prepared professionally to meet these delegated challenges. This means that they have proactively participated in continuous learning of the most advanced knowledge in their field of work, have increased their problem-solving and decision-making skills and capabilities and have developed their emotional and motivational relationship competencies to function as more effective collaborative team partners.

A collaborative organization fully supports these efforts by promoting continuous learning opportunities and providing the most advanced learning tools for professional and personal career growth. In this process the collaborative organization builds trust with all its members and creates a more trusting culture.

However, in reality the greater the challenges, the greater the risks of mistakes, setbacks and even failures. The true test of trust depends on how the senior leadership responds to such results and the individuals involved. Are lessons learned, mistakes rectified, failures taken as feedback for creating new directions and new organization competencies developed? Or are individuals involved personally blamed for the mistakes and failures and made scapegoats? This is an oversimplification of a complex process, but the point being made is that how senior leadership responds determines whether trust becomes a lived core value or is degraded to a token phrase that leads to mistrust and cynicism throughout the organization.

The manager holds the pivotal position in how quickly and effectively individuals who report to them will become successful self-managers and self-leaders. If the organization was strongly command and control, managers may be reluctant to give up control, one of their main functions in the hierarchical organization, and support the growing independence of those who report to them. In this case, managers must first be trained and coached in how to delegate. They must have the appropriate skill sets and motivation to effectively manage the change process to a more democratic and empowering work environment. If managers are not themselves motivated for this change, it will not occur. They may pay lip service to the principles of collaboration, but individuals will not risk acting independently under such a manager.

4. Goals

If an organization is to work together collaboratively to achieve its goals, then those goals should be set collaboratively. This will require a great deal of rethinking about how goals are set, as well as about a major logistic problem of how to solicit input from so many players. The best way to begin would be to work through a process whereby the current goals of the organization are reevaluated and reaffirmed or revised. Once the members of an organization have participated in such an exercise they will be more motivated and inspired to achieve those goals. By participating in the exercise to reevaluate, reaffirm or revise the goals of the organization, the various sectors that make up the organization as a whole will have a better idea of where they fit into the overall structure of things.

Goal setting must be coordinated throughout the organization. A process must be put in place that ensures that, as goals are set in various subdivisions of the organization, they are aligned at all levels of the organization, from the enterprise as a whole to each organizational division right down to the level of working groups and individuals. Developing team goals becomes more democratic as individuals gain skilled knowledge in collaborative goal setting and decision making. As individuals are expected, or even required, to become more participatory, their personal goals to increase emotional and motivational competencies take on renewed importance. These divisional, working group and individual goals must be closely aligned with the overall organizational goals.

In addition to setting business goals to realize the overall vision of the organization, the process goal of becoming an effective collaborative organization should become a major goal in itself. By setting collaboration as a goal in itself, the members of the organization will become more attuned to the value of collaboration and as a result more willing to make the effort to realize this goal. Naturally, building in rewards for achieving this goal will certainly accelerate the process.

Some authors have argued that collaboration should be focused on business goals and that collaboration for the sake of collaboration is not a valid business goal, albeit perhaps a desirable social goal. We agree with the first part of the statement but not the second. Collaboration should be focused on business goals for two reasons:

1. Business goals are important because they sustain the company and therefore should be the focus of all activity within the company, including collaboration, and

2. By focusing on business goals the motivation to achieve the process goal of collaboration is greater.

But we cannot agree with the assertion that collaboration for the sake of collaboration is not a worthwhile goal. We not only believe that collaboration helps to better achieve business goals, as does every one else, but we also believe that it leads to the formulation of business goals that might not have been formulated otherwise. Collaboration is not merely a process goal but it is also a core value, which like honesty makes for greater success in business in the long run. Collaboration makes for a positive qualitative improvement in business life as well as a quantitative one. The qualitative improvement indirectly leads to a quantitative one because it gives greater satisfaction to the employees and improves their morale, leading to increased productivity. This is the point we made when we talked about how organizational change and vision could be arrived at collaboratively through large-scale collaborative processes as developed by Ion Global Australia (www.sitescape.com, 2003) and Dannemiller Tyson Associates (2000). There was additional value in the process. The same is true of collaboratively setting strategies (the subject of the next section).

5. Strategies

As was the case with setting goals, formulating strategies collectively builds greater commitment and cultivates alignment and collaboration more easily. Organizational strategies usually require the coordination and input of various sectors of the organization, and therefore a collaborative organization is in a better position to formulate and execute its strategies. This has been the experience at Hill & Knowlton with offices across the globe serving clients in many different markets, as reported by H&K's Ted Graham:

> There's somewhat of a trade-off in strategy formulation. You still need someone who is strong in terms of taking a strategic direction and establishing it. However, I think as you engender more and more collaboration when you are servicing clients you often are consensus building across international geographies to harmonize strategies, not necessarily make one homogenous strategy. I guess that would be the best point to make. You are really trying to see where strategies from one part of the world can work with other strategies, rather than dictating one from a central part of the world by sending people a memo and saying "Implement this." So it's much more interactive in nature; strategies often will evolve based on the realities of what's happening. Change information now goes up the chain of command much faster and strategies are changed appropriately. (Interview, 2003)

Developing a Strategy for Building a Collaborative Organization

In addition to developing strategies to realize its business goals, an organization that wishes to become a collaborative organization must develop a strategy for the process goal of collaboration. Because a discussion of the particulars of strategy to realize a business goal is dependent on the particulars of the organization in question, we will focus in this section on what a strategy for collaboration might look like. The transition to a collaborative organization requires a carefully planned and implemented total strategy because it is a significant culture change involving the personal and professional beliefs of all organization members. It directly affects the work habits and interactive relationships of everyone in the organization. An enterprise-wide culture shift of this magnitude must have the full support of the senior executives and a proactive human resource implementation strategy that addresses the essential issues involved in this transition to a more collaborative culture. An ill-planned or poorly implemented strategy can lead to cynicism and greater mistrust of the organization—the exact opposite of the result intended. Having individuals collaborate in the development of the strategies for achieving the collaborative goals is in itself an important step in the cultural transition process.

How to develop the transition strategy in stages from an internal competitive environment to a more collaborative work environment depends on many factors. We have therefore developed a blueprint for a comprehensive strategy consisting of nine steps or elements. This strategy for collaboration will not happen by chance nor succeed by isolated pockets of collaborative initiatives scattered throughout the organization. These initiatives must be coordinated. Although described in a linear order below, all nine elements of the strategy need to be developed together. From a timeline perspective the different elements of the strategy will overlap to varying degrees in the implementation process. The nine-element strategy for building the collaborative organization that we are proposing consists of the following steps:

1. Choose appropriate business projects or accounts as primary collaborative prototypes,

2. Develop ways to identify and overcome barriers to collaboration,

3. Establish a comprehensive continuous learning program with an emphasis on the skills required for collaboration,

4. Senior management needs to develop a communication program extolling the benefits of collaboration,

5. Create organization-wide and local collaboration forums,

6. Establish an effective Internet-based collaboration network,

7. Establish new guidelines for the realignment of decision-making responsibilities and accountability,

8. Develop a human resource strategy for the recognition and reward of collaborative contributions and results, and

9. Create the position of the Chief Collaboration Coordinator (CCC).

1. Choose Appropriate Business Projects or Accounts as Primary Collaborative Prototypes

The more a collaborative spirit imbues the process of developing the collaboration strategy, the more successful will be its implementation. This, of course, does not mean that every single individual in the organization is involved in every decision—that would be impractical. But it does mean that all individuals participate at their level in collaboratively arriving at local impact decisions and that they are appropriately represented by selected representatives for higher level decisions.

In developing a strategy for collaboration, it is also important to note that not all goals need to be achieved in a collaborative way every time. Collaboration has been an underutilized strategic organization process in our culture. But the solution is not to set up a strategy to dramatically swing to an exclusive collaboration style. The organization's business conditions may not support the total change and partners might not be receptive. The strategy is to develop a more successful organizational culture that can collaboratively interact internally and with appropriate external partners, and at the same time be intensely competitive in asserting itself in the global market arena. Other leadership modalities and relationship styles still remain valuable and effective when used appropriately. This is an important point in a cultural transition phase since an attempt to develop a strategy to make everything fit into a collaborative process, even if inappropriate, will diminish those collaborative interactions that are of value to the organization.

The first projects in which the collaborative methodology is to be introduced in the organization should be high-profile ones so as to serve as a role model for future collaborative projects. These initial projects should also be chosen so that a quick and measurable success may be achieved to support the culture change to a collaborative organization. During any major organizational transformation, there is reluctance to change from previous behavior patterns; individuals need to experience success in working together collaboratively to sustain their motivation in the process. These prototype collaborative business projects then need to be monitored and evaluated on a regular basis from both the standpoint of the business success that results and the progress that is made from introducing collaborative techniques into the way the organization does business.

2. DEVELOP WAYS TO IDENTIFY AND OVERCOME BARRIERS TO COLLABORATION

In any major cultural transformation it is inevitable that resistance and barriers to change will occur. There are many reasons why individuals may be hesitant or even hostile to work with their co-workers and management in sharing and creating knowledge together. Some reasons might be personality related and some career-oriented based on rewards or punishments for past behavior.

The only important issue is: Does the organization have an integrated strategy developed to resolve resistance and remove these barriers in the most efficient and consistent way possible? An initial internal and external collaboration assessment is necessary to determine the current strengths of the organization to act collaboratively and to identify and prioritize major organizational collaboration gaps. We introduce the notion of such an instrument, the Collaboration Quotient, in the next chapter. With the information collected with such an instrument, a comprehensive and effective strategy can be developed.

Many issues can become barriers that impede collaboration efforts at local levels, such as manager reluctance or even hostility to implementing collaborative practices, incompatible technology communication linkups and more. Major resistance can come from managers who are reluctant to share more responsibility with their staff by delegating meaningful tasks and supporting their growth as self-leaders. In most cases, it is very risky for any manager's staff to go over them and lodge a complaint within the normal channels. Establishing a separate strategy for dealing with collaborative process resistance and barriers can be very important, depending on the culture of the organization.

3. ESTABLISH A COMPREHENSIVE CONTINUOUS LEARNING PROGRAM WITH AN EMPHASIS ON THE SKILLS REQUIRED FOR COLLABORATION

As we have argued previously, a successful collaborative organization depends on all its members becoming effective self-leaders and self-managers. Management has a responsibility to provide their employees with the skills and competencies needed for collaboration. A comprehensive online and offline learning strategy should be implemented so that all organization members have easy access to the most advanced learning technologies to:

1. Augment their skills in emotional and motivational competencies that support trust and collaborative relationship building,

2. Enhance their cognitive creative thinking and decision-making competencies to become better problem solvers, and

3. Keep up-to-date with the most advanced IT techniques for capturing, storing and sharing knowledge.

In a major cultural change, advanced proactive training is necessary to bridge any competency or skills gaps staff may have. Continuous learning, one of the five messages of the Internet, is not just a metaphor. It is a practical methodology essential for developing collaborative skills.

Organizations that have as one of their goals to be an effective learning organization support the organization's members' goals of professional development. Reciprocally, this leads to increased motivation by the organization's employees to support the company's goals. As employees increase their competencies, managers and team leaders have more opportunities to delegate challenging and professionally rewarding work that is motivating. In the knowledge economy, most organizations have flattened their hierarchy of management levels. This is especially true in collaborative organizations where individuals are expected to be self-starters within their functional teams. From a motivational perspective, this also means there are fewer management positions that one can move into for career advancement. Motivation must come from the challenging work one does and the continuous learning of new skills so that lateral promotions can be achieved.

Collaboration depends on competent people to increase their intellectual and emotional value to the organization. Knowledge professionals, in turn, have as one of their key personal goals to continually develop their competencies to stay at the forefront of their respective fields. An easy system for augmenting technical or professional proficiencies as well as creative and analytical thinking and problem-solving skills on an ongoing basis is essential. The Logan-Stokes Collaborative Knowledge Network (LSCKN), which will be described in Chapter 8, enables the organization to implement an efficient collaborative knowledge networking system. The LSCKN system makes it easy for individuals to improve on those competencies that maximize their personal professional strengths and optimize their collaborative contribution to their projects. The LSCKN also provides each member of the organization with access to the knowledge competencies and skills of all of their co-workers.

4. Senior Management Needs to Develop a Communication Program Extolling the Benefits of Collaboration

The senior leadership of the organization should develop a highly visible, ongoing communication program explaining the benefits of collaboration. Middle managers and staff need to have the confidence that the transition to a collaborative organization is supported by senior management as a real culture change and is not merely the latest management fad. The successes from the initial collaboration projects should be fully described.

A major part of the communication program should entail the ways collaborative attitudes and processes are being incorporated into the internal and external working procedures and relationships of the organization. A significant culture change takes a significant period of time measured in months, even years, to become established. Senior management must be prepared to publicly support this transition over the "long haul." Continuous, consistent and well-publicized support for the collaborative vision provides the organizational clarity that helps individuals align their personal career goals with the organization. As you will recall, alignment is one of the five messages of the Internet.

In implementing a collaborative knowledge strategy it is important that employees see that the tasks they perform and the effort they exert to capture, store and share knowledge or information to benefit others is meaningful and will benefit them and their organization in the long run. Too often they look upon these tasks as extra work not directly related to their function or responsibility within the organization.

Management has a responsibility to demonstrate the importance of collaboration and knowledge management to their staff.

5. CREATE ORGANIZATION-WIDE AND LOCAL COLLABORATION FORUMS

In addition to taking part in a robust communication program, employees need to be involved in active dialogue about the business rationale for making the transition to a collaborative organization through local and organization-wide collaboration forums. This collaborative process-oriented strategy is an essential first step in enrolling the organization's members to develop a collaborative culture. This process provides senior leaders, management and staff the opportunity to personally experience the benefits and challenges of engaging in collaborative dialogue. One of the outcomes of the dialogue should be a decision-making process that strives for consensus as a key process objective.

Initially focusing on the internal collaborative process, individuals and working groups can learn how to apply collaborative processes to current accounts or business projects to increase innovation and productivity. From this initial account work, collaborative best practice principles can begin to be formulated and business projects or accounts evaluated for selection for the next phase of prototype accounts collaboration with key customers (as described in element 1 above). In this way all collaborative process training activities can have direct business application.

Through this organization-wide dialogue, cultural values of trust and respect can be reinforced as the foundation of the organization's core values, further reinforcing the vision of the company as a fully integrated collaborative organization. Task groups can be established to collaboratively work on the specific building blocks of vision, trust, leadership, goals, strategies and tactical objectives. Through this process, individuals will have the opportunity to voice their concerns about change and barriers to success. Two-way communication, a key message of the Internet, becomes established as a vital process for dialogue throughout the organization.

Local and organization-wide forums provide the opportunity to bring together people from different functional groups to build cross-departmental collaboration. How these groups would be configured depends on the organization's business strategy and goals. These collaborative dialogues become the models for how teams can effectively collaborate. This strategy helps strengthen community, another one of the five messages of the Internet.

6. ESTABLISH AN EFFECTIVE INTERNET-BASED COLLABORATION NETWORK

A strategy for the optimization of Internet infrastructure and technology is indispensable for any organization in today's knowledge economy. The more all members of the organization can easily and quickly access relevant knowledge and include collaborating partners, the more innovative and effective problem solving will be. A plan for expanding or upgrading the organization's Internet infrastructure and collaboration software must be implemented in timely stages. This provides essential two-way communication and ease of access to knowledge that supports the daily ongoing collaborative dialogue. The LSCKN provides an important online system for accessing individuals throughout the entire organization who would have the skills and competencies required for collaboration on a particular project. This system provides the ease of access to information (another message of the Internet) about individuals for collaborative team involvement or support.

Hill & Knowlton adopted a strategy of establishing an effective Internet-based collaboration network and found that it helped them to realize their vision of fielding "best teams" for their clients.

> In the late '90s we really had a vision that supported the idea of best teams within our consultancy. And those best teams included the best teams within our firm and also the best joint teams as our firm collaborates with our clients. That vision has not changed but HK.net has just made attaining that vision that much more real. We are not limited to how much travel we can afford to get people to see each other face to face. Our company is now more capable of having more touch points because we are enabling our clients to have contact virtually with any of our people from around the world who are contributing their intelligence to their projects. (Graham, interview, 2003)

Internet-based collaboration also allows H&K to strengthen customer relations. "HK.net, powered by Intraspect, demonstrates the effectiveness of using collaboration to manage our most strategic accounts. It is essential in providing our team and clients with immediate access to information, past work and resources throughout the agency" (www.intraspect.com, 2003).

7. Establish New Guidelines for the Realignment of Decision-Making Responsibilities and Accountability

One of the key distinctions between a strict hierarchical organization and a collaborative organization is the sharing of responsibility and accountability in the decision-making process. Power and authority no longer derive strictly from hierarchical position, but from the shared consensus of all those collaborating in solving the business problem or meeting the challenge. A strategy must be developed for how this important shift in power, authority, responsibility and accountability will be promulgated throughout the organization. Managers have to be trained and coached on how and when to share or delegate decision making. Staff has to be trained and coached on how to apply good decision-making principles and how to take on the responsibilities and accountability for making those decisions. The best strategy for achieving this will vary according to organizational factors unique to each company. The key guiding principle for any strategy developed is that the organizational guidelines for responsibility and accountability must be clearly understood by all who will be involved in the new decision-making process.

8. Develop a Human Resource Strategy for the Recognition and Reward of Collaborative Contributions and Results

Individuals act in specific ways when positive behavior is reinforced and negative behavior is discouraged. The most direct ways to influence individual motivation is through rewards and recognition for positive behavior. To bring about a cultural transition to a collaborative working environment, collaborative behaviors leading to results need to be rewarded in significant ways to positively establish these behaviors as the new ways of doing business. Depending on the organization, and even on the cultures of the distinct functional units and divisions, different recognition and reward strategies may be called for. Some strategies will focus on financial rewards, some on nonfinancial recognition; some strategies will be implemented as a total package, others will be introduced in phases. All strategies will need to address the relationship of organization, division, working group and individual components of any reward and recognition system. Whatever strategies are developed, it is imperative that they are clearly communicated to all members of the organization. Without a clear understanding of the new behavior expectations, individuals will continue their previous behaviors and hold back on embracing new activities until they become more certain about what is expected of them in a changing environment.

The importance of a system of rewards and incentives is underscored by Dale Hoopingarner, director of advance systems at EMC Corporation. EMC is a world leader in information storage systems, software, networks and services that makes use of the collaborative software of Primus, namely, eServer, eSupport and Interchange to bring about customer collaboration.

> A big part of the success of an implementation does not revolve around the technology but around the cultural issues. Lack of attention to the cultural change required leads to project failures even when the technology works just fine. New staff and managers are not used to providing support by using a knowledgebase and have to be educated on the disadvantages of "knowledge hoarding." At the same time, managers must change their method of rewarding staff. Instead of praising an employee for solving a problem when no one else could, managers should reward staff for sharing knowledge by contributing to and using the knowledgebase. Managers and executives should be prepared to do frequent coaching to build a successful knowledgebase and an efficient, happy team of customer service representatives, says Hoopingarner. (www.primus.com, 2003)

Another example of a simple way of recognizing the collaborative efforts of staff has been devised by Hill & Knowlton by publicizing the collaborative successes of their staff with their customers.

> Our people are more willing to share and collaborate internally when they see their client responding to their work by saying, "I'm very impressed with how, even though it was not invented in your own local office, you are able to take an idea from your worldwide knowledge base and reuse it for the betterment of us as your client." And because our people see their ultimate customers responding to it, they are more apt to see the rewards themselves. I think where a lot of these collaboration systems kind of fall down is that the individuals using them don't see that kind of reward or recognition that really matters to them. You may get some recognition within your office or from an HR manager, "I saw you are using the system, great." But when their client is telling their boss that, "This consultant is really effectively working with their colleagues and that's helping our business"—that's when it makes a real difference.
>
> The geographic boundaries in our company are starting to break down more than we had seen them in the past when people were unsure

about the skill sets of people in other parts of our worldwide network. Many people only knew their colleagues as a name on an email message. We've tried to do some things that help them see the long-term benefits of how we can change to serve our clients better by working together more collaboratively. For example, we do things like having a "Best Sellers" list of contributions on the HK.net system, where people can see the contributions their fellow employees have posted and shared whether they are from Oslo, or Singapore or San Francisco. Through the Best Sellers program they get to see how much the documents they have contributed are being reused over and over again by their peers, commented on and shared within another business context. I think this has a tremendous positive motivating impact as it helps employees feel, "I am building a merit-based reputation in the firm." It does not matter if someone does not see this individual every day, because they now know they are aware of their contributions. Also employees are more likely to pick up the phone and collaborate with another person who has contributed because they've got something, some background or some context of who they are and what they do, and what they are capable of. (Graham, interview, 2003)

9. CREATE THE POSITION OF THE CHIEF COLLABORATION COORDINATOR (CCC)

One possible strategy for building a collaborative organization is to appoint a senior person to be the Chief Collaboration Coordinator (CCC) to maintain the focus on and momentum of the collaboration process. Their role would also be to act as the point person to assist in removing organizational and systemic barriers that transcend group or department authority or influence. This would require a commitment of resources to support collaborative activities on the individual and working group levels.

The person chosen for the position of CCC must be a skilled diplomat and a "people person." The CCC should have high visibility and acceptance within the organization and be an active role model and mentor for collaboration through his or her own actions. If the person in this position acted in an authoritative control approach, this position itself would become a barrier to collaboration.

With a visible and accessible proactive CCC and an appropriate communication process in place, issues can be carefully researched and effectively resolved. It is essential that barriers be quickly removed so that the momentum of change is not diverted or blocked.

For example, individuals who have autocratic managers will be reluctant to exhibit self-directed behaviors. Instead, they will hold back and maintain the status quo until they perceive that a more supportive environment for collaboration has emerged.

The success of the work of Ion Global Australia (www.sitescape.com, 2003) and Dannemiller Tyson Associates (2000) that we reported earlier indicates that a CCC can be quite effective in promoting collaboration within an organization. Ion Global and Dannemiller, although they were outside the organizations they worked with, effectively played the role of a collaboration coordinator. We therefore strongly recommend that organizations wishing to increase the level of collaboration within their organization appoint someone as their Chief Collaboration Coordinator or at least bring someone from the outside to perform that role and then train someone within the organization to take over that role.

6. Tactical Objectives

Tactical objectives that are specific, measurable, actionable, realistic and timely give reality to the goals and strategies for establishing a collaborative organization through the implementation process with actual business accounts and projects. Tactical objectives formulation must take into account the many current realities impacting on any business project—internal resources, customer expectations, time pressures, production schedules, competitive challenges and price constraints—with one additional parameter, namely how collaboration can add to the effectiveness of any particular tactical objective. Formulated at the front-line level by project teams, tactical objectives are the powerful tools necessary for achieving results. Collaborative team practices create the most effective tactical objectives because all relevant stakeholders, including customers or suppliers, are involved in creating the critical tactical objectives so that all parties achieve maximum benefit.

A collaborative organization works towards consensus decision making as an organizational principle. There are no hard and fast rules that apply to all decision-making circumstances within an organization, but there is a general principle to be followed. The more that appropriate stakeholders are involved in the decision-making process and the greater the level of consensus, the more alignment and the deeper the sense of community and commitment that will be achieved. This is also true for joint project objectives with suppliers and customers. Their collaborative involvement in tactical objective development is a key factor for success.

How specific objectives are decided and implemented becomes a practical real-life differentiator between a command-and-control organization and a collaborative one. In the command-and-control model, decisions are made by senior executives or managers and are translated into objectives that are then executed by subsequent lower organizational levels without input or questioning. In the full consensus decision-making model, all involved parties must agree on the decision and objectives before they can be implemented.

In developing the mutually agreed-upon tactical objectives for a working group or a project team, optimal collaboration is required between co-workers who are professional specialists in their respective fields of knowledge. This requires that each participant is both competent and comfortable in making decisions and accepting personal responsibility for their decisions.

If and when to use a consensual decision-making model in developing objectives needs to be explored as to their appropriate use. Certainly, not all problems can be approached nor can all decisions be made in a full collaboration mode. There are varying degrees of collaboration called for depending on the challenges at hand. But it is certainly true that problems, decisions and the formulation of tactical objectives can be dealt with in a more collaborative way than is currently done. The collaborative approach would maximize the organization's inherently rich human resource assets, the key value-creation resource in every organization.

In Chapter 1 we reviewed the Collaboration in Product Development (CPD) activities of Ford (www.documentum.com, 2003), Elkay and APTEC (www.cocreate.com, 2003), Teleflex and APTEC (ibid.) and Eli Lilly (www.accenture.com/Outlook, 2002). Each of these case studies are examples of how tactical objectives were arrived at collaboratively and implemented successfully with savings in both time and cost. Another example of collaboration on developing tactical objectives is the case of international investment banking firm Rothschild, Inc. These investment bankers had trouble assembling complex deals because of "the inability to effectively access and share financial models, agreements, reports and market data." The situation was resolved with iManage's WorkSite suite of collaborative software products. As a result, bankers, analysts and researchers were able to collaborate on developing the optimum tactical objectives for their clients (www.iManage.com, 2003).

Tactical Objectives for Supply Chain Management

Another area where pursuing tactical objectives can have a handsome ROI is in supply chain management. Here is a list of some simple effective low-cost tactics that can have significant payoffs:

- Attracting new customers with collaborative IT. As reported earlier, Ted Graham from Hill & Knowlton described how their use of collaboration software with customers helped them to land many new accounts (Graham, interview, 2003).

- The customized customer. Success can be achieved by creating individual Web sites for each key customer for communication and coordination of their needs, as National Semiconductor did (www.vignette.com, 2003).

- Providing customers with access to part of one's intranet. Haimila (2001b) reported the successful use of this no-cost, simple tactic with a number of companies.

- Meeting customers' needs by collaborating up the chain as well as down the chain. This tactic is exemplified by the collaboration of APTEC and Teleflex with Elkay (their supplier) in which Elkay helped APTEC and Teleflex create products to meet the needs of their customers (www.cocreate.com, 2003).

- Building customer loyalty as did Otis Elevator by providing customers with a wide array of services (www.vignette.com, 2003). Hill & Knowlton built loyalty by archiving their interactions with customers and thereby being able to provide their customers with valuable information when they lost a staff member to turnover (Graham, interview, 2003).

- Working with the customer, not for the customer, requires trust, openness and, in most cases, a culture change.

Tactical Objectives for Realizing Organizational Goals and Strategies

We now turn our attention as to how the goals and strategies for collaboration may be reached by choosing the appropriate tactical objectives for collaboration. To that end we have developed a set of key tactical objectives corresponding to each of the nine elements that make up the strategy for collaboration we formulated above.

Strategy 1. Choose appropriate business projects or accounts as primary collaborative prototypes.

- Evaluate and prioritize current business accounts and projects for immediate introduction of collaborative working arrangements involving senior managers and all key staff involved in either the business account or project.

- Choose potential prototype business accounts and meet with these customers to gather their input and secure their commitment to participate as collaborative partners.

- Create specific key business objectives with all key players that are challenging, achievable and amenable to collaboration.

- Ensure all project team members receive training and coaching in collaborative competencies to maximize their participation and contribution to the project.

- Evaluate and report, on an ongoing basis, the business results and progress with establishing collaborative interactions evaluating both personnel performance and the effectiveness of the IT being used.

Strategy 2. Develop ways to identify and overcome various barriers to collaboration.

- Find and resolve issues or situations that create barriers or resistance to collaborative interactions.

- Encourage and reward suggestions that identify and/or neutralize barriers to collaboration.

Strategy 3. Establish a comprehensive continuous learning program with an emphasis on the skills required for collaboration.

- Assess the motivation and emotional competencies for collaboration using an instrument like the Collaboration Quotient described in the next chapter.

- Identify skills gaps that could make collaboration difficult and remedy them.

- Review in-house training programs for effectiveness in addressing gaps in the emotional, motivational and cognitive skill areas.

- The training department should work collaboratively with managers and staff representatives to develop, deliver and evaluate the most effective and comprehensive training programs required for developing collaboration skills.

Strategy 4. Senior management needs to develop a communication program extolling the benefits of collaboration.

- Senior leaders should make clear statements about their deep commitment to the organization's change to a collaborative culture.

- Senior leaders should collaborate with managers and staff representatives to develop and publicize organizational core values of trust and respect as the foundation for a collaborative culture.

- Senior leaders should work collaboratively with managers and staff representatives to develop communication and dialogue programs on the benefits of collaboration.

- Set up a committee or working group with representation throughout the organization to focus on communicating about collaboration.

Strategy 5. Create organization-wide and local collaboration forums.

- Establish a forum where representatives from different collaborative working groups can compare their experiences and learn from each other.

- Use facilitators who are collaboration experts to moderate forum meetings.

- Facilitators should provide feedback on collaborative process experiences to all project teams and individuals for continuous learning improvements.

- Develop group meeting environments that are conducive to collaborative interactions, incorporating online or video conferencing facilities to include distant team members.

Strategy 6. Establish an effective Internet-based collaboration network.

- Determine gaps in Internet collaborative communication processes and technologies through manager and end-user assessment processes.

- Review the organization's existing intranet-based communication network to determine the optimal architecture for knowledge creation and collaboration (see Chapter 8 for a prototype architecture).

- Monitor the use of the organization's knowledge network and evaluate its usefulness for collaboration.

Strategy 7. Establish new guidelines for the realignment of decision-making responsibilities and accountability.

- Conduct a review of how decisions are made in the organization and to what extent there is input from those with relevant information or expertise.

- Take steps to correct any information or knowledge gaps in decision making.

- Establish clear guidelines for authority and responsibility for collaborative decision making within working group structures.

- Develop decision-making authority transfer guidelines for individuals in an interdisciplinary or cross-functional team so they have clarity as to what decision authority they can exercise on their own and when they need to obtain additional approvals.

- Develop an active delegation program where managers report on how they are realigning decision making in their department through increased assignments of job responsibilities to appropriately prepared staff.

Strategy 8. Develop a human resource strategy for the recognition and reward of collaborative contributions and results.

- Determine best practices in collaborative behavior that would warrant special recognition and/or reward in addition to performance result rewards.

- Design recognition and reward processes that provide incentives for collaborative performance at the individual or working group level.

- Develop new or expanded measures for collaborative performance activities based on feedback from working group members or customers.

- Have collaborative performance award ceremonies and publicity as early as possible after evaluating the collaborative prototype business account or project results to support the culture change.

- Move recognition and reward decisions down to the working group level for individual collaborative activities.

- Develop special award and recognition programs for best practice collaboration activities.

Strategy 9. Create the position of the Chief Collaboration Coordinator (CCC).

- Find a highly motivated champion of collaboration within the organization with a high level of organizational skills and strong social skills to be the Chief Collaboration Coordinator.

- Give this person the authority, the profile, the prestige and the resources to get the job done.

7. Action and Implementation

Taking action to implement the mutually agreed-upon tactical objectives is the final building block to be put in place in order to build the collaborative organization. There are three basic ingredients required to make sure that action is taken and carried out vigorously. They are motivation, coordination and communication. Motivation is required to make sure that agreed-upon action plans are carried out with enthusiasm. Coordination is required to make sure that the actions taken by different elements of the organization are integrated, aligned and coherent to maximize their effectiveness. And, finally, communication between all personnel of the organization is required to assure collaboration and coordination.

Collaborative relationships are important for the implementation process because they can overcome unexpected problems that could otherwise derail successful implementation. The common adage "the devil is in the details" or Robbie Burns' famous adage, "the best laid plans of mice and men often go astray" poetically express what many of us have experienced in most major project initiatives. In our complex changing world unforeseen and unforseeable changes occur, which even the best-laid contingency plans cannot account for. The integrated resources of collaborating partners, however, still offers the best means of dealing with and overcoming unexpected problems.

It is essential to have readily available, easy-to-use field support systems that support collaboration throughout the implementation process. An Internet-based network provides a medium for instant communication and the resolution of implementation issues on a real-time basis as they arise. Internal collaboration during implementation between an organization's different divisions and external collaboration with customers, suppliers and business partners of mutual action plans is one of the most immediate and effective benefits of creating such support systems. The Logan-Stokes Collaborative Knowledge Network described in Chapter 8 is an example of such a network, which facilitates communication, motivates employees and coordinates implementation of action plans (see also Skyrme, 2001).

Both virtual and physical group work environments must be created that directly foster collaborative knowledge co-creation. Physical face-to-face meetings are a powerful collaboration opportunity for multisensory co-creation between internal and external participants. Meeting facilities need to be set up to facilitate knowledge creation between members with both low-tech collaboration tools, such as graphic mind-mapping processes and the ubiquitous flip charts and/or high-tech interactive computer systems specifically designed to cultivate interactive creative processes. A designated team facilitator or collaboration coordinator will keep the meeting focused on collaboratively achieving the specific project objectives. This focus keeps the dynamic group energy moving forward in a purposeful way.

Effective collaborative meeting practices should:

- Gather input beforehand with email or telephone surveys,

- Involve all members in collaboratively prioritizing issues,

- Have clear intentions about project outcomes,

- Make sure all presentations are interactive with active participation,

- Capture all relevant meeting information to build the group mind,

- Make certain everyone participates in building and committing to coordinated action steps,

- Identify any obvious barriers and discuss ways around them,

• Review all major group decisions, making sure all internal and external participants have input into the decision and that they commit to it, and

• Create clear action steps with timelines and checkpoints so everyone knows what do to "Monday morning."

Any large implementation project must also have an Internet space for sharing and networking with all collaborating partners. This system provides real-time ability to collaborate with accurate up-to-date information. There are a number of collaboration software solutions available that can be utilized based on the organization's collaborative networking needs. (Appendix 4 – Descriptions of the Software and Consulting Companies Whose Case Studies Were Used, and the KM World Web site, www.kmworld.com/100.cfm, for the latest listings of software products to facilitate collaboration.)

Collaboration always has a purpose. Effective implementation teams are composed of passionate individuals aligned with the organization's vision. When that purpose has been fulfilled, that particular implementation team will disband. Members will then reconstitute as new collaborative teams to tackle other pressing business and organization challenges. In a Knowledge Era organization environment, this refocusing and group reformatting is one of the most important ways to cross-fertilize the entire organization through modeling successful collaborative behaviors.

There are many applications that collaborative software can facilitate, from design engineering of new products, customer relationship management and supply chain integration to mergers and acquisitions and many more. In all these collaborative applications a culture change from the previous processes and methodologies takes place. Emotional attitudes toward change, trust, sharing, diversity and similar issues are best addressed prior to any major technology implementation. Depending on the organization's culture, implementation strategies need to include assessments of current culture practices and beliefs held that will support or act as barriers to the transition to a more collaborative process.

For an example of how collaborative software can facilitate project implementations we turn to a case study in the volunteer sector (Hurst, interview, 2002). The Taproot Foundation, launched in 2001 in the San Francisco Bay Area by Aaron Hurst, is redefining volunteering by combining the efficiencies of traditional volunteer matching services with the quality management practices of leading business consulting firms. Using Internet and Web-based collaborative technologies, Taproot has developed a successful online application and project implementation process for both volunteers and the participating nonprofit organizations. This online volunteer process makes it easy for full-time professionals to integrate volunteer service into their careers and ensures that their skills and experience will be fully leveraged to provide meaningful support for critical nonprofit organizations. By enlisting thousands of trained and experienced business professionals in the community, Taproot is working to ensure that all nonprofits have access to the same professional skills as do corporations.

Using basic collaboration tools, the Taproot Foundation has created an Internet-based model for teams of volunteers from the business community to help local nonprofit organizations develop their marketing and technical infrastructure. Collaboration technology allows the foundation to expand the scope of traditional volunteerism and provide nonprofit organizations with new solutions for increasing their capacity to serve the public. Taproot's growing success is based on its committed use of technology for collaboration between the Taproot volunteers and the participating nonprofit organizations and between the Taproot volunteers who work together on the virtual project teams. Also, through the growing number of Taproot project volunteer email (Internet) user groups, organizations are starting to share information in ways that they never did before, breaking down the many silos of valuable knowledge scattered throughout the nonprofit community. By using Internet technology to create transparency between volunteer organizations, the Taproot collaborative process removes inefficiencies in the nonprofit sector, which better serves the community at large.

How the Five Collaborative Messages of the Internet Support the Seven Building Blocks

1. Two-Way Communication

Two-way communication is not just a matter of sending and receiving reciprocal messages, whether by email, telephone or other electronic means, because, most importantly, it involves dialoguing as the basis for the co-creation of knowledge. Dialoguing means a spirit of receptivity to the ideas of others, especially to those whose ideas are different from our own, as individuals collaborate together. Dialoguing most essentially means that individuals have a real opportunity to express themselves, their views, hopes, concerns, fears and ideas, on a timely basis so that all interested parties have input into the knowledge creation and decision-making process and are listened to, even if they are not necessarily involved in the final decision-making process. To ensure two-way communication facilitates collaboration, it is necessary that all relevant stakeholders have an opportunity to work together in jointly solving complex problems through shared critical and creative thinking processes. At the individual level it is important that each member of the team feels free to express themselves openly and to stand up for their rights but be sensitive to the need of others to do the same. Face-to-face meetings facilitate dialoguing, as do other electronic means of communicating informally. We provide a list of possible face-to-face and virtual collaborative forums where individuals have a chance to think and act in concert with each in the next section: Collaborative Meetings and Forums.

Two-way communication is critical for the collaborative development of the organization's vision, goals, strategies, tactical objectives, action plans and their dissemination once formulated. Conversely, the vision, goals, strategies, tactical objectives and action plans of the organization must include two-way communication to ensure collaboration throughout the organization. Organizational leaders need to be visible and willing to dialogue in open communication with all levels of the organization, demonstrating a true spirit of collaboration. Trust building depends on open communication and active listening skills to support authentic dialogue.

2. Ease of Access to Information

An intranet is the ideal medium for disseminating information throughout the extended organization, but it does not necessarily guarantee it. To ensure the ease of access to information necessary for effective collaboration on a continuing basis, there are two conditions that must be met in addition to using an intranet and other media to distribute information. They are:

1. A concerted effort must be made to collect, capture, refine, organize, store and format information and explicit knowledge that will be useful to organization members depending on their organizational role, and

2. Senior managers and front-line managers must trust the mem-
    bers of their organization to use the information that they are
    provided in a responsible manner so that all relevant informa-
    tion is readily available to appropriate individuals.

These are essential management decisions to foster the spirit of collaboration throughout the enterprise. There are, of course, appropriate
bounds on the sharing of information to protect the privacy of individuals and the proprietary information of the organization. We are not
proposing that The Coca-Cola Company divulge its secret recipe for
its syrup nor that a company publish its confidential business strategies
or health records of its employees. However, we believe that there is
substantially more information that an organization can make available
to its members to create a greater feeling of trust, community and a
sense that every member of the organization is valued and an integral
part of the whole organization. Most importantly, this open access provides the information that will allow greater co-creation of new
knowledge.

Ease of access to information is critical for the collaborative development of the organization's vision, goals, strategies, tactical objectives,
action plans and their dissemination once formulated. And the vision,
goals, strategies, tactical objectives and action plans of the organization
must include ease of access to ensure collaboration throughout the
organization.

Senior managers need to make certain that all employees can
access the same information on which decisions are based at the senior levels of the organization. Unless information is shared on a timely
basis with all members of the organization, an atmosphere of mistrust
will develop.

3. Continuous Learning

All organization members should be actively encouraged to continue
their professional education and learning process to expand their personal value to any collaborative task. This means providing individuals
with the time and resources to update their business-relevant skills and
knowledge, both for their current and future positions. It means putting mechanisms and forums in place so that knowledge can be shared
among organization members and so that new sources of knowledge
from outside the organization can be introduced to the community.

Peter Senge (1990), whose work we referred to in Chapter 3, has provided many ideas and examples of how to create a learning organization, which we will not repeat here. There is one more component, however, that should be incorporated into a learning program geared to collaboration. We believe that the skill set for collaboration should include creative thinking skills, analytical critical thinking skills, social relationship skills and self-motivational skills. They should be part of every member's education in addition to traditional information-processing skills. Since collaboration does not come naturally to everyone, those who possess collaboration skills should be encouraged to share and impart their knowledge to their co-workers through workshops and informal exchanges of ideas.

Continuous learning is critical for the collaborative development of the organization's vision, goals, strategies, tactical objectives, action plans and their implementation once formulated. At the same time, the vision, goals, strategies and tactical objectives of the organization must include continuous learning to ensure the organization's actions are all up to date. All individuals need to learn how to increase their leadership skills if they wish to achieve collaboration throughout the organization.

4. Alignment

Collaboration cannot take place unless the values and objectives of the parties are aligned. This condition pertains both internally with co-workers and externally with customers, suppliers and business allies. Teamwork is the tactical alignment of actions, whereas collaboration also entails an alignment of the knowledge resources of those collaborating.

Alignment is critical for the collaborative realization of the organization's goals, strategies, tactical objectives and action plans and depends on the existence of a climate of trust and community. The vision, goals, strategies, tactical objectives and action plans of the organization, on the other hand, must be aligned with the personal careers and aspirations of the organization's stakeholders. This point is illustrated by the experience at Turner Construction, which in planning its implementation of its knowledge network, the TKN, took into account the requirement to align the needs of the organization and the personnel with positive implications for recruitment, employee retention and staff development.

When we did the original TKN business plan, we really needed to align our business strategy with our learning strategy. There were three drivers; one was retention, one was recruitment and the other was development of staff. Let's take them one at a time. Let me take recruiting first of all because recruiting is not just new hires out of college, but it is also experienced hires out of industry. And we developed our knowledge network and its learning process because one of the consistent findings that came out of surveys for the last 20 years is that what people want is training. While our colleges and universities do a wonderful job of preparing people to think, they don't necessarily give them what they need from a practical side on how you build buildings. So this becomes a tremendous recruiting tool since we can increase the quality of the recruits that are coming into our company. Also it's a great recruiting tool for experienced hires because there are not too many companies that have this kind of vision that Turner has and what we have been able to create in the last couple of years.

It's also a big tool for retention because when our staff have been with us for four or five years, they actually become pretty valuable in the industry. They get hit by recruiters and headhunters all the time. Our concept here is "think twice" before you say, "I'm going take that next $10,000 in salary and I'm going to leave." We want them to think whether their next company is going to have the kinds of resources that they are going to really need to develop their careers. So that's a big part of the retention issue. And we're measuring all this so we can see over a long period of time whether or not we're making an impact.

The third thing was the development of staff. And now if we can get a young man or woman to become a superintendent, engineer or project manager to a level of competency or proficiency in 10 years instead of, say, 12 years, then we've done something not just for the individual in terms of their career, but also for ourselves as a company. We have done something good; plus they are better skilled, they are more knowledgeable. (Mitnick, interview, 2003)

5. Community

The analytic and technical skills needed for collaboration can be taught as can certain social skills, such as understanding group dynamics and relationship building. The motivation to collaborate and share one's knowledge cannot be taught, but it can be nurtured and encouraged.

This is why community and the sense of community are essential to create a fertile environment for collaboration. Each of the other four messages—two-way communication, ease of access to information, continuous learning, especially through knowledge sharing, and alignment—all contribute to building community.

Community also requires providing opportunities for professional and social interactions so that employees and managers can develop their relationships and build their sense of community. The building of social capital requires an investment, but the spirit of collaboration that increased social capital makes possible can provide a readily justifiable ROI.

A shared vision and goals gives rise to a sense of community, and a vision and goals that include a sense of community will reinforce collaboration within the organization. The greater the sense of community that can be created, the less dependent an organization is on leadership to foment a collaborative environment. Trust is the bedrock foundation upon which community is built; there can be no sustainable community without trust between its members. A community is basically a society in which individuals trust each other and wish to collaborate with each other. The power of community is enhanced when all members of the organization are included and feel personally committed to achieving the objectives.

Collaborative Meetings and Forums

The implementation of collaborative goals, strategies and tactical objectives requires people coming together to share their ideas, thoughts and knowledge. Throughout our discussion of the seven building blocks of a collaborative organization we have stressed the need for collaborative meetings and forums. In the final section of this chapter, we describe a number of relationship-building processes and venues to bring people together to collaborate and search for consensus.

Chief Collaboration Coordinator (CCC)

We have already described in the section on the strategy block the role that the Chief Collaboration Coordinator (CCC) can play to facilitate the organization of collaborative meetings and forums.

Informal Social Meetings

Informal lunchtime or after-work meetings where individuals can get together socially to come to know each other better are extremely effective for the exchange of tacit knowledge and the discussion of problems that need to be addressed collaboratively. A lunch-and-learn environment can be created for informal sharing of individual or team information that is of general interest. Another important feature of this program is providing a time period and opportunity for developing and expanding relationships informally.

Large-Scale Collaborative Meetings

Important objectives that require the collaborative input of a large number of individuals can be accomplished through a specific, large group, collaborative workshop process along the lines developed by Dannemiller Tyson Associates. The main defining factors for success are the intentions and commitment of senior management to the collaborative process and the alignment of the expectations of all the participants. There are different facilitation processes that can engage large numbers of organization members as collaborative participants in discussing, analyzing and making decisions on major issues. These processes employ trust-building and open-dialogue meeting techniques in which individuals:

- Feel empowered to discuss and align their personal visions for their work and the organization,

- Are encouraged to demonstrate their passion to important organization goals through open dialogue in self-forming groups,

- Have the opportunity to collaborate with other passionate individuals and co-create specific tactical objectives to achieve those goals, and

- Participate in creating action plans relevant to their work to achieve those objectives.

There are different electronic technologies that can be deployed for real-time polling of large groups. Direct feedback can be obtained on group recommendations or by voting on options that senior leadership present. The most critical factor for success in this process is the follow-through by senior leadership with the feedback from many organization members. Misaligned expectations can wreck havoc within an organization, for example, if participants expect acceptance and implementation of their recommendations and senior management only treat them as information for consideration. Clear communication about expectations of the process and the results are essential for it to be successful. These are very powerful enterprise-wide tools that can provide important opportunities to develop a collaborative culture (Allee, 2003, pp. 137-38).

Conferences and Workshops

In an Internet-connected organization environment, information and knowledge can be co-created and shared online throughout the organization anywhere in the world. Therefore, one of the key objectives for having individuals physically come together in conferences or workshops is for relationship and trust building through face-to-face collaborative activities. This can be done within the format of skills and knowledge training development sessions. Conference and workshop facilitators must ensure that collaborative relationship development has a high priority within the specific group process activities. Based on a prior assessment of the emotional and motivational competency needs of the individuals, specific competencies such as adaptability, self-confidence, managing change and empathy, to name a few, can be planned for within group problem-solving sessions.

Knowledge Networks

A knowledge network is an excellent tool for sharing and co-creating knowledge. It allows users to identify the expertise they need to collaborate with. It also can be a learning tool with online diagnostic tools and courses. In Chapter 8 we will fully develop the design for a knowledge network. David Skyrme has devoted an entire book entitled *Knowledge Networking* (2001) to this subject.

Virtual Meeting Places

Advances in information technology have certainly made collaboration between co-workers easier, especially for those who are not co-located. As powerful as these technologies are, they cannot replace the intimacy of face-to-face meetings and should never be used instead of them. They are excellent tools, however, to bridge the gaps between face-to-face meetings and therefore should be part of the IT arsenal for collaboration, which includes:

- Personal email exchange,
- A listserv serving a group of users with a common interest such as a community of practice,
- A project chat room,
- Video or telephone conference calls,
- Intranet-based knowledge networks, and
- Web-enabled collaborative tools.

Spontaneous virtual meetings cannot be mandated by the organization, but they can be supported and encouraged so that individuals take the initiative to develop collaborative exchanges where topics are chosen according to the passionate interests of the participants.

Web-Enabled Collaborative Tools

The Internet technology for collaboration within a company, and between companies and their suppliers and customers, has become increasingly sophisticated and readily available on a national and global scale. A number of companies have created Internet based-collaboration enabling software widely used throughout North America and the world. (See Appendix 4 – Descriptions of the Software and Consulting Companies Whose Case Studies Were Used, and KM World Web site, www.kmworld.com/100.cfm, for the latest listings of software products to facilitate collaboration.) However, as we have discussed above, the enabling technical hardware and software issues of collaboration are only part of the solution. They provide the necessary technological infrastructure but depend on the member's attitudes and motivations to actively exploit the software to develop a sustainable collaborative culture.

A First-Hand Report of Virtual Collaboration

Jon Wagner, president of J. Wagner Consulting Inc., is very much a virtual worker with a passion for IT-assisted collaboration. Jon has had the challenge of helping to build, lead and sustain numerous high-performance virtual and remote teams at Hewlett-Packard and Agilent Technologies over the past 15 years. He was a member of leadership teams for large business units, managed teams that delivered HR services, led virtual project teams and consulted to business leadership teams. Team members were geographically dispersed across Europe, Asia and the Americas and came from many different time zones, cultures and languages. For much of the last decade, Jon telecommuted nationally and globally from his home office located north of Toronto, Canada. He was able to successfully communicate and collaborate online globally with minimal face-to-face meetings. Here is Jon's story of virtual collaboration by making use of a variety of Web-enabled collaboration tools as described above:

> I helped lead research into Remote Leadership with a consortium of companies, which also found that remote management and geographically dispersed and virtual teams had become a critical issue. We found managers and leaders of virtual and remote teams have many of the same challenges and require the same skills of all successful leaders, but there are several areas that need special attention:
>
> * Leading with purpose, vision and goals,
> * Building and maintaining trust,
> * Communicating and providing access to information,
> * Providing coaching and timely feedback,
> * Creating a sense of "team,"
> * Using travel effectively,
> * Using technology effectively, and
> * Orienting new employees.
>
> As a member and leader of many virtual teams, I had embraced interactive Web technology at the same time as being committed to building collaboration. Building a shared vision is important for all leaders, but a remote leader especially cannot be effective without each and every team member knowing what success will look like, and ultimately how it will be measured.
>
> Virtual teaming is a day-to-day thing. Sensitivity to time zones and cultural differences are extremely important. Quarterly "coffee talks" using interactive Web conferencing allows the leadership team to communicate stories about progress towards the vision, highlight key contributions, poll for real-time results, and respond to pressing critical questions. Web conferencing tools also enable interactive team meetings for collaborating on document creation and revision, while information sharing is efficiently

done by email and audio conferences. Limited travel is used most effectively to launch the team, orient new team members, develop a shared vision and build trust and relationships.

Effective use of technology actually allowed remote and virtual teams to outperform co-located teams by working on projects around the clock, maintaining key documents in "eRooms," with everyone having access to continuously updated documents. A discipline was developed in the team through "operating agreements" where the team documented how they planned to work together. Agreements covered such things as the understanding that all emails would be responded to within 24 hours, a process for dealing with conflict and disagreements and a process for managing meetings. Living up to these agreements is the cornerstone for building trust.

Regular communications with each team member is especially important for virtual leaders. As a best practice with my teams, I scheduled a monthly one-hour one-to-one teleconference to acknowledge contributions and review the next month's priorities and issues with each person on the team. A face-to-face meeting was planned for at least once per year.

Creating a sense of team must be a priority and takes effort that is well worth it. A critical success factor is having clear, documented goals, well-defined roles and agreed-upon processes for working together. Building and maintaining trust and relationships requires regular two-way communication, both formal and informal. We used regular virtual "watercooler" teleconferences that allowed for informal chats, much like the ones that spontaneously happened at Hewlett-Packard in offices—only these had to be planned so everyone "showed up" at the virtual watercooler to celebrate birthdays, catch up on what's new and get into engaging discussions for a brief weekly break that built trust and enhanced relationships. (Wagner, private communication, 2002)

The Logan-Stokes-Wagner Collaboration Matrix

Together with our colleague Jon Wagner we created a cubic matrix (see Table 6.1), which lists various forms of communication and identifies the ones that can lead to collaboration. We classify communication media first in terms of whether or not they permit two-way communication and, hence, whether or not they can be used for collaborative interactions, as two-way communication is a prerequisite for collaboration. We then classify the media in terms of whether they are synchronous, i.e., occurring at the same time, or asynchronous, i.e., occurring at different times. Finally, we classify the media in terms of whether the participants are in the same place location or whether they are in different locations.

Table 6.1: Logan-Stokes-Wagner Collaboration Matrix

Examples	Collaborative Space with Two-Way Communication	Time	Physical Locality
Face-to-face meetings Lecture/presentation (with question period)	Yes	Same	Same
Telephone Web-enabled collaborative tools WebEx Net Meeting Video conferencing	Yes	Same	Different
Interactive bulletin board	Yes	Different	Same
email Listserv Chat rooms e-room e-bulletin e-commerce/ c-commerce	Yes	Different	Different
Non-collaborative command-and-control directive/order Lecture/presentation (without question period)	No	Same	Same
TV Radio	No	Same	Different
Public notice bulletin board Traffic signals/signs	No	Different	Same
Written orders Books Reports	No	Different	Different

Notes:

- If there is a shared collaborative cyberspace, it implies two-way communication

- Each modality has a role when used appropriately
- Time:
  - Same: when everyone can participate at the same time
  - Different: when you can't all be together at the same time

A Multidimensional Approach to Creating Collaborative Space

Northrop Grumman is a premier aerospace systems integration enterprise for a number of strategic military aircraft programs in the U.S. and abroad. With nearly 96,000 employees and operations in 44 states and 25 countries, Northrop Grumman places a great deal of importance on collaboration. In an interview, Dr. Scott Shaffar and Jerry Garcia, project managers for KM, outlined their organization's multidimensional approach to collaboration, which combines virtual and physical environments as follows:

> The main barriers to collaboration, if you are geographically separated, is how do you know there are others out there to collaborate with? How do you find them? Then how do you build those trust relationships that are needed since you don't normally see those people on a daily basis or work with them?
>
> We are developing different communities of practice as our main approach in building trust. We believe that trust is basically built by creating the opportunities for personnel to share information and work together on some project and that typically takes time.
>
> Even in the world of the Internet, we still see a lot of face-to-face meetings. Having initial face-to-face meetings has been our going-in position. I think you need to look at it from the standpoint that the virtual meetings and the collaborative spaces really give you that ability to keep things moving after you've had the face-to-face and you've developed that initial level of trust. We have communities of practice that will have virtual meetings on a more frequent basis than they have actual face-to-face meetings in part because of budget constraints. Their face-to-face may only happen once a year, but they have routine meetings all the time that are done through virtual collaborative spaces.
>
> We have found five major issues for increasing collaboration through collaborative software implementation, which is essential for enterprise-wide collaboration within the company and with our business partners and suppliers.

User Learning Curve. The first issue is the general user learning curve. People have to learn how to use any collaboration software application and this takes time; not everyone learns at the same speed. We have found that the learning curve is aided for the most part not by any formal classroom training but by others helping others—peer-to-peer learning.

Behavior Change. The second issue, which is probably the most important one, is behavior change. Patience is really the key word here because as change agents, we realized over time that people don't accept change easily. You need to change the culture to the new way of thinking. Once you get the process going and you show people the benefits of this new way of doing business, it really starts taking off on its own.

Leadership. What drives the change in behavior most effectively is leadership—mandating that everyone use that new collaborative technology, saying, "That's the only way we're going to work as a team." Leadership drives the change in behavior. That's what we have seen to be most effective.

Work Integration. The fourth issue is to integrate the collaboration software application with normal work.

The Importance of Collaboration Meeting Spaces. One of the other issues that we are pursuing on the topic of collaboration is actually in the area of physical office environments. We think they have a great impact on team collaboration on a daily basis. Over the past 20 to 25 years we have been organized by cubicles. We have been moving towards a more open-plan environment that is laid out to support teams. Within that open-plan environment we have small centralized areas that are shared team space that are specifically there for promoting short, impromptu team meetings. We've done some surveys that show that these environments are definitely increasing collaboration and communication.

Physical space has a very significant impact. People work in the areas that surround the collaborative environment with its conference table and chairs in the center. We have white boards, tack boards and embedded high-tech tools. On that conference table are the LAN connections so people will sit down with their laptops and plug in, we have our projector, our pull-down screen and speakerphone. So this is where we do our Net meetings, etc. Effective collaboration for us is not based on just one approach, it's multidimensional. (Shaffar and Garcia, interview, 2003)

Having developed the seven building blocks for creating the collaborative organization, we next turn to a consideration of how to measure the level of collaboration in an organization in the next chapter where we introduce the Collaboration Quotient Tool.

The Collaboration Quotient (CQ)

Measuring the Collaborative Capacity of an Organization and Its Personnel

It is a well-known adage in business that once something is measured people pay attention to it. Measuring the ability of individual employees to collaborate is the first step towards building a collaborative organization. Collaboration requires motivated personnel with the requisite emotional and intellectual skills and access to needed tools and information. We have developed a methodology for measuring the collaborative capacity of an organization and its personnel. Every organization has achieved a certain level of collaboration just to have survived; the question is to what degree. Any program to increase the level of collaboration in an organization must start with an assessment of the existing level of collaboration and attitudes towards it among the staff and management. It is also important to determine the level and effectiveness of the organizational infrastructure that could support collaboration, as well as the ability of the organization to collaborate with customers, suppliers and partners.

An initial assessment of the collaborative culture of the organization, as well as its systems, procedures and processes, is essential in planning a successful collaboration implementation process. Understanding the reality of the organization's culture, as expressed by its constituent members and in its vision, practices, processes and procedures, will give us the necessary understanding of the collaboration gaps across the entire organization, including all of its personnel. With this information one can determine the priority and sequencing of measures to create a successful collaborative organization. While some organizational processes or procedures can be modified relatively easily, other processes can take considerably longer. The same holds true for cultural mind-set changes—some may take place quickly, while others will take much longer.

The Logan-Stokes Collaboration Tool, which includes the Collaboration Quotient, (CQ), is a suite of collaborative KM-measuring instruments that allow an assessment of an organization's readiness for collaboration. The information gathered using this tool makes it possible to make the appropriate decisions for building a collaborative organization. The suite of collaboration tools consists of the following four elements:

1. The Collaboration Quotient (CQ), which measures the willingness and ability of individual employees to collaborate in co-creating and sharing knowledge.

2. The Managers' Collaboration Quotient (MCQ), which measures the level of support and encouragement for collaboration from senior executives and the middle managers.

3. The Organizational Collaboration Quotient, which measures the degree to which the organization's current systems, policies, procedures and infrastructure support collaboration.

4. The Collaborative Commerce Quotient, which measures the organization's readiness to enter into collaborative relationships with customers, suppliers and potential business partners.

The Collaboration Quotient (CQ)

The most fundamental building blocks of a collaborative organization are the interpersonal relationships between the members of the organization. In order to measure the willingness and ability of each member of the organization to collaborate, we make use of an instrument that we call the Collaboration Quotient (CQ).

The CQ assesses individuals through a series of questions within the framework of the five collaborative messages of the Internet and the seven collaborative building blocks of the organization. A CQ profile provides information on the individual's collaborative strengths and weaknesses and, hence, identifies developmental gaps in their behavior and attitude that need to be addressed. It also determines each individual's perception of the collaborative capability of the organization.

By aggregating the CQ scores of individuals, the readiness levels of working groups, departments, divisions and the organization as a whole can be determined and compared. Through a series of questions about their own performance, that of their colleagues and the collaborative infrastructure, the staff provide a picture of the current status of collaboration within the organization from their perspective.

An analysis of responses will provide a sense of the strengths and weaknesses of the organization's collaborative capacity. From this information one will be able to determine what goals, strategies and tactical objectives the organization needs to take to optimize its potential for becoming a more collaborative organization. The full collaboration assessment process also creates an awareness among participants of the value of collaboration.

The Collaboration Quotient is divided into three basic components corresponding to the cognitive, emotional intelligence and motivational aspects of collaboration as outlined in Chapter 5. This will generate three measures:

1. The intelligence quotient, or IQ, which measures the cognitive skills required for collaboration,
2. The emotional intelligence quotient, or EQ, which measures the social skills required for collaboration, and
3. The motivational quotient, or MQ, which measures the motivation to collaborate.

From the three measures of IQ, EQ and MQ we can generate two versions of the collaboration quotient, one which we call the average collaboration quotient and denote by CQav and the other the effective collaboration quotient, which we simply denote as CQ. We obtain the average collaboration quotient by adding the IQ, EQ and MQ measures and dividing by three so that

$$CQav = (IQ + EQ + MQ)/3$$

The effective collaboration quotient, on the other hand, is the product of IQ, EQ and MQ so that

$$CQ = IQ \times EQ \times MQ$$

The values of IQ, EQ, MQ and CQav provide information on how well and where progress is being made by individual employees. The CQ or the effective collaboration quotient, composed of the product of IQ, EQ and MQ, however, gives a measure of the effectiveness of the collaboration contribution for each individual. Because collaboration must be balanced, an individual must possess all three skill sets to be effective. If any one of the skill sets has not been developed to an adequate level, then that individual's ability to collaborate is compromised. Without cognitive skills the individual has little of substance to offer. And without social skills, even if they have something to offer, their contribution will be compromised because of their inability to work with others. And finally, if someone is socially skilled and has good ideas but is not motivated to share with others, very little or no collaboration will take place. It therefore follows that a successful collaborator must score high in all three quotients, IQ, EQ and MQ, and therefore the product of these three quotients is a measure of collaboration effectiveness.

The Collaboration Quotient instrument is specifically designed to assess the most relevant behaviors and attitudes of an individual to be an active collaborating member of an organization. We do not directly assess any specific emotional or motivational competencies per se, but only indirectly insofar as these competencies support collaborative behaviors. As we have discussed in the previous chapter, different authors on emotional intelligence have identified, named and organized their versions of the important emotional and motivational competencies from their different theoretical perspectives. Appropriate competency categories from these different models, along with additional competencies that we believe are essential for building a collaborative organization, have served as important references in our design of the Collaboration Quotient.

The Collaboration Quotient instrument is also used to probe the opinions of the staff as to the effectiveness and availability of the organization's collaborative and organizational infrastructure. This information is then matched with the information gathered using the Organizational Collaboration Quotient instrument.

The Collaboration Quotient Instrument, the Five Messages of the Internet and the Seven Building Blocks of a Collaborative Organization

The Collaboration Quotient instrument is divided into 12 sections, corresponding to the five collaborative messages of the Internet (two-way communication, ease of access to information, continuous learning, alignment and community) and the seven building blocks of a collaborative organization (vision, leadership, trust, goals, strategies, tactical objectives and implementation). We use these categories to probe because they form the basis of our model of collaboration first presented in Chapter 4 and elaborated on in Chapters 5 and 6. The five messages and the seven building blocks metaphorically form the warp and woof of collaboration. Without these essential, interwoven, enabling elements there cannot be a functioning collaborative organization in the knowledge economy.

Some of the questions we ask will determine the IQ, EQ and MQ measures and some of the questions will pertain to the existence and effectiveness of the organization's infrastructure and procedures for collaboration. We will indicate for the sample questions we now present which measure is being probed by using the following codes: IQ, EQ, MQ and INF (for infrastructure). The distribution of IQ, EQ, MQ and INF questions will be different for the 12 categories (five messages and seven building blocks) as each requires a different mix of characteristics. The questions we present are representative of our instrument, but they do not represent the complete set. The responses to the questions that will be requested will be valued on a Likert scale of 1 to 5, where 5 denotes almost always, 3 denotes 50% of the time, 1 denotes hardly ever and 2 and 4 are intermediate values. The weighting of each question will vary, as some factors can be determined with a single question and others with two or more questions.

1. Two-Way Communication

IQ
- Is the information and knowledge you bring to your work and your working group discussions appropriate, current and complete for the task at hand or the problems being examined?

- Do you clearly articulate and explain your position so that others can easily understand you?

EQ
- Do you take into account the needs of your co-workers when communicating with them?

- Do you find that diversity in opinions causes more richness as opposed to more strife in group discussions?

MQ
- Do you feel that management and your organization listen to you and your working group's ideas?

- Do you reach out to others and stimulate and generate two-way communication?

- Does your manager keep you informed of important and current information?

INF
- Is the communication infrastructure in your organization adequate to provide you with meaningful collaborative communication with all members of your organization?

2. Ease of Access to Information

IQ
- Do you frame, organize and communicate your ideas and thoughts in such a way as to make them easily accessible to others?

- Do you know how to readily access the information you require to do your job?

INF
- Do you have the level of access to the information you require to do your job?

- Do your customers have access to the information they need so that you can serve them better?

- Do you have the ability to search and access information at your desktop from both organizational and worldwide resources?

3. Continuous Learning

IQ
- Do you know how to organize and build knowledge structures with others and independently?

- Do you know how to evaluate your own competencies and those of others?

- Can you source the knowledge you require but might not possess?

MQ
• Do you value learning and are you disciplined to do the work necessary for effective learning?

INF
• Is continuous learning encouraged, facilitated and provided by your organization?

4. Alignment

IQ
• Are you able to share and integrate your knowledge with others easily?

EQ
• Are you aligned with your working group's vision?

• Are you aligned with your organization's vision?

MQ
• Are the objectives of the group well defined and understood by all the working group members, and aligned with your values and theirs?

• Are you motivated to find and enhance the common elements between your individual goals and those of your organization?

INF
• Do you find there is alignment and integration of the data, information and knowledge available to the group?

• Are all the members of your working group aligned to work together collaboratively?

5. Community

EQ
• Do you feel supported by your workplace community?

MQ
• Do you enjoy your community of colleagues at work?

• Do you have an enthusiastic willingness to work with others versus working on your own?

INF
- Are there sufficient opportunities for face-to-face meetings and regularly scheduled events to meet with co-workers?

- Are face-to-face meetings supplemented by electronic communications?

- Do your co-workers consistently provide support and advice to you and others?

- Do you believe that your co-workers have a sense of allegiance and loyalty to the organization as a whole and to each other?

6. Vision

IQ
- Do you feel you have the analytical and creative thinking skills to contribute to a vision of your working group and your organization?

- Do you have a clear vision of your own professional career?

EQ
- Do you strongly believe in the organization's vision?

- Do you find that the organization's vision is a lived dynamic vision as compared to static words?

MQ
- Does the organization's vision capture your imagination and passion, your heart and soul and inspire you to greatness?

INF
- Does there exist a clearly defined vision for your organization's operations?

- Is there a common set of values shared by the members of your organization?

- Does the visioning process include you and all the organization's members through an ongoing communication process?

7. Leadership

IQ
- Do you feel you have the necessary decision-making skills to take an active and effective leadership role in your team?

EQ
- Do you avail yourself of the opportunity to be a self-leader by taking self-initiated actions appropriate to your position and experience?

MQ
- Are you willing and prepared to take on more responsibilities in your current position?

- How committed do you feel senior management is to making your company a collaborative organization?

- Does your manager encourage you to become more innovative and take a more active role in presenting your ideas?

INF
- Are you and your working group given the opportunity to make important work decisions and initiate strategic actions?

- For your position, does your company provide you the opportunity for online and/or workshop training in leadership skills?

8. Trust

IQ
- Do you trust that the members of your team, internal and/or external, have the skills and abilities to overcome the challenges that the team faces to achieve its objectives?

EQ
- Do you trust the members of your working group to behave in a reliable manner?

- Do you trust the members of your working group to be supportive and not take advantage of your vulnerabilities?

MQ
- Does your manager trust the quality of your work by giving you increasingly challenging work assignments?

INF
- Do you feel that your organization treats you fairly?

- Do you feel that trust and respect are true core values of your company that the organization lives by?

9. Goals

IQ
- Are you clear about the goals you and your working group are working to achieve?

MQ
- Do you feel personally committed to achieving the goals of both your working group and your organization as a whole?

INF
- Are you actively involved in setting the goals you are responsible for achieving?

- Does your working group set its goals collaboratively as compared to the goals being imposed from above?

- Do you feel free to voice your opinions about how your working group's goals are determined?

10. Strategies

IQ
- Do you proactively involve your customers in jointly developing your business strategies?

- Do you have a clear understanding of the business strategies of your organization as a whole?

- Do you have a clear understanding of the business strategies of your working group?

INF

- Are your working group's strategies for achieving its goals arrived at collaboratively?

- Is there an adequate communication flow between different working groups in developing and executing overall organizational strategies?

- Are the strategies of the working groups and departments of the organization aligned and coordinated?

11. Tactical Objectives

EQ
- Does your team encourage all members to actively participate in creating the project or account objectives?

MQ
- Do you have an active role in formulating the project or account objectives that you are responsible for achieving?

INF
- Are the tactical objectives of individual working groups communicated to each other?

- Are the tactical objectives of individual working groups coordinated?

- Are the tactical objectives of your organization clearly defined and communicated?

- Does your team have the resources necessary to achieve the tactical objectives you are responsible for?

12. Implementation

IQ
- Do you feel you have gaps in the technical skills needed to adequately carry out your responsibilities?

EQ
- Do you find it easy to work with your co-workers in day-to-day operations?

MQ
- Do you find your day-to-day work exciting and challenging?

- Is every team member encouraged to voice their views on how the project is going so the team is quickly alerted to any potential problems in the implementation process?

INF
- Do you have the communication and collaboration tools to work effectively with your team members throughout the organization on a daily basis?

The Managers' Collaboration Quotient (MCQ)

In the transition from a hierarchical organization to a more collaborative one, senior executives and middle managers play a pivotal role by encouraging and coaching the employees for whom they are responsible and by delegating appropriately challenging work. Managers and executives are therefore asked to respond to the same Collaboration Quotient instrument as their staff and then respond to an additional instrument, the Managers' Collaboration Quotient (MCQ). The MCQ deals with their role in stimulating and supporting collaboration within the working unit for which they are responsible or, in the case of senior executives, for the organization as a whole. The MCQ also deals with the executives' and managers' vision and strategy for the successful transformation of their organization into a collaborative culture.

The different members of a working group can assess their own collaborative CQ scores and compare their own profile to the working group's composite collaborative profile. This provides the working group and working group leader with a dynamic assessment of the working group's current collaborative reality as the essential first step in enhancing the quality of collaborative relationships. Comparisons can also be made between different working groups and/or divisions of the organization. By having all members of the organization, including middle managers and senior executives, evaluate the overall collaborative culture of the organization, a valuable 360-degree evaluation is realized.

MCQ questions are presented in an interview format to establish dialogue and to stimulate a process of self-reflection. Here is a sample of some of the questions we ask.

- Do you proactively dialogue with and seek out the ideas, opinions and feedback of those who report directly to you, as well as other members of the organization?

- Do you share your knowledge with your direct reports and colleagues on a regular basis?

- Do you encourage open communication between yourself and your direct reports and are they free to speak their mind with you?

- Do you make information to which you are privy available to your direct reports on a regular basis?

- Do you demonstrate the value of continuous learning by actively and publicly learning new skills and competencies?

- Do you actively encourage and support continuous learning of direct reports by organizing access to education and/or training courses, by providing time off from regular duties for learning and by recognizing learning achievements of your staff?

- Do you actively coordinate and align the efforts of those who report to you so that they are working together coherently?

- Do you develop activities that build community in the working group, division or organization for which you are responsible?

- Do those for whom you are responsible have a vision of their role in the organization and is it reviewed periodically?

- Do you encourage those for whom you are responsible to take a stronger leadership role in initiating actions and making decisions without "micro-managing" them?

- Do you delegate challenging and critical work goals to those for whom you are responsible and allow them to make decisions as to how they will achieve those goals?

- Do you encourage input and feedback from all quarters in developing the goals, strategies and tactical objectives of the working group or division for which you are responsible?

The Organizational Collaboration Quotient

The Organizational Collaboration Quotient instrument is a detailed survey that is completed by senior executives to determine whether the organization has the appropriate communication facilities, access to information, continuous learning facilities, effective knowledge networks and all the tools and infrastructure it needs to become a collaborative organization. A cross-check on the effectiveness of the collaboration infrastructure can be made by comparing the results of this instrument with the response of individual employees to those questions in the Collaboration Quotient instrument that deal with infrastructure. This analysis will provide valuable insights as to how the organization's current systems, policies, procedures and infrastructure to support collaboration can be improved. Sample questions that are part of the instrument include the following queries:

- Is the organization's Internet or intranet an effective channel for two-way communication?

- Can one access relevant organizational databases through up-to-date search engines to find accurate information for creating strategies and making effective decisions?

- Does the organization have an effective intranet so one can communicate easily and on a timely basis with anyone in the organization anywhere in the world?

- Is the intranet structure extremely user friendly so that one can find needed information and knowledge easily without a great deal of effort?

- Are the information systems designed to distribute accurate information quickly throughout the entire organization?

- Are there organizational online learning systems that are organized to make it easy to learn in a just-in-time mode?

- Are there continuous learning programs that encourage individuals to learn or enhance work-related skills during work time or with tuition reimbursement for off-time courses?

- Is the collaborative learning and knowledge networking aligned and integrated with the product support and distribution function?

- Do you find the collaborative learning programs aligned and integrated with the needs of the marketplace?

- Is the Internet used to create a sense of community among employees, customers and suppliers?

- How much trust is there that the technology infrastructure will be maintained and upgraded to support the collaboration initiative enterprise-wide?

- Are there reward and recognition systems in place that compensate teams and individual members for successful collaborative achievement of goals?

- Is there a secure information database about key customers and main competitors that is continually updated and accessible to authorized individuals?

- Are the goals, strategies and tactical objectives of the various working groups, divisions and the organization as a whole readily accessible and understood by all employees?

- Does anyone in the organization fulfill the role of the Chief Collaboration Coordinator?

The Collaborative Commerce Quotient

The Collaborative Commerce Quotient is a far-ranging appraisal instrument to determine if an organization is in a position to develop collaborative relationships with customers, suppliers and potential business partners (i.e., external organizations) and to conduct collaborative commerce. The scope of collaboration can range from working with customers or suppliers to develop new products or services to entering into joint ventures with third parties, even competitors. The Collaborative Commerce Quotient can also provide a focus on the relationships with specific key customers or suppliers with the goal of improving specific collaborative partnerships. Here is a sample of some of the questions we ask.

- Do individuals at all levels of the organization understand the objectives of collaboration with external organizations and the importance of their role in the well-being of the organization?

- Is communication currently open and frank between your personnel and that of the external organizations with which you are working?

- Are systems and processes in place to ensure appropriate access to current information between organizations?

- Do the personnel in both organizations have direct access to pertinent information (as opposed to rumors) about the collaborative partnership and how it impacts them?

- How well do the organization partners understand each other's core businesses?

- Have lessons learned from previous collaborative partnerships been shared with all members of your organization?

- To what extent are collaborative relationships being built at multiple levels throughout both organizations?

- How much do the two organizations' current visions overlap? How much potential overlap is there?

- Is a new shared vision for the collaboration of the two organizations being developed collaboratively?

- How committed are the senior leaders of both organizations to collaboration?

- Have the goals of the collaborative venture been made specific?

- Are the goals of approximate equal parity and importance for the two participating organizations?

- Are tactical objectives collaboratively developed by individuals from both organizations?

- Is there a joint administrative structure to ensure that challenges and barriers that may arise between the two organizations will be quickly resolved?

- Are there regularly scheduled review and analysis sessions to resolve tactical objectives issues or problems?

Conclusion

By responding to these questions the reader can begin to assess the level of collaboration within their organization. For a more complete analysis of an organization's collaborative capacity the full Logan-Stokes Collaboration Tool is recommended.

The Logan-Stokes Collaborative Knowledge Network (LSCKN)

An Internet-based knowledge network is an excellent tool and platform for most KM activities. In the majority of organizations, a knowledge network or intranet is used for acquiring, collecting, organizing and applying information and explicit knowledge. As we have stressed throughout this book, this is only half of the KM mandate. In this chapter we will describe a knowledge network that can be used to do all of the above and also aid in the creation of new knowledge, facilitate the sharing of tacit knowledge and serve as a medium for collaboration. Tacit knowledge cannot by definition be shared directly over the Net because it requires personal contact. Only explicit knowledge can be packaged into a format that can be shared over the Net. A knowledge network, however, can serve the function of identifying and finding those individuals within the organization and among its customers and suppliers with whom one would want to develop a personal relationship for the purposes of collaborating and sharing tacit knowledge. A knowledge network can be organized not only to answer the question of "know what" but also the question of "know who."

The Logan-Stokes Collaborative Knowledge Network (LSCKN), which we will present in this chapter, is an architectural design of a knowledge network that is both a tool and a platform to facilitate the process of innovation and collaboration that an organization requires to compete in the Knowledge Era. We shall explore how Internet technology provides an ideal environment for the actualization of the key elements of collaborative knowledge management that we have identified throughout this book. We see the Internet as a powerful medium that supports, enhances and facilitates collaborative knowledge management. An Internet-based knowledge network is an ideal medium for knowledge networking and dynamic teaming. It facilitates the development and cultivation of the intangible assets of intellectual capital and in particular the way in which human, structural and external intangible assets can be coherently marshaled to achieve organizational objectives. It provides a medium for capturing group memory, which is the essence of organizational knowledge. The organization's capacity to recall its past events, actions and results and to apply them to a new situation saves both time and money, as valuable lessons do not have to be relearned. The culture of an organization is not just its social and business practices but also its organizational knowledge. Many firms talk about how much they value their organization's culture but forget to develop a strategy to capture and increase their organizational knowledge. The great value of human culture is that a child born into a culture does not have to go through the painful experience of relearning the many lessons that have been embedded in the culture. A company, like a society, that has invested in retaining its organizational memory does not have to relearn the painful lessons of the past and as a result can use its resources more productively.

Knowledge networking is an excellent tool for the conversion of tacit knowledge into explicit knowledge and is at the heart of Nonaka-Takeuchi's model of knowledge creation. "Knowledge can be amplified or crystallized at the group level through dialogue, discussion, experience sharing and observation....Team members create new points of view through dialogue and discussion" (Nonaka and Takeuchi, 1995, pp. 13-14). Dialogue is essential to knowledge creation because no one person holds the key to knowledge. New knowledge does not arise in isolation but in communities of interest or practice. People create new knowledge by organizing their experiences in new ways that build on the experiences of others but still reflect their own personal perspectives and insights. Dynamic teaming is group thinking and creative collaboration, which results in knowledge co-creation. A knowledge network allows members of an organization to identify each other to create a community of practice. It also allows members of the community of practice to remain in touch with each other between face-to-face meetings.

In addition to its role in the creation of new knowledge, a knowledge network has another an important function, namely the application of that knowledge to achieve the organization's objectives. "The economic problem of society is thus not merely a problem of how to allocate 'given' resources...it is a problem of the utilization of knowledge not given to anyone in its totality" (Hayek, 1945).

It is not only the products of knowledge networking, i.e., new knowledge and the application of knowledge to practical problems, that are of value, but the process itself has a value for the organization. "The so-called 'Hawthorne' experiments showed that social factors such as morale, a 'sense of belonging' to a work group, and interpersonal skills to understand human behavior improved productivity" (Nonaka and Takeuchi, 1995, p. 36).

The Internet already functions as a global knowledge network for those users who know how to exploit its rich resources. Intranets can function like the Internet but still provide a secure private environment and platform that permits full connectivity to all knowledge resources within an organization, including knowledge and data banks, online training tools and personnel, including collaborating colleagues, experts, coaches and mentors as well as suppliers, customers and other partners.

The architectural design of a generic collaborative knowledge network we present here is based on our experiences working with former clients. The principal ideas for the LSCKN came out of two projects we worked on. One was a preliminary design for an internal knowledge network for Siemens AG and the other was a collaboration of a number of companies who wanted to share their initial experiences with implementing KM initiatives within their separate organizations. The Millennium Project (so called as it was initiated shortly before the turn of the millennium) was headed by Charles Savage and linked at different times to personnel from Intel, Siemens and a number of KM practitioner-consultants. We would like to acknowledge at this point in our text the contribution of Dr. Charles Savage to our ideas.

The LSCKN is composed of three basic components—a learning system, a sharing system and a measuring system (see Figure 8.1). We believe that to be successful, a knowledge network must possess all three of these components. The learning and sharing systems are obviously essential elements of collaborative knowledge management as they are essential for the acquisition of new knowledge and the sharing of existing knowledge. The sharing system also functions as a platform for the co-creation of new knowledge. The role of the measurement system is also an important component as the measurement and publication of certain key parameters will motivate individuals to be more collaborative.

Figure: 8.1: Logan-Stokes Collaborative Knowledge Network

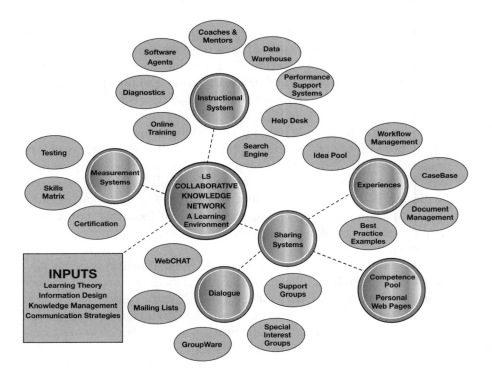

The design of the LSCKN is not based on any particular product or service that was available in the marketplace at the time of publication but rather the design is based on generic elements that we believe provide the right mix of functionality for a collaborative knowledge network. There now exists on the market literally hundreds of tools that can be used to build a collaborative knowledge network. As mentioned in Chapter 1, KM World in 2000 listed 100 of what they considered to be the top companies providing "KM-related products and services" (Taylor, 2000) and have updated the list yearly and published it on their Web site (www.kmworld.com/100.cfm). As well, we have listed a number of software companies that have been identified in our case study excerpts in Appendix 4. Because new products and services have emerged since the list was compiled and will continue to emerge, we have mapped out a generic architecture that can take advantage of products already on the market, those that will appear in the future and some that are probably already in use in your organization.

The particular choices of software are not essential to the architecture of the LSCKN. We like to joke that the design we have developed does not even require Internet technology but could be implemented with telephones and three-ring binders. In actuality the LSCKN was designed for workstations linked by the Internet, intranets or wide area networks and powered by software and/or groupware, which facilitates knowledge harvesting, sharing and creation and, naturally, communication.

The LSCKN is designed with the Internet and Web pages in mind, but it cannot function solely in cyberspace. In order to be successful the IT component must be supplemented by face-to-face meetings, telephone conversations and other electronically configured interactions of the members of the network. As we have stressed throughout this book the employees' values, their trust in each other and the culture within which they operate are all crucial to the success of any collaborative effort and certainly to an Internet-based collaborative knowledge network like the LSCKN described in this chapter.

A collaborative knowledge network is always a work in progress in that it is never finished, and that certainly is the case with the LSCKN we present here. We have developed a design that should meet the basic collaboration and KM needs of most organizations. But as the reader well knows, there is no such thing as a generic organization. Each one is unique and each one has its own peculiar collaboration and KM needs. The LSCKN presented here should therefore be considered as a basic system to which specialized modules can be added. As the reader will soon discover, the LSCKN has a modular design, making it easy to snap in new modules as needed.

In designing a collaborative knowledge network from scratch or modifying the LSCKN to meet an organization's needs, it is important that the organization's objectives, strategies and tactics are well understood and shared by both management and employees, a point made by Nonaka and Takeuchi (1995, p. 74): "The knowledge spiral is driven by organizational intention, which is defined as an organization's aspiration to its goals....The most critical element of corporate strategy is to conceptualize a vision about what kind of knowledge should be developed and operationalize it into a management system for implementation." Many organizations have trouble making explicit their aspirations or their goals and, hence, what kind of knowledge should be developed. Although this is crucial for the final design of a knowledge network, it is sometimes necessary to start to build the network before the aspirations and the kind of knowledge needed have been fully formulated. Once the knowledge network is up and running, it can be used as a tool to better define aspirations and the kinds of knowledge needed, which can then be used to refine the network. In other words, formulating clearly defined objectives and building a knowledge network is an iterative process, and an initial knowledge network like the one we present here is an appropriate way to begin the process. In order to do this, two forms of action will be required:

1. The development and implementation of a knowledge sharing and co-creation architecture making use of tools already available on the market and customizing them for the organization's specific needs, and

2. Explicitly formulating the organization's goals of knowledge creation in the organization within the context of an initiative to build a tool similar to the LSCKN described below.

It has been our experience in building knowledge networks for our clients that almost all of the participants in the projects were convinced that there was a need for a knowledge network, but approximately half indicated that they wanted more direction and guidance from senior management as to what was to be achieved by the knowledge network itself. It is rather ironic that these people were, for the most part, those that worked daily with the practical requests and needs of the customers, yet they still wanted concrete objectives and goals to be formulated for them.

The project team that builds the knowledge network must partner with the end users to best determine their needs. A sensible start to this would be to engage those managers and employees who are enthusiastic about the idea of knowledge networking in a dialogue to get their ideas and then to formulate some preliminary goals or at least some parameters for defining more detailed goals. After the first round of goal formulation, the next step is to go out to a wider audience to survey potential users for their reactions to the preliminary formulation of knowledge-creation goals. The survey should also contain an open-ended section so that suggestions from this larger cohort of employees can be collected and analyzed. It is in this manner that the goals of the knowledge network can be "bootstrapped" and formulated in such a way that members of the knowledge community will always feel comfortable adding new goals and altering older ones.

The Purpose of a Collaborative Knowledge Network

The purpose of a collaborative knowledge network is to create a knowledge community and a learning organization. The knowledge network should contribute to creating a non-threatening, supportive, convivial environment where individual members of the organization can realize their personal potential and goals as well as those of their firm, so that by working together they can transform their knowledge into wealth. In terms of functionality, the collaborative knowledge network is an organization-wide tool that facilitates the accession, sharing, utilization and creation of knowledge in which all of the organization's stakeholders can participate. Another goal of a knowledge network is to allow the dynamic teaming and collaboration of specialists so that the finely structured division of labor that is required in an age of sophisticated technology does not prevent an organization from realizing its full potential. The realization of this goal will have a number of desired outcomes for the organization, its staff, its customers and its suppliers:

1. Openness within the organization and between the organization and its customers and suppliers,

2. The empowerment and involvement of all of the organization's stakeholders,

3. The bridging of the gaps between departments and working groups, i.e., organizational cohesiveness,

4. The elimination of bureaucratic barriers and organizational friction,

5. An environment that is conducive to creativity and allows participants to think outside the box and at the same time work cooperatively with their colleagues,

6. Reduction of the time it takes to bring new products and services to market and to more quickly to satisfy the needs of customers, i.e., hasten the pace of innovation, and

7. The ability to harvest the knowledge of all stakeholders in the organization, including employees, managers, customers, suppliers and partners.

Turner Construction Company created the TKN using Open Text's Livelink collaboration and KM software. The TKN was rolled out in March 2002 to 5,000 employees and 1,500 contractors and has had a number of positive impacts. "Supporting employee development and training, the TKN is a reflection of Turner's continuous dedication to improving service quality and enhancing the overall project experience for each of its valued partners and shared clients. Through the TKN, Turner is creating a more efficient and conscientious workforce—both internally and among its extended team of owners, architects, engineers and subcontractors. The result of this innovative solution includes faster, more consistent employee growth and development; enhanced recruiting, retention and development; cost savings and increased value to customers" (www.opentext.com, 2003). The TKN has become a major resource for online training not only for its own staff, subcontractors, customers and partners but for large segments of the construction industry through its association with McGraw-Hill and the National Safety Council.

Another success story with a knowledge network is the experience of Lockheed Martin who created the "my e-Portal" network for its 40 business units using Vignette's Application Portal. The network allowed Lockheed Martin to provide specialized portals for each of its 40 business units and at the same time allow the exchange of ideas and resources within and across business units. "The easy-to-use portal network serves as a hub to increase employees' awareness of the Web-based resources they might otherwise not have known about. Increased awareness of key resources translates to extensive use of these resources and increased productivity.... The portal network, in serving as the single point of entry for employees to access Intranet/Internet applications and content, offers a collaborative work environment in which employees can exchange ideas and resources. 'my ePortal' enables employees to access email and work collaboratively through discussion forums and shared documents" (www.vignette.com, 2003).

Hill & Knowlton has also found that a collaborative knowledge network increased their productivity. Deployed across H&K's extended global enterprise, HK.net combines elements of KM, document management and project tools with a robust search engine into a collaborative enterprise application that enables employees and clients to access and store important information. HK.net helps make employees more productive by leveraging the existing body of knowledge and project work and it establishes a standardized business workflow for coordinating global accounts and completing daily tasks such as press release writing and "pitch" development.

An Overview of the LSCKN

LSCKN is not a software product—it is an intranet-based system for the management of expertise and knowledge. It is also a learning environment providing access to online courses, help desks, coaches and mentors. Most importantly the LSCKN mediates the interactions between the individuals within an organization and provides easy access to the information and explicit knowledge in their organization's Information System. The sharing of tacit knowledge requires, for the most part, personal face-to-face encounters, but the intranet-based tool can help users to find the people with whom they can collaborate. It can also sustain the personal interactions in the time periods between face-to-face encounters. It should be said that a number of individuals have reported excellent collaboration with people they never met face-to-face. We believe, however, that face-to-face encounters wherever and whenever possible can only enhance collaboration that takes place in cyberspace.

In this overview we describe the functions, applications, benefits and components of the LSCKN.

Primary Functions

- •A medium for the development of a knowledge community through internal dialogue and information/knowledge sharing,

- •A KM tool for the development of the organization's human resources,

- A delivery mechanism and brokerage for online training and education, and

- A medium for storing organizational memories and hence enriching the organization's culture.

Principal Applications

- Diagnose employee skill level, identify their training needs and identify the appropriate training courses,

- Identify the need for new online training courses or modules,

- Deliver online training modules using leading-edge Internet tools,

- Provide a medium and tools for the in-house generation of online courses from existing training source materials,

- Maintain a database of available offline courses to supplement online training,

- Provide online help desks,

- Generate and maintain a directory of coaches and mentors within the organization,

- Provide a forum for staff to share learning experiences and convert these experiences into corporate knowledge,

- Maintain an inventory of cases studies, best practices and staff skills and experiences, and

- Manage documents needed by staff to keep information current.

Benefits

KNOWLEDGE MANAGEMENT BENEFITS

- Create an inventory of the current knowledgebase of the organization,

- Develop an understanding of the knowledge creation and sharing processes of the organization,

- Identify areas where new knowledge is needed,

- Document and archive organizational learning and experience,

- Build understanding of the total knowledge resources of the organization (including external stakeholders, such as customers and suppliers), through information gathered in the casebase forum,

- Offer insights into the firm's organizational thinking and behavior,

- Promote organizational and individual commitment to lifelong learning and growth and evolution into an organic learning organization and knowledge community,

- Nurture improvement and revitalization of interactions and communication within the enterprise,

- Provide a reading on the organization's ability to adapt to change, create new ideas and access the wealth of knowledge inside the organization and in the marketplace, and

- Develop greater sensitivity to the changing dynamic of the marketplace and a more proactive response to those changes.

ONLINE TRAINING BENEFITS

- Reduce costs and inefficiencies associated with traditional computer-based and/or classroom training,

- Deliver uniform training and learning,

- Integrate readily with other training delivery methods,

- Allow easy, ongoing update/revision of courses and information,

- Support integration and alignment of organizational activities,

- Promote peer learning and interactions,

- Promote coaching and mentoring,

- Create performance support systems for individual employees, and

- Provide support and help to all employees.

Components

This overview describes the contents of the LSCKN and complements the bubble diagram shown in Figure 8.1. The objectives and approach of each of the components of the LSCKN system are described, as well as the way they contribute to transforming an enterprise into a knowledge community and a collaborative organization. The LSCKN system can be divided into three basic components, namely the instructional, the sharing and the measurement systems, each of which enhance learning and collaboration.

I. THE INSTRUCTIONAL SYSTEM

The instructional system contains both formal explicit and informal tacit content, consisting of:

- The Diagnostic Tool—an online tool to determine training and/or coaching needs that contains a catalogue of the learning and training resources available to members of the organization.

- Online Training Courses—the basic instructional content of the system (the explicit knowledge).

- Help Desk—an online synchronous help facility to provide immediate advice and direction.

- Coaches and Mentors—online access, or directory of coaches and mentors to provide guidance and encouragement as well as the sharing of tacit knowledge or the tips of the trade.

- Software Agents—which exploit Artificial Intelligence (AI) techniques to search the Internet for needed information.

- Data Warehouse—to store vital data and information for future reference.

- Search Engine—to help users locate detailed information anywhere within the LSCKN system and hence anywhere in the organization's Information System.

- Performance Support System—by combining the online training courses with a search engine, users are able to access information just in time to support their on-the-job performance.

2. SHARING SYSTEM

The sharing system allows an enterprise to become a knowledge community and a collaborative organization. Wealth is created by sharing and co-creating knowledge. The Sharing System provides a forum for developing, sharing and floating new ideas and consists of three subsystems: A. The Players, B. Sharing and Cataloging Experiences and C. Sharing Through Dialogue.

A. The Players

- The Competence Pool—a personal Web site for staff to describe and share their competencies, personal interests, concerns and aspirations.

B. Sharing and Cataloging Work and Experiences

- Workflow Management Facility.

- Idea Pool—an environment for sharing new ideas and useful suggestions.

- Document Management Facility—a facility to manage the organization's documents, including the Best Practice Examples and Casebase Forum described below.

- Best Practice Examples—a collection of the best practices of the organization.

- Casebase Forum—a collection of cases that describes the outcomes of projects, including difficulties that were encountered and overcome. The background as to how best practices were arrived at is as valuable and informative as the Best Practice Examples themselves. The casebase should include histories of interactions with customers, suppliers and strategic partners.

C. Sharing through Dialogue

- Listservs,

- Groupware,

- Chat groups,

- Special interest groups, and

- Support groups.

3. MEASUREMENT AND PUBLICATION SYSTEM

This section not only serves as a tool to control quality but also as a medium to publicize the accomplishments of all members of the organization.

- Testing—a feature of all online training courses for the purposes of certification and to measure results.

- Certification programs—to publicize and record the achievements of staff and track their skills.

- A Skills/Knowledge Matrix—a catalogue of the skills and/or knowledge within an organization that lists all the people within the organization with a particular skill or knowledge set. The skills/knowledge matrix is both a catalogue of all the skill and knowledge sets in the company, plus who possesses those skill or knowledge sets. It contains the same information found in the Competence Pool except it is organized or catalogued by the skills or knowledge sets. In the Competence Pool the information is organized or catalogued by each individual in the enterprise. The Skills/Knowledge Matrix is basically what others call a knowledge map, except we believe that both skills and knowledge sets should be catalogued.

Conclusion

The implementation of a collaborative knowledge network similar to the one we have outlined in this chapter is just one element in developing an overall strategy in building a collaborative organization. In closing, we remind the reader that an IT tool like a collaborative knowledge network will not by itself create a collaborative organization. The human side of the equation, in which attention is paid to vision, trust and leadership, is at the heart of a collaborative organization.

Internet as a Marketing and Sales Tool

Further Considerations

Marketing has proven to be one of the most effective uses of the Internet. The first instinct was to use the Net as an advertising medium, that is, using the old media of magazines and television as the content for the new medium of the Internet. This approach is not very effective because it does not take advantage of the interactivity that the Net offers. The traditional use of media for display ads in print media and spots in broadcast media have lost their effectiveness. After almost 50 years of being bombarded by rapid-fire sound bites and flashy images, the public has become fairly immune to the effects of traditional advertising. To have an impact today, a superficial hit will not work; it is necessary to educate one's potential customers about the advantages of the product or service one is offering.

This is why the use of the Internet for marketing, which takes advantage of its potential for interactivity, can be such a powerful strategy. By providing information with which potential customers can interact, companies can allow individuals to learn about a product or service on their own terms without feeling that they are being manipulated. Customers can and will sell themselves on the advantages of a company's products or services on the basis of this information. By providing such information as product announcements, newsletters, frequently asked questions (FAQs), corporate profiles, pricing, product descriptions and so on, in an interactive format, one is basically narrowcasting to potential customers and at the same time unobtrusively making a large amount of data available to them, allowing them to customize the information to suit their needs and interests. Because the Internet is already segmented into micromarkets, it is easier to narrowcast one's message.

The challenge of using the Internet for marketing is to get people to visit one's Web site. One cannot rely on the Internet itself to do this job because the ethos of the Net frowns upon direct advertising and solicitation. Instead, one must deploy other, more traditional information channels to make potential users aware of one's Web site. Having a telephone is an indispensable part of running a business, but one does not rely on the telephone to inform potential clients of one's telephone number. The same applies to the Internet. If one creates an interesting site that has information of relevance to some audience, however, word will soon spread and people will flock to the site.

Nine Internet Marketing Models

In a recent study of life insurance Web sites sponsored by the Life Insurance Marketing Research Association International (Baranoff et al., 1997) we identified a number of different models for the use of the Internet for marketing:

1. The Traditional Model, in which the company disseminates information about its products and services.
2. The Corporate Relations Model, in which a multinational uses a Web site to link the activities of its various subsidiaries.
3. The Lead Generation Model, in which the Web site is used to generate leads that a salesforce then follows up on using traditional means of communication such as snail mail or telephone.
4. The Direct Sales Model, in which the visitor to the site is given the opportunity to buy and/or order a product or service online.
5. The Personalized User Model, in which a customer has a personalized folder on the Web site of the provider of a service or a product.

6. The Corporate Intranet Model, in which a supplier is able to place Web pages on the intranet of a customer so that employees of the customer can access their services or products.
7. The Industry Extranet Model, in which a group of collaborating organizations collaborate with each other and coordinate their commercial activities.
8. The Electronic Commerce Distribution or Portal Site Model, in which third party marketing arrangements through electronic commerce intermediaries provide a comprehensive set of related products and services.
9. The Information Model, in which an organization, by providing valuable information either through an electronic magazine (e-zine) or an educational Web site, attracts visitors and is able to introduce their products or services in an unobtrusive manner.

E-Commerce and Direct Sales

Examples of all these models can now be found on the Internet. The one that is causing the most excitement at this early juncture in the history of the Internet is the direct sales model. Many sales organizations are attempting to fulfill sales and find new customers with a Web site through portals sites and direct sale Web pages on their own sites. A portal site is a site that focuses on a particular vertical market niche and offers the products and services of third parties to the portal site visitor. The reason these sites are successful is that the Internet is becoming so large and unwieldy that surfers prefer to go to a site that focuses on their particular interest and search a site that has human scale rather than surf the whole Internet which no longer possesses human scale.

Sales on the Internet started very slowly, but are now threatening to change the nature of commerce. Cars, computers, consumer goods, books, business supplies, electronic components, etc., are all being sold on the Internet. There are auction sites and online garage sales such as at uBid.com and eBay.com, where one-of-a-kind items are bought and sold. The Internet is being used to sell real estate and rent apartments. Consumer spending over the Internet has shown tremendous growth.

The U.S. Census Bureau, which has been tracking retail consumer spending over the Internet reported that in 1999 the total sales were US$15 billion, that it increased to US$36 billion in 2001 and reached US$45.5 billion in 2002 (E-stats U.S. Dept. of Commerce, March, 2003). Jupiterdirect.com (2003) reported that online advertising was US$5.6 billion for 2002.

The statistics provide one indication of the way the Internet has changed the nature of business; the following experiences of a number of different companies provides a qualitative description of this change. We begin with Dell Computers, which sells directly to its customers who are able to design and customize the computer system they wish to buy. Dell created a new computer sales channel through direct selling to the consumer to become one of the biggest computer companies in North America, and is a well-known, unparalleled success story in the computer industry. Creating an ordering system that allowed the consumer to customize the computer that they purchased within a realistic range of upgrade choices was an innovative and bold marketing move. This direct customer interaction started by phone and fax even before the Internet was widely installed. From our perspective, Dell's outstanding success was based on fulfilling the five collaborative messages of the Internet, even in the pre-Internet era.

They created a direct two-way communication channel between the purchaser and a specific account sales representative who worked with the caller about potential upgrades before taking the final order. Alignment was skillfully achieved through the making of the many upgrade choices available, since the computer purchased was custom built to personal specifications (within a range of realistic choices). And for follow-up, the purchaser could call tech support for help and keep the two-way communication channel open. Information was easy to access through being on their faxed, now emailed, new product distribution list. In a more public domain of access, full-page ads in prominent national newspapers, as well as their Web site, always made information easy to access. Their constant upgrading of products and services maintained a continuous learning environment. Community was also established through extended warranty programs and guaranteed services and online tech support, so that the purchaser did not feel isolated, but rather a part of a supportive technical community that cared about the quality of the Dell computer.

Toyota of Australia developed a model similar to Dell's, which allows its customers to personally customize the vehicle they wish to buy. "Vignette's technology made it possible to use the Prius site as a highly-effective lead generator, first by creating a compelling interactive customer experience, where a customer can build a Prius to match their needs, obligation free" (www.vignette.com, 2003). *The Wall Street Journal*, another Vignette customer, created a customization capability for its subscribers to provide "better access to content, more relevant content and consistent, 24-by-7 service tailored to individual needs" (www.vignette.com, 2003).

Another form of customization of customer's needs was developed by National Semiconductor.

> To better serve their existing clients, National developed private Web pages for major customers within the Vignette environment. These sites deliver specific, detailed account information via a 24-hour online channel. A distributed model allows National to delegate those pages to the appropriate person to fill in the content. National has successfully developed more than 120 private Web sites which serve as information conduits for customers. In addition to contacting their sales representatives, customers can obtain immediate, online service. These private sites help sales representatives reach and influence additional levels of engineering, purchasing and executive management within customers companies, in addition to their day-to-day contacts. (www.vignette.com, 2003)

A direct sales operation that changed the nature of the retail book trade was the initiative of Amazon.com. Amazon allows people to buy their books online from their homes, choose from hundreds of thousands of titles on their computer screens, read sample pages of the book itself, read professional and personal reviews and have the book delivered to their homes, often shipped out in 24 hours. Many traditional, local, general bookstores disappeared because they couldn't carry the same range of titles, nor compete with the discounts Amazon was able to offer. But it was more than discounts and ease of shopping that has made Amazon so successful. Based on our five collaborative messages of the Internet, we find that Amazon has been so successful because it has created a new collaborative relationship with viewers that changed their book-buying experience. Instead of finding a clerk in a store and then waiting for them to check on a book title, a viewer could now browse for books themselves by key words, author's name, type of content and find tens or hundreds of book titles to review (ease of access to information). Individuals could read other readers' personal reviews of the book they were thinking of buying and then have the opportunity to evaluate whether that review was helpful to them. They could even write a review of the book themselves and list their own Web site if people wanted to contact them (two-way communication).

Amazon collected information about individuals' book-buying preferences and used that information to suggest other books that other individuals who had bought this book had ordered (alignment of interests). Through the reviews, sample pages and access to comparable books, Amazon created a continuous learning environment for the viewer. And in the process of collaboration, a virtual online community of like-minded readers evolved for those with similar interests. The "bricks and mortar" bookstore model did survive in its response to Amazon by going in two opposite directions. In one direction, the mega book store with thousands and thousands of titles incorporated reading lounges and even coffee shops to create a browse-and-relax buying experience. In the other direction, small bookstores that specialized in specific categories of books for a very targeted market survived.

However, the mega bookstores also have to have their own online presence so that they can capture both market segments. Barnes & Noble in the United States and Chapters Indigo in Canada compete head to head with Amazon for the online market. Borders, on the other hand, has partnered with Amazon for its online service.

As our final example of the way in which the Internet has changed business, we consider eBay.com, which created a new business sector on the Internet that was not possible with any other previous communication medium. eBay's astounding success is based on its ability to elicit ongoing collaborative behaviors of most of its buyers (called winners!) by asking them to rate their experience of completing their full transaction with the seller. Based on a very simple measurement of satisfaction or dissatisfaction, eBay maintains a permanent buyer evaluation history of each seller for all eBay auction transactions. This becomes the eBay user's official "reputation." Any potential bidder can review a seller's track record of satisfying previous buyers before they consider bidding on the seller's current auction offerings.

The success of eBay, we believe, is based on its ability to fully exploit the five collaborative messages of the Internet to create a viable Internet trust and credibility process that builds and sustains a virtual public community. Buyers and sellers are actively involved in two-way communication through their bidding and evaluation processes; they have instant access to information about their bids throughout the entire process; they are aligned with other virtual members in providing valuable information of their personal experiences with sellers to benefit others; and they are continually learning about new items and services and through seller evaluation updates.

eBay is well aware of the critical importance that trust and the sense of community has for its success. In their welcoming statement they proclaim, "Welcome to the eBay Community; eBay is a community that encourages open and honest communication among all its members."

Just to make sure all users comply with their call for open and honest communication eBay enforces one strict rule—that all evaluations, positive and negative, remain in the seller's cumulative history and cannot be taken off once posted except under very strict circumstances. Recognizing that misunderstandings do occur between buyer and seller, eBay has provided an independent online Mediator service that sellers who obtain negative evaluations can appeal to for a fee to expunge their negative evaluations through either mediation or review. This mediated two-way communication achieves alignment between individuals to maintain the overall trust levels essential to a functioning virtual community.

Five Economic Eras

Further Considerations

Collaboration: An Ancient Tradition Dating Back to the Hunting and Gathering Economy

The history of hunting and gathering predates human existence. It was a mode of existence that we inherited from our hominid ancestors and dominated human commerce until the advent of agriculture a mere 10,000 years ago. Human survival for hunters and gatherers was totally dependent on cooperation and collaboration in terms of food sharing, tending the hearth to keep the home fires burning, large-scale coordinated hunting and the sharing of child-rearing duties when a newborn child and its mother were dependent on the community for survival. A measure of the importance of this cooperation is that during this period the punishment of banishment was literally a death sentence.

The only medium of knowledge sharing and co-creation was speech, which also served as a medium for abstract thinking and conceptualization. Practical and abstract knowledge was passed along from generation to generation by children working by the side of their parents and by traditional story telling. Speech was the first "Internet," the first tool for networking and the exchange of information. With the advent of speech a conceptual-based culture emerged, which allowed the lessons of survival learned by one generation to be passed on to the next. Culture not only shortens the time it takes for an individual to learn the lessons of the past, it also provides a base from which new knowledge can be created. This basic mode of human learning through culture and story telling is as applicable in today's business organization as it was at the dawn of human history. Collaboration is as old as human speech and culture, and although there are now many more media of communication and information storage, the basic principles are the same—sharing, cooperating and working to common goals of mutual benefit. It should also be noted that competition for scarce resources also dates back to our pre-hominid days. But back then and for a long time thereafter it was always a question of either/or, i.e., either collaboration or competition.

The Agricultural Economy

It was some 10,000 years ago at the end of the last Ice Age that the domestication of plants and animals appeared simultaneously around the world, with the cultivation of wheat and barley in Southwest Asia, coconuts and taro in Southeast Asia and yams in West Africa (Mithen, 1996, p. 219). The knowledge of farming was traditional and was handed down from father to son or mother to daughter in the course of their working together in their fields. This mode of knowledge sharing and the form of cooperation and collaboration in the early stages of the Agricultural Age was similar to that which took place in the hunting and gathering society.

As the agricultural-based economy prospered and the population grew, a more intensified form of agriculture was needed that required irrigation systems and other forms of public works, such as terracing, market systems, trade cartels and the secondary processing of agricultural products, such as the milling of grain and the pressing of olive oil. These developments became "possible only with the increasing involvement of leadership, with its concomitants of increasing dependence and political development" (Johnson and Earle 1987, p. 15). It is at this stage in the evolution of human commerce and politics that a system based purely on cooperation and collaboration through familial ties gave way to one in which non-democratic, top-down hierarchical economic and political leadership emerged. In all of these subsequent economic systems, whether they are characterized by the big man or chief of a tribe, the lord of a manor or estate or the ruler of an agrarian state, such as a king, a pharaoh, or an emperor, ownership and decision making is concentrated in a very exclusive elite, with the rest of the society following and respecting the edicts of those in charge. The only collaboration that takes place is within the small circle of the elite when different polities agree to cooperate or enter into trade agreements. By and large the elite ruled by fiat and their regimes were often tyrannical and always authoritarian or command and control.

Another consequence of large-scale agriculture and the need for political and economic administration was the invention of writing and mathematical notation in Sumer in 3100 BC as has been recounted in *The Sixth Language* (Logan, 2000). Writing and numbers were invented for accounting purposes to keep track of the tributes paid by farmers to the administrators of the irrigation systems. Writing and math gave rise to the first formal schools where young people were taught the three Rs: reading, writing and arithmetic. Up until this point in history all knowledge sharing was done through the apprenticeship form of instruction or on-the-job training. Schools with formal lessons had to be organized to teach literacy and numeracy because these skills cannot be learned by watching someone else do them. The student has to learn the secret code of what the symbols mean and how they can be used. The preparation of lessonware led to scholarship and some of the schools for teaching basic literacy and numeracy developed into institutions of higher learning and centers for research and the development of science, engineering and medicine. It was in these fields that collaboration resurfaced as scholars shared their learning with each other.

The Industrial Era

Industrialization required a certain way of organizing information, knowledge, engineering processes and economic transactions in order to successfully carry out its program of the machine production of wealth. Toffler identified the elements of this program in his book *The Third Wave* (Toffler, 1980, pp. 46-60) as follows: standardization, specialization, synchronization, concentration, maximization (or economy of scale) and centralization. These forms of organization optimized efficiency of the machinery used to manufacture goods and generate wealth. They did not apply just to the physical aspects of industry, i.e., the management of the raw materials, finished goods and the equipment and machinery used for manufacturing and transportation but also applied to the organization of personnel, information and knowledge.

As envisioned in Adam Smith's *Wealth of the Nations*, work should be divided and subdivided into tiny steps. In this way it would be easy to train a worker to repeat the same step time after time. His pin-making factory became the prototype for the Industrial Era. Workers were deskilled so that their role in the factory system was to perform one simple task over and over again in a mind-numbing manner, in sharp contrast to earlier times when workers possessed a number of skills, some of which were general and some of which were specialized for their particular trade. In the hunting and gathering period each member of society was a highly skilled generalist who was expected to perform all of the tasks necessary for survival. In the Agricultural Age, highly skilled specialists emerged to cope with tasks that had become more difficult and complicated. The deskilling of industrial workers served two purposes: Firstly, it was more efficient to perform the same task over and over again, and secondly, it was imperative that the workers could learn their task quickly so that they could be replaced immediately if they were sick or injured. There was no need to have an informed workforce but rather one that was docile, uniform and interchangeable like the components of the manufactured goods they produced.

The Industrial Era was made possible by the science of Newton and the engineering of Watt, as well as advances in the financial system. This allowed the wealth under the earth in the form of raw materials to be exploited by lending capital to purchase machinery. The most valuable asset in the industrial plant was therefore the capital-intensive machinery whose well-being was far more important than that of the workers. A top-down, hierarchical, command-and-control form of management was implemented to synchronize the action of the workers with that of the machinery. Industrial workers had even less freedom than agricultural workers. Their work was totally circumscribed by the need to maximize the return on investment of the capital-intensive equipment that made industrialization possible.

Manufacturing during the Industrial Era was concentrated and centralized in a small number of factories, often in a small number of industrial centers. In a similar way, knowledge in industrial firms was also concentrated and centralized with a small number of senior managers who set the overall direction of the company. The overwhelming majority of the employees had no need to access this knowledge, as they were expected to perform very simple tasks requiring little skill. They were expected to be obedient and follow the orders of their superiors like soldiers during the time of war.

The only exception to this rule was the technical staff who designed the manufactured products and/or the processes for manufacturing. Although the knowledge work of the R&D departments of manufacturing firms played a key role in the success of a company, there was not a great deal of interaction between the research team and the operational workers. Once the engineers had designed a product and/or a manufacturing process, the rest of the organization manufactured and distributed the product with virtually no interaction with their knowledge workers. It's as though they lived in two separate worlds. In the next round of product/process design there might be some gathering of data from the sales and marketing or manufacturing departments but basically the specialists relied on their own expertise as to what was the best possible product or process they could design. In sum, the Industrial Era organization was a collection of non-collaborating cells of specialists who worked largely independent of each other and whose activities were coordinated by a few senior managers who ran the organization in an autocratic manner.

The Information Age as a Neo-Industrial Phenomenon

The system of industrialization, in which natural resources are converted into mass-produced manufactured goods, thrives on innovation and new forms of knowledge. Industrialization coupled with the capitalist's economic system based on the competitiveness of the marketplace puts a premium on developing cheaper and more efficient forms of production due to economies of scale. This competitiveness has motivated new scientific and technological breakthroughs. With the development of the assembly line and the unprecedented large numbers that this system of manufacture entailed, the control of information became essential for success. A similar pressure to work with large numbers and complex data banks was also being felt in various fields of science and technology. The scientific motivation combined with the financing of industry and government led to the invention of computers and the advent of the Information Age. With the introduction of computers and automation, the mass production of manufactured goods still remains the principal form of production. With automation, however, manufacturers were able to create variety through mass customization.

Information Age organization and structures are similar to Industrial Era ones in many ways. Hierarchical command-and-control non-collaborative structures remain in place. The linear assembly line used to process natural resources into manufactured goods was supplemented with an equally linear process for transforming data into information. The Information Age economy is in fact a neo-industrial phenomena. It is due to the extreme mechanization of all aspects of industrial activity, including management functions (Toffler, 1980), that the computerization and automation of functions could take place in the Information Age. It also explains why so many features of the Industrial Era have been retained.

To illustrate our point, let us consider the reasons why Microsoft is the world's largest and perhaps most successful knowledge-based company. The secret of Microsoft's success is not the excellence of its R&D efforts, as good as they are, but rather the way in which it is able to monopolize its field using the standard Industrial Era techniques of standardization, specialization, synchronization, concentration, maximization and centralization (Toffler, 1980, p. 153). Microsoft's maximization, concentration and centralization of software production has led to charges that Microsoft is a monopoly. Microsoft's chief defense against this charge, somewhat justified, is the claim that their products benefit the computing community because they contribute to the standardization and synchronization of computing. Despite all the talk about the need for customization, which is true, in the end companies and computers also need to talk to each other. This is the reason that the computing community has settled on the Microsoft standard ever since IBM introduced its line of personal computers using MS-DOS as its operating system. Microsoft then ensured its position as the standard-setter of microcomputing by introducing MS Windows. It is attempting to do the same, with less success, with the Internet by introducing MS Explorer. Fortunately for those opposed to the total hegemony of computing by Microsoft, Netscape, the first to introduce a commercial Internet browser, is still holding its own and new browsers, such as Opera, are making a dent in the marketplace. There is also the whole phenomena surrounding Linux, which is an alternative operating system developed collaboratively within the programmers' community.

The paradox of Microsoft and other large Information Age companies like Adobe, Intel, IBM and Hewlett-Packard is that while the focus of their activity and the products they provide concern themselves with information and software, they still make use of Industrial

Era forms of organization. The content of their activities is information, but the modes of operation or the medium is industrial. It is for this reason that we regard the Information Age as a neo-industrial phenomenon. In other words, although the products and focus of attention of Information Age companies have more to do with information than hard goods, their way of doing business does not differ all that much from classical Industrial Era manufacturing firms.

The layering of Industrial Era techniques on Information Age companies parallels the way in which industrialization made use of Agricultural Age patterns of specialization, centralization and economies of scale. One could also claim that the knowledge required for agriculture derived itself from the detailed knowledge that hunter and gatherers had of the plants and animals in their environment. Each new economic era builds on the practices of the previous one and vestigially retains elements from it. The evolution of the economy follows a pattern similar to that of the evolution of biological species and the evolution of languages.

Contributions from Our Collaborative Partners on Collaboration

The following contributions are from colleagues with whom one of us, Dr. Robert K. Logan (RKL), has had the good fortune to work with over the past seven years. Some of the ideas that emerged in this study are a result of various forms of collaboration that developed between RKL and Verna Allee, Debra Amidon, Charles Armstrong, Karl Erik Sveiby and Charles Savage. We have asked each of them to provide us with a sample of their thinking that connects with our topic of collaboration. Being the outstanding collaborative partners they are, they all consented. We are delighted by their contributions because they reinforce the ideas and themes that we have attempted to develop in our book. The usual practice is to ask colleagues to write a foreword to one's book. We have deviated from the norm by presenting our colleagues' ideas in this appendix as background to how our ideas developed and as backup for some of our ideas. We thank our friends for their contributions, which greatly enrich our book.

The Future of Knowledge: Increasing Prosperity through Value Networks

Verna Allee's recently published book contains an approach to knowledge sharing that illustrates the importance of developing collaborative relationships because they entail not only the exchange of the tangible items but, more importantly, the exchange of intangibles. We thank her for giving us permission to reproduce an edited excerpt from her book.

> A value network is any web of relationships that generates both tangible and intangible value through complex dynamic exchanges between two or more individuals, groups, or organizations. People in organizations and enterprise networks engage in many different types of business interactions other than just exchanges of goods, services and revenue. They also exchange knowledge and other intangibles such as favors and benefits in order to build relationships and ensure that everything runs smoothly....

An Example

Our example is a fictitious pharmaceutical company, PharmCo. In this instance, the people in the Sales and Marketing group would like to improve their ability to use customer feedback in developing new products.

The first step in the modeling process is to consider all the groups, both internal and external, that play key roles in the activities of the Sales and Marketing group. In this case, the four key groups (Participants) inside the company are Sales and Marketing, Research, Product Development, and Manufacturing. Key Participants outside the company are Patients, health care Providers such as doctors, Payers such as insurance companies, and Regulators. We then arrange these Participants as "nodes" for the network diagram as shown in Figure A3.1.

Mapping Tangible Transactions

First we will want to think about tangible exchanges that take place between the Participants. What are the core money-related Transactions? What are the tangible Deliverables in the system? Figure A3.1. shows the tangible Deliverables such as product candidates, process specifications, claims, payments, orders, and so on. In this case, the communication channel is considered a tangible Deliverable because it consists of data links, Web sites, and call centers that are paid for and hosted by PharmCo as part of the expected customer service support.

Figure: A3.1: Tangible and Intangible Exchanges

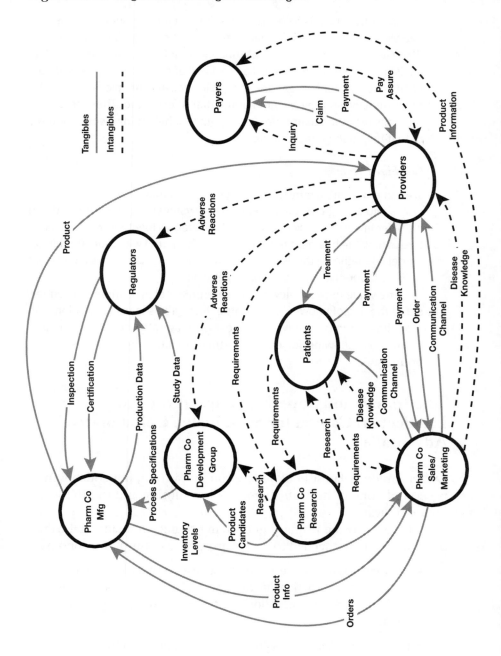

Mapping Intangible Transactions

For PharmCo, one intangible is patient requirements. Another is disease knowledge, which PharmCo makes available through publications and its Web site. Others are informal assurances that Payers make to Providers advising that a new product will be covered, and reports to the Regulators of adverse reactions. These are intangibles because people do not pay for them directly, so they are not contractual or expected. They are extras, offerings extended to another Participant that help things work smoothly or that help build relationships.

Combined View

We can now pull together a whole-system view that shows how both tangibles and intangibles are working in the system (see Figure A3.1). When we diagram all these exchanges and Deliverables together, we have a picture of how the business really operates. Compared with more traditional modeling methods, this is a much truer picture. (It also shows along what lines collaborative relationships might develop.)

The value network view of the enterprise helps us more fully understand the role of knowledge and other intangibles in value creation. The modeling process maps the most strategically critical intangible exchanges, allowing for easy targeting of value opportunities (2003, pp.192-99).

The Innovation Superhighway: Harnessing Intellectual Capital for Sustainable Collaborative Advantage

Debra Amidon's latest book focuses on innovation, but collaboration is certainly one of her sub-themes as her subtitle and the following quotes indicate:

There are three primary underlying themes fundamental to the new infrastructure needed to create prosperity in this new economy:

- Knowledge is the new, expandable source of economic wealth. There is an emerging recognition that the inherent intellectual assets, effectively exploited through innovation, are the most valuable resource of any country.

- Innovation encompasses the full spectrum, from creative idea generation through full profitable commercialization. Successful innovation depends on converting knowledge stocks and flows into marketable goods and services.

- Collaboration replaces the competitive (win/lose) paradigm, which is prevalent in many businesses today, with win/win benefits based on pooling competencies: knowledge, know-how, and skills....

- Collaboration can provide a synergistic win/win in which opponents and partners develop a shared understanding of what's possible and make decisions on what might be created (and actualized) in concert with one another, rather than as separate entities. (2003, pp. 9-10)

Collaboration plays a central role throughout Amidon's study of innovation. We thank her for permission to reproduce the following table, The Evolution of Thought, from her latest book.

Table A3.1: The Evolution of Thought

50's - 70's	70's - 90's	21st Century
Data	Information	Knowledge
Product	Solution	Innovation
Competition	Cooperation	Collaboration

Collaborative Climate and Effectiveness of Knowledge Work: An Empirical Study

The following is an excerpt from the paper "Collaborative Climate and Effectiveness of Knowledge Work: An Empirical Study" of Karl Erik Sveiby and Roland Simons, which appeared in the *Journal of Knowledge Management:*

In 1999 Drucker postulated that the most urgent management issue for the 21st century is to make the knowledge worker more productive. A term more conducive to value creation in knowledge work would probably be "effective." In the last few years it has been argued that the effectiveness of knowledge work has to do with how the creation of new knowledge and transfer of existing knowledge is organized (Nonaka and Takeuchi, 1995). Practitioners claim that underutilized knowledge is the largest hidden cost in organizations (c.f. the CEO of HP Lew Platt lamenting: "if HP only knew what HP knows").

The organization's ability to transfer knowledge from one unit to another has been found to contribute to the organizational performance of firms in both the manufacturing (Epple et al., 1996) and service sectors (Darr et al., 1995). The benefits of knowledge sharing have been documented in many settings (Stewart, 2001), but the effectiveness varies considerably among organizations (Argote and Ingram, 2000).

What is it that makes some knowledge transfer and creation processes more effective in creating value than others? Clearly, process design, office design, information sharing software, etc. help effectiveness and anecdotes about "best practice" abound in knowledge management circles. But careful design and IT do not help if the willingness to share with each other is not there. Although Buckman Labs has been a heavy user of IT infrastructure since the mid 1980s, earlier president Bob Buckman attributes his company's more than doubling of introduction of new products from 14 per cent of sales to 34 per cent to an improved climate of trust and increased willingness to collaborate.

The trouble is that knowledge is not a discrete object and that the most valuable knowledge—tacit knowledge—is embedded in people and so difficult to transfer outside the immediate context that it becomes a major competitive advantage. In their theoretical paper, Argote and Ingram (1999) argue that companies can utilize this feature strategically by embedding knowledge in interactions involving people.

However, also internal knowledge transfer is very difficult to achieve. Executives cite the internal "culture" of resistance to sharing as the hardest barrier to overcome in implementation of KM. In a Conference Board Report by Hackett (1999) managers identify the major obstacles to knowledge management. The second biggest hurdle (after "perceived need for KM") is "a culture of knowledge hoarding." The culture is also where the surveyed managers believe the best opportunities will be found in the five years to come.

Scholars tend to define culture as the deeper level of basic values, beliefs and assumptions that are shared by an organization's members. The values, beliefs and assumptions are influenced by members' activities and can be observed in behaviours (Laine-Sveiby, 1991). That a culture of trust and collaboration improves knowledge sharing and organizational effectiveness in general is argued by several authors, who also link trust, collaboration and knowledge sharing. Urch-Druskat and Wolff (2001) argue that trust, identity and efficacy are the core elements for team collaboration. Also Huener et al. (1998) regard the level of trust in the organization as the most important factor affecting the willingness to share knowledge.

Although seemingly self-evident, there is scant empirical evidence for such assertions. Tschannen-Moran (2001) has made one of the few empirical studies on the topic and found evidence that the level of collaboration in schools was related to the level of trust. She found a significant link between collaboration with the principal and trust in the principal, collaboration with colleagues and trust in colleagues, and collaboration with parents and trust in parents.

Still, even if we can accept that effective knowledge sharing relies on trust and collaboration, which is more effective for creating value, competition or collaboration? Since the birth of the market economy, competition has proven its worth. Can collaboration be more effective? Although anecdotal evidence and some empirical studies suggest that trust and collaboration are essential ingredients for the willingness to share knowledge, information and ideas, there is no empirical evidence that more collaboration is 'better', i.e., creates more value than competition.

Collaboration and trust can be seen as elements of an organization's culture, but the concept of culture is contested and too broad to be a good foundation for large-scale empirical studies. We are interested in only one specific aspect of culture: the values, beliefs and assumptions that influence the behaviours and willingness to share knowledge. We decided to call this aspect *collaborative climate* defined by behaviours that people can observe, "what people do around here."

With this in mind we identified some 50 factors mentioned in the literature on culture and employee attitude as influencing knowledge sharing, trust and collaboration. The first selection of survey items was derived from research into the nature of teamwork and knowledge sharing in research and development teams found in the literature....

The final set of factors influencing knowledge sharing was grouped into four clusters: One group of questions that describes the respondent's own attitude, employee attitude; one that describes the knowledge sharing behaviour of the individual's nearest colleagues, Work Group Support; one that describes the behaviours of the immediate manager, named Immediate Supervisor; and finally one of leadership factors outside the individual's nearest working environment, which we named Organizational Culture....

The Findings

We have found that collaborative climate tends to improve with age, educational level and managerial role. Contrary to 'common sense' collaborative climate also seems to improve with organizational size at least up to mid-size, an inverted U-shape. We have further found that employees tend to experience a U-formed appreciation of the collaborative climate; very positive at recruitment, then deteriorating during the first five years and later improving again closely correlated with seniority in the organization. We have to some degree confirmed theories proposing that people reach a 'professional plateau' after around 15 years in the same profession when they begin to rate lower than in their earlier years what they learn, what they receive from their nearest work environment and their managers. We have also confirmed earlier empirical evidence that distance is bad for collaboration. We have found that gender has no impact on the perceptions of collaborative climate. Finally, we have found collaborative climate in the private sector to be generally better than in the public sector. (2002, Vol. 6, no. 5)

The Value and Values of Collaborative Teaming: The Key to the Knowledge Economy

The following excerpt from Charles Savage's article "The Value and Values of Collaborative Teaming: The Key to the Knowledge Economy" is important because of the way in which he ties collaboration to values.

Dawn of the Knowledge Era

The knowledge economy can only succeed if we learn to be collaborative and imaginative together in teams within and between organizations. Instead of power and control over others, we will need to learn how to value and energize one another. We will not only create new "things" but we will be co-creating one another in the process. These developments will not be possible unless we redefine and deepen our personal ethics and the values that shape the work context.

Signs of the Knowledge Era

Early signs of the emerging knowledge economy are already with us. A language is evolving to describe the elements and dynamics of the knowledge economy. We know the value of explicit data, but are coming to value the power of tacit knowledge and experience. Subjective insights, intuitions and hunches are as valuable as the facts. We understand that knowledge is not just a thing moved on the Internet, but it is a process, a process of seeing things in new ways because we are able to shift mindsets and values. There is even a shift in our prepositions. Instead of focusing on whom I work "for," there is more interest in those "with" whom I work. Words beginning with "co" are more common now: collaboration, coordinate and co-create to mention just three.

Instead of dividing and subdividing work, we are teaming and re-teaming professionals around whole assignments. Instead of paying people for what they do, we will also need to pay them for what they know. Instead of fitting people to jobs, people will team with others to seize emerging business opportunities. Instead of closely controlling people, we will set cultural norms and values and trust people. And instead of assuming blind self-interest, we find interest in others which sets a whole new dynamic of creativity in motion. This last point is key to opening up the knowledge era.

Now I need to be able to discover your talents, your capabilities and aspirations, if I want to work with you as individuals or companies. By trusting and valuing you, we are able to combine our abilities in new and co-creative ways, generating possibilities no one dreamed of. This then becomes the engine of innovation and economic activity that propels us into the next millennium. This can not be possible until people understand and internalize the ethics of valuing and trusting.

Indeed, it is trust that brings forth the value of knowledge, the new source of wealth and opportunity. The dynamics of the knowledge era bring exciting new meaning and possibilities to individuals and companies, from knowledge management over the Internet to the leveraging of our intellectual capital. Our talents, our integrity, our abilities, our values and our visions will count like they have never counted before, driving the new economy, the knowledge economy, forward.

While still producing products and services bound to necessities of life (the economy of scarcity) like houses, telephones and automobiles, we will also co-create conditions for people to better discover themselves as individuals and communities (the economy of abundance) like drama, family celebrations, life-long-learning opportunities and cultural events.

The Value of Collaborative Teaming

Too often people have posed the dilemma of the individual versus the team. If I join the team, I will lose my individuality. Why?

Our experience with sports teams has conditioned our thinking in this regard. In a truly delightful book by James Carse (1986), we learn that finite games are games played at a specific time, at a specific place with known rules, and with the object to win, like sports teams. Infinite games are played all the time and everywhere and the task is to continually rewrite the rules to keep the game going in a collaborative manner. Most people think teaming is like a finite game, whereas the teaming in business is really an infinite process. Our challenge is to continually imagine new possibilities.

My work over the last twenty years has convinced me that excellence in teaming makes it possible to tap the best in the individual. As individuals on a team authentically trust and value one another's capabilities and aspirations, they discover together wonderful talents. In the quality interaction, they are able to create and weave together unexpected combinations of ideas, feelings and experiences. The whole person is involved, emotions and intellect.

In terms of clear human values, the Industrial Era really had few. If the Knowledge Era is to take hold, it will be because we have convincingly built the case for and implemented a culture of values and valuing. This is why the work at the Centre for Human Values at the Indian Institute of Management in Calcutta is so critical, not just for Indian leaders, but for world leaders. The legacy of Aurobindo, Tagore and others is a world treasure. Why? Because their legacy opens us to our souls and spirits. Work in the knowledge economy is not just about efficiency and productivity, but it is about the soul discovering itself in community.

I see our efforts in the West as simply the beginning of a long process that will take many years to understand. The foundations for a new value of teaming is beginning to take shape, but there is still a lot of hard work ahead. It is truly difficult to unlearn the assumptions and values of the Industrial Era because they are so subtle and ubiquitous. Our accounting systems, our language, our reporting hierarchies and our reward systems all collude to keep us captive to an old way of thinking and being.

Nevertheless, as we prepare for the next millennium, we will begin to feel the excitement, the energy and the drive to build an economy that is truly co-creative of one another. We will come to understand that we need one another's acknowledgment, encouragement, and challenge if we want to be all we can be. We will indeed move from self-interest to self-knowledge to knowledge of other selves, and ultimately to an acknowledgment of the unknown and ineffable in others. Instead of power

over, we will celebrate energy with one another as we participate in creating and shaping a world truly worthy of humankind and the spirit of life.
Ethics and Values will no longer be felt as a constraint, but as opening new
visits of possibilities for us to learn who we are and what we can become
in a collaborative community with other selves. (1998)

KNOW Inc. (www.knowinc.com):
A Source of Collaboration Tools

We have attempted in this last section of Appendix 3 to bring to the
reader information regarding the most recent initiatives in collaboration studies, mostly in the form of books and articles. We now turn to
an innovative portal Web site that supports collaboration and organizational development. KNOW Inc., based in Toronto, operates the
portal www.knowinc.com. For more than five years KNOW has been
developing Web-based tools to support collaborative KM initiatives.
Although they are advocates of technology to support KM, they consider the human network to be the most significant contributing factor
to developing collaboration.

Their mission statement is: "To provide the intangible assets community with the means to accelerate the value adding capabilities of
their assets for community interaction, co-creation, legal security,
access, distribution, deployment and developmental improvements."

Their key advisors are international practitioners who are also
developers of knowledge assets frameworks and hence "knowinc.com
is a vertical and role-based portal designed for and by the KM community." As a viable alternative to the traditional expert consulting,
KNOW collaborates with KM practitioners to develop tools that help
managers, consultants and CKOs implement KM concepts in practice.
These tools are available through individual "Toolkits," which are e-
learning modules that support knowledge strategy implementations.
KNOW believes tools and simple models to be far more effective than
lectures or information as methods for transferring knowledge.
KNOW, through its e-commerce outlet www.knowledgeshop.com,
distributes books and software that support their Toolkits series. Their
Web sites are worthy of a visit.

Descriptions of the Software and Consulting Companies Whose Case Studies Were Used

Accenture

Accenture is the world's leading management consulting and technology services company. Committed to delivering innovation, Accenture collaborates with its clients to help them realize their visions and create tangible value. With deep industry expertise, broad global resources and proven experience in consulting and outsourcing, Accenture can mobilize the right people, skills, alliances and technologies. Accenture has more than 75,000 people in 47 countries. For more information, visit www.accenture.com.

Centra

Leading with an undisputed track record of helping millions of users to increase revenue and improve overall business performance, Centra Software Co. enables global corporations, government agencies, and universities to drive greater productivity and lower costs through the industry's most extensible enterprise software application for real-time business communication and collaboration. Today more than 1,000 organizations across every industry and market sector choose Centra, including Cadbury Schweppes, Citigroup, AT&T, Procter & Gamble, McKesson, Nationwide Insurance, Sysco, and Stanford University.

Centra's products are bolstered by a vital ecosystem of strategic partners, including Deloitte Consulting, EDS, Microsoft, Siebel, Cisco,
and Oracle. Headquartered in Boston, Centra services a worldwide
customer base throughout the Americas, Europe, Asia and Australia.
For more information, visit www.centra.com.

CoCreate

CoCreate Software produces CAD and Collaboration software to help
companies design products, share ideas, and manage data. Its One-
Space Designer CAD products include 2D drafting, 3D modeling and
data management tools. Its OneSpace Collaboration products let people interactively share documents, 2D drawings and 3D designs
online—whether those designs were created with CoCreate's CAD systems or those of other companies. CoCreate products foster innovation
and communication across the extended development team, empowering people with various interests, skills and talents to join together to
explore ideas and to make more rapid and better decisions. CoCreate
can be found in more than 30 countries. For more information, visit
www.cocreate.com.

Documentum

Documentum, Inc. provides enterprise content management solutions
that enable organizations to unite teams, content and associated business processes. Documentum's integrated set of content, compliance
and collaboration solutions support the way people work, from initial
discussion and planning through design, production, marketing, sales,
service and corporate administration. With a single platform, Documentum enables people to collaboratively create, manage, deliver and
archive the content that drives business operations, from documents
and discussions to email, Web pages, records and rich media. The Documentum platform makes it possible for companies to distribute all of
this content in multiple languages, across internal and external systems,
applications and user communities. As a result, Documentum's customers, which include thousands of the world's most successful
organizations, harness corporate knowledge, accelerate time to market, increase customer satisfaction, enhance supply chain efficiencies
and reduce operating costs, improving their overall competitive advantage. For more information, visit www.documentum.com.

Hummingbird

Headquartered in Toronto, Canada, Hummingbird Ltd. is a global enterprise software company employing 1,300 people in nearly 40 offices around the world. Hummingbird's revolutionary Hummingbird Enterprise, an integrated information and knowledge management solution suite, manages the entire lifecycle of information and knowledge assets. Hummingbird Enterprise creates a 360-degree view of enterprise content with a portfolio of products that are both modular and interoperable. Today, five million users rely on Hummingbird to connect, manage, access, publish and search their enterprise content. For more information, visit www.hummingbird.com.

iManage

Headquartered in Foster City, California, iManage Inc. is a leader in collaborative content management software that enables businesses to efficiently manage and collaborate on critical business content across the extended enterprise. iManage WorkSite delivers document management, collaboration, workflow and knowledge management accessible through an integrated portal in a single integrated Internet solution. This results in significant improvements in communication and process efficiency, faster response times and a rapid return on investment. More than 500,000 professionals in 1,200 businesses have transformed their organizations with iManage WorkSite. For more information, visit www.imanage.com.

Intraspect

Intraspect Software, Inc. is the leading provider of enterprise solutions that power complex business processes, manage content lifecycles and enhance internal and external collaboration. More than 200 companies use Intraspect's solutions to increase productivity and enhance customer satisfaction, including Bank of America, Barclays Global Investors, BearingPoint, Cadence, GE Capital, Hill & Knowlton, J.P. Morgan Chase, LSI Logic, Ogilvy, Sun Microsystems and Reed Elsevier. For more information, visit www.intraspect.com.

J.D. Edwards

J.D. Edwards makes customers stronger, enabling them to solve their most important business challenges. The company offers collaborative enterprise software as well as consulting, education and support services. J.D. Edwards' offerings are differentiated by a deeply ingrained attitude of listening to customers, innovating on their behalf, and delivering solutions as part of a results-oriented relationship. Founded in 1977 and headquartered in Denver, J.D. Edwards focuses on long-term business partnerships and helping its 6,600 customers in more than 110 countries collaborate electronically to manage their business processes, supply chains, enterprise assets, and supplier and customer relationships. For more information, visit www.jdedwards.com.

Open Text

Since 1991, Open Text Corporation has delivered innovative software that brings people together to share knowledge, achieve excellence, deliver innovation and enhance processes. Its legacy of innovation began with the successful deployment of the world's first search engine technology for the Internet. Today, as the leading global supplier of collaboration and knowledge management software for the enterprise, Open Text supports 15 million seats across 10,000 corporate deployments in 31 countries and 12 languages throughout the world. As a publicly traded company, Open Text manages and maximizes its resources and relationships to ensure the success of great minds working together. For more information, visit www.opentext.com.

Primus

For more than a decade, Primus Knowledge Solutions, Inc. has provided knowledge management software solutions that help companies define, meet, and exceed the productivity and quality goals of their contact centers, help desks, and Web self-service environments. Businesses around the world use Primus software to increase customer satisfaction, improve employee efficiency and lower operating costs. Primus customers include such industry leaders as 3Com, Airbus, The

Boeing Company, Concord Communications, EMC, Enterasys, Ericsson, Inc., Fujitsu Limited, Inc., IBM, Motorola, Novell, T-Mobile, and VeriSign. For more information, visit www.primus.com.

Siebel

Siebel Systems, Inc. is a leading provider of eBusiness applications software, enabling corporations to sell to, market to, and serve customers across multiple channels and lines of business. With more than 3,500 customers worldwide, Siebel Systems provides organizations with a proven set of industry-specific best practices, CRM applications, and business processes, empowering them to consistently deliver superior customer experiences and establish more profitable customer relationships. Siebel Systems' sales and service facilities are located in more than 28 countries. For more information, visit www.siebel.com.

SiteScape

SiteScape, Inc. produces Web-based collaboration software and services that allow employees, customers, business partners and suppliers to easily communicate and share information in a secure, Web-based environment. SiteScape's products facilitate business processes such as knowledge management, program management, communities of practice, workflow and e-learning. The company has numerous Fortune 500 and Global 2000 customers, clustered in a variety of industries, including government, DoD, aerospace, oil and gas, construction, high tech, automotive, trade associations, and education. For more information, visit www.sitescape.com.

Vignette

Vignette Corporation enables enterprises to achieve real-time advantage by rapidly building, deploying and optimizing enterprise Web applications. Vignette powers the Web applications of more than 1,600 leading organizations and is headquartered in Austin, Texas. Vignette has offices located throughout the Americas, Europe, Asia and in Australia. For more information, visit www.vignette.com.

Bibliography

Allee, Verna. 1997. *The Knowledge Evolution: Expanding Organizational Intelligence*. Boston: Butterworth-Heinemann.

_____. 2003. *The Future of Knowledge: Increasing Prosperity through Value Networks*. Boston: Butterworth-Heinemann.

Amidon, Debra. 2003. *The Innovation Superhighway*. Boston: Butterworth-Heinemann.

Argote, L. and P. Ingram. 2000. "Knowledge transfer: a basis for competitive advantage in firms." *Organizational Behaviour and Human Decision Processes* 82, no. 1. May: pp. 150-69.

Argyris, Chris. 1993. *Knowledge for Action*. San Francisco: Jossey-Bass.

Armstrong, Charles. 2002. Private Communication.

Athey, Robin. 2002. *Collaborative Knowledge Networks: Driving Workforce Performance through Web-enabled Communities*. New York: Deloitte Research.

Austin, J.E. 2000. *The Collaboration Challenge: How Nonprofits and Businesses Succeed through Strategic Alliances*. San Francisco: Jossey-Bass.

Austin, James E. and Frances Hesselbein. 2002. *Meeting the Collaboration Challenge: Developing Strategic Alliances between Nonprofit Organizations and Businesses*. San Francisco: Jossey-Bass.

Axelrod, R. 1984. *The Evolution of Cooperation*. New York: Basic Books.

_____. 1997. *The Complexity of Cooperation: Agent-Based Models of Competition and Collaboration*. Princeton: Princeton University Press.

Baranoff, R., M. Logan, R. Logan, P. Michalak and P. Ryan. 1997. *The Strategic Uses of the Internet as a Business Tool*. Hartford: LIMRA International.

Bar-On, R. 2000. "Emotional and social intelligence: insights from the Emotional Quotient Inventory." Edited by Reuven Bar-On and James D. A. Parker. *The Handbook of Emotional Intelligence: Theory, Development, Assessment, and Application at Home, School, and in the Workplace*. San Francisco: Jossey-Bass.

Bar-On, R. 2002. *Bar-On Emotional Quotient Inventory (EQ-i): Technical Manual*. Toronto: Multi-Health Systems.

Bar-On, R. and J.D.A. Parker (eds). 2000. *The Handbook of Emotional Intelligence: Theory, Development, Assessment, and Application at Home, School, and in the Workplace*. San Francisco: Jossey-Bass.

Berners-Lee, Tim. 1999. *Weaving the Web*. San Francisco: Harper.

Bertels, Thomas and Charles Savage. 1998. "Tough questions on knowledge management." Edited by G. von Krogh, J. Roos and D. Kleine). *Knowing in Firms*. London: Sage.

Beyerlein, Michael, Sue Freedman, Craig McGee and Linda Moran. 2003. *Beyond Teams: Building the Collaborative Organization*. San Francisco: Jossey-Bass Pfeiffer.

Botkin, James W. and Jana B. Matthews. 1992. *Winning Combinations: The Coming Wave of Entrepreneurial Partnerships between Large & Small Companies*. New York: John Wiley.

Carse, James. 1986. *Finite and Infinite Games: A Vision of Life as Play and Possibility*. New York: Free Press.

Cauley de la Sierra, M. 1995. *Managing Global Alliances: Key Steps for Successful Collaboration*. England: Addison-Wesley.

Cherniss, C. and D. Goleman (eds). 2001. *The Emotionally Intelligent Workplace: How to Select for, Measure, and Improve Emotional Intelligence in Individuals, Groups, and Organizations*. San Francisco: Jossey-Bass.

Cronin, Mary. 1994. *Doing Business on the Internet*. New York: Van Nostrand Rinehold.

Dannemiller Tyson Associates. 2000. *Whole-scale Change: Unleashing the Magic in Organizations*. San Francisco: Berret-Koehler.

Darr, E., L. Argote and D. Epple. 1995. "The acquisition, transfer and depreciation of knowledge in service organizations: productivity in franchises." *Management Science* 24, no. 11: pp. 1750-62.

Davenport, T. and Prusak, L. 1998. *Working Knowledge: How Organizations Manage What They Know*. Boston: Harvard Business School Press.

De Bono, Edward. 1985. *Six Thinking Hats*. New York: Penguin Books.

Donald, Merlin. 1991. *The Origin of the Modern Mind*. Cambridge: Harvard University Press.

Drucker, Peter. 1994. "The age of social transformation." *The Atlantic Monthly*, November 1994.

_____. 1999. *Management Challenges for the 21st Century*. New York: Harper Business.

Dyer, J.H. 2000. *Collaborative Advantage: Winning through Extended Enterprise Supplier Networks*. New York: Oxford University Press.

Edvinsson, Leif and Michael S. Malone. 1997. *Intellectual Capital: Realizing Your Company's True Value by Finding Its Hidden Brainpower*. New York: Harper Business Press.

Eisenstein, Elizabeth. 1979. *Printing Press as an Agent of Change*. London: Cambridge University Press.

Epple, D., L. Argote and K. Murphy. 1996. "An empirical investigation of the micro structure of knowledge acquisition and transfer through learning by doing." *Operations Research* 44: pp. 77-86.

E-stats U.S. Dept. of Commerce. 2003. *U.S. Dept. of Commerce News*, March 2003.

Frydman, B., I. Wilson and J. Wyer. 2000. *The Power of Collaborative Leadership: Lessons for the Learning Organization*. Boston: Butterworth-Heinemann.

Gardner, H. 1983. *Frames of Mind: The Theory of Multiple Intelligences*. New York: Basic Books.

Garten, J.E. 2001. *The Mind of the CEO*. New York: Basic/Perseus Books.

Genefke, J. and F. McDonald. 2001. *Effective Collaboration: Managing the Obstacles to Success*. Great Britain: Palgrave.

Gerstner, L.V. 2002. *Who Says Elephants Can't Dance?: Inside IBM's Historic Turnaround*. New York: HarperBusiness.

Goleman, D. 1995. *Emotional Intelligence*. New York: Bantam.

_____. 1998. *Working with Emotional Intelligence*. New York: Bantam.

_____. 2001. "An EI-based theory of performance." Edited by Cary Cherniss and Daniel Goleman . *The Emotionally Intelligent Workplace: How to Select for, Measure, and Improve Emotional Intelligence in Individuals, Groups, and Organizations*. San Francisco: Jossey-Bass.

Graham, Ted. 2003. Hill & Knowlton, Worldwide Director of Knowledge Management Services. Private Communication-Interview.

Gundry, L. and L. LaMantia. 2001. *Breakthrough Teams for Breakthrough Times: Unlocking the Genius of Creative Collaboration*. Chicago: Dearborn.

Hackett, B. 2000. *Beyond Knowledge Management: New Ways to Work and Learn*. New York: Conference Board Report.

Haimila, Sandra. 2000. "Betting on collaboration." *KM World*, Dec. 13, 2000.

_____. 2001a. "Shell creates communities of practice." *KM World*, Feb. 19, 2001.

_____. 2001b. "Consultant: advise thyself." *KM World*, April 4, 2001.

Hammer, Michael and James Champy. 1993. *Business Process Reengineering*. New York: HarperBusiness.

Hargrove, R. 1998. *Mastering the Art of Creative Collaboration*. New York: McGraw-Hill.

Hayek, F.A. 1945. "The use of knowledge in society." *American Economic Review* 35, no. 4: pp. 519-30.

Herzberg, F., B. Mausner and B.B. Snyderman. 1959. *The Motivation to Work*. New York: John Wiley.

Horibe, F. 1999. *Managing Knowledge Workers: New Skills and Attitudes to Unlock the Intellectual Capital in Your Organization*. Toronto: John Wiley.

Hudson, W.J. 1993. *Intellectual Capital: How to Build It, Enhance It, Use It*. New York: John Wiley.

Huener, L., G. von Krogh and J. Roos. 1998. "Knowledge and concept of trust." Edited by G. von Krogh, J. Roos and D. Kleine. *Knowing in Firms, Understanding, Managing and Measuring Knowledge.* London: Sage.

Hurst, Aaron. 2003. Founder and President of the Taproot Foundation. Private Communication-Interview.

Huseman, R.C. and J.P. Goodman. 1999. *Leading with Knowledge: The Nature of Competition in the 21st Century.* Thousand Oaks, CA: Sage.

Huxham, C. (ed). 1996. *Creating Collaborative Advantage.* London: Sage.

Johnson, Allen W. and Timothy Earle. 1987. *The Evolution of Human Societies: From Foraging Group to Agrarian State.* Stanford: Stanford University Press.

Jupiterdirect.com. 2003. Jupiter Direct.

KM World Editorial. 1999. "The interactive enterprise: end-to-end interactions define performance." *KM World*, Sept. 27, 1999.

_____. 2001a. "Click and track." *KM World*, June 18, 2001.

_____. 2001b. "Project management potion for pharmaceutical firm." *KM World*, Aug. 20, 2001.

_____. 2001c. "Mills speeds lease process." *KM World*, Aug. 27, 2001.

_____. 2001d. "Proctor & Gamble pampers R&D with a bounty of knowledge-sharing power." *KM World*, Sept. 5, 2001.

_____. 2001e. "Smooth operator." *KM World*, Oct. 10, 2001.

Kostner, J. 1994. *Virtual Leadership: Secrets from the Round Table for the Multi-Site Manager.* New York: Warner Books.

_____. 2001. *Bionic eTeamwork: How to Build Collaborative Virtual Teams at HyperSpeed.* Chicago: Dearborn Trade.

Kuhn, Thomas. 1972. *The Structure of Scientific Revolutions.* Chicago: University of Chicago Press.

Laine-Sveiby, K. 1991. "Företagil kulturmöten. Tre findlänska företag och ders svenska dotterbolagen etnologisk studie." (dissertation) Akademitryck Edsbruk.

Leonard-Barton, D. 1993. *Wellsprings of Knowledge: Building and Sustaining the Sources of Innovation*. Boston: Harvard Business School Press.

Levi-Strauss, Claude. 1960. *The Savage Mind*. London: Weidenfeld & Nicolson.

Logan, Robert K. 1986. *The Alphabet Effect*. New York: Wm. Morrow Publishing. (The second edition will appear in 2003, published by Hampton Press.)

_____. 1995. *The Fifth Language: Learning a Living in the Computer Age*. Toronto: Stoddart Publishing.

_____. 2000. *The Sixth Language: Learning a Living in the Internet Age*. Toronto: Stoddart Publishing.

Lucier, Charles E. and Janet D. Torsilieri. 2001. "Can knowledge management deliver bottom-line results?" Edited by I. Nonaka and D. Teece. *Managing Industrial Knowledge*. London: Sage Publications.

Mandell, M.P., (ed). 2001. *Getting Results through Collaboration: Networks and Network Structures for Public Policy and Management*. Westport, CT: Quorum.

Manville, Brook. 2003. Private Communication.

Maslow, A. 1954. *Motivation and Personality*. New York: Harper & Row.

Mayer, J.D. and P. Salovey. 1993. "The intelligence of emotional intelligence." *Intelligence* 17: pp. 433-42.

Mayer, J.D., P. Salovey and D.R. Caruso. 2000. "Emotional intelligence as zeitgeist, as personality, and as a mental ability." Edited by Reuven Bar-On and James D.A. Parker. *The Handbook of Emotional Intelligence: Theory, Development, Assessment, and Application at Home, School, and in the Workplace*. San Francisco: Jossey-Bass.

Mayo, George Elton. 1933. *The Human Problems of an Industrial Civilisation*. New York: Macmillan.

McClelland, D.C. 1961. *The Achieving Society*. Princeton: Van Nostrand.

McClelland, David C., John W. Atkinson, Russell A. Clark and Edgar L. Lowell. 1953. *The Achievement Motive*. New York: Appleton-Century-Crofts.

McGregor, D. 1960. *The Human Side of Enterprise*. New York: McGraw-Hill.

McLuhan, Marshall. 1962. *Gutenberg Galaxy*. Toronto: University of Toronto Press.

_____. 1964. *Understanding Media*. New York: McGraw-Hill.

McLuhan, Marshall, and R.K. Logan. 1977. "Alphabet, mother of invention." *Etcetera* 34: December.

McLuhan, Marshall, and Bruce Powers. 1981. "Ma Bell minus the Nantucket gam: or the impact of high-speed data transmission." *Journal of Communication*: Summer 1981.

Mertins, Kai, Peter Heisig and Jens Vorbeck (eds). 2001. *Knowledge Management: Best Practices in Europe*. Berlin: Springer.

Mithin, S. 1996. *The Prehistory of the Mind*. London: Thames & Hudson.

Mitnick, James. 2003. Senior Vice-President, Turner Construction Company. Private Communication-Interview.

Moore, G.A. 1995. *Inside the Tornado: Marketing Strategies from Silicon Valley's Cutting Edge*. New York: HarperBusiness.

Morey, D., M. Maybury and B. Thuraisingham (eds). 2002. *Knowledge Management: Classic and Contemporary Works*. Cambridge: MIT Press.

Nonaka, I. and H. Takeuchi. 1995. *The Knowledge Creation Company*. New York: Oxford University Press.

Nonaka, I. and D.J. Teece (eds). 2001. *Managing Industrial Knowledge: Creation, Transfer and Utilization*. London: Sage.

Paivio, A. and I. Begg. 1981. *Psychology of Language*. Englewood Cliffs, NJ: Prentice-Hall.

Plunket, A., C. Voisin and B. Bellon (eds). 2001. *The Dynamics of Industrial Collaboration: A Diversity of Theories and Empirical Approaches*. Great Britain: Edward Elgar.

Pogson, Philip. 1999. "The university and intellectual capital" presented at 6th AHED International Conference, Adelaide, July 1999 (published on the Internet).

Porter, Michael. 1985. *Competitive Advantage: Creating and Sustaining Superior Performance*. New York: The Free Press.

Preiss, K., S.L. Goldman and R.N. Nagel. 1996. *Cooperate to Compete: Building Agile Business Relationships*. New York: Van Nostrand Reinhold.

Prigogene, Ilya and Irene Stengers. 1984. *Order Out of Chaos*. New York: Bantam Books.

Roethlisberger, F.J. and W.J. Dickson. 1939. *Management and the Worker*. Cambridge: Harvard University Press.

Saarni, C. 1999. *The Development of Emotional Competence*. New York: Guilford.

_____. 2000. "Emotional competence: a developmental perspective." Edited by Reuven Bar-On and James D.A. Parker. *The Handbook of Emotional Intelligence: Theory, Development, Assessment, and Application at Home, School, and in the Workplace*. San Francisco: Jossey-Bass.

Saint-Onge, H. and D. Wallace. 2003. *Leveraging Communities of Practice for Strategic Advantage*. Boston: Butterworth-Heinemann.

Salovey, P. and J.D. Mayer. 1990. "Emotional intelligence." *Imagination, Cognition, and Personality* 9: pp. 185-211.

Sapir, Edward. 1921. *Language*. New York: Harcourt, Brace.

Savage, Charles. 1996. *Fifth Generation Management*. Boston: Butterworth-Heinemann.

_____. 1998. "The value and values of collaborative teaming: the key to the knowledge economy." Munich: KEE, Inc.

Schrage, M. 1989/1995. *No More Teams: Mastering the Dynamics of Creative Collaboration*. New York: Currency Doubleday.

Senge, Peter. 1990. *The Fifth Discipline*. New York: Doubleday.

Shaffar, Scott and Jerry Garcia. 2003. Project Managers, Knowledge Management: Integrated Systems Sector, Northrop Grumman Corporation. Private Communication-Interview.

Skyrme, David. 2001. *Knowledge Networking: Creating the Collaborative Enterprise*. Boston: Butterworth-Heinemann.

Stalk, G., P. Evans and L. Shulman. 1992. "Competing on capabilities." *Harvard Business Review*, March/April 1992: pp. 57-69.

Stein, S.J. and H.E. Book. 2000. *The EQ Edge: Emotional Intelligence and Your Success*. Toronto: Stoddart Publishing.

Stewart, Thomas. 1991. "Brainpower." *Fortune*, June 3, 1991: pp. 40-56.

_____. 1995a. "Trying to grasp the intangible." *Fortune*. Oct. 2,

1995: pp. 105-8.

_____. 1995b. "Mapping corporate brainpower." *Fortune*, Oct. 30, 1995: pp. 151-3.

_____. 1996. "The coins in the knowledge bank." *Fortune*, Feb. 19, 1996.

_____. 1997. *Intellectual Capital: The New Wealth of Organizations*. New York: Currency Doubleday.

Straus, David. 2002. *How to Make Collaboration Work*. San Francisco: Berrett Koehler.

Sveiby, Karl Erik. 1997. *The New Organizational Wealth: Managing and Measuring Knowledge-Based Assets*. San Francisco: Berrett-Koehler.

Sveiby, Karl Erik and T. Lloyd. 1987. *Managing Knowhow: Add Value by Adding Creativity*. London: Bloomsbury.

Sveiby, Karl Erik, et al. 1988. *Den Nya Arsredovisningen (The New Annual Report)*. Stockholm: Affarsvarlden.

Sveiby, Karl Erik, et al. 1989. *Den Osynliga Balansrakningen (The Invisible Balance Sheet)*. Stockholm: Affarsvarlden/Ledarskap.

Sveiby, Karl Erik and Roland Simons. 2002. "Collaborative climate and effectiveness of knowledge work—an empirical study." *Journal of Knowledge Management* 6, no. 5.

Takeuchi, Hirotaka. 2001. "Towards a universal management concept of knowledge." Edited by I. Nonaka and D. Teece. *Managing Industrial Knowledge*. London: Sage.

Tapscott, Don and Art Caston. 1993. *Paradigm Shift*. New York: McGraw-Hill.

Taylor, Bruce. 2000. "100 Companies that matter in DM, WM, CM, KM and BI." *KM World*, May 15, 2000.

Taylor, F.W. 1911 (reprinted 1967). *The Principles of Scientific Management*. New York: W.W. Norton.

The New Lexicon Webster's Dictionary. 1988. New York: Lexicon Publications, Inc.

Thomas, K.W. 1976. "Conflict and conflict management." Edited by M. Dunnette. *The Handbook of Industrial and Organizational Psychology*. Chicago: Rand McNally.

Thomas, K.W. and R.H. Kilmann. 1974. *Thomas-Kilmann Conflict Mode Instrument*. Xicom: Consulting Psychologists Press.

Tiwana, A. 1999. *The Knowledge Management Toolkit*. Upper Saddle River: Prentice-Hall.

Toffler, Alvin. 1970. *Future Shock*. New York: Random House.

_____. 1980. *The Third Wave*. New York: William Morrow.

Toffler, Alvin and Heidi Toffler. 1990. *Powershift*. New York: Bantam.

Tschannen-Moran, M. 2001. "Collaboration and the need for trust." *Journal of Educational Administration* 39, no. 4: pp. 308-31.

Turner. 2003. News Release, www.turnerconstruction.com, March 4, 2003.

Urch-Druksat, V. and B.S. Wolff. 2001. "Building the emotional intelligence of groups." *Harvard Business Review*, March 2001.

VanGundy, A.B. 1992. *Idea Power: Techniques & Resources to Unleash the Creativity in Your Organization*. New York: AMACOM.

Vine, David. 2000. "Starting small: first steps towards KM orchestration." *KM World*, Dec. 6, 2000.

Von Grogh, G., J. Roos and D. Kleine (eds). 1998. *Knowing in Firms*. London: Sage.

Wagner, Jon. 2002. Private Communication.

Warnecke, H.J., transl. by Maurice Claypole. 1993. *The Fractal Company*. Berlin: Springer Verlag.

Weinberger, David. 1999a. "Webby collaboration." *KM World*, April 1, 1999.

_____. 1999b. "David Weinberger speaks." *KM World*, Sept. 27, 1999.

Weisinger, Hendrie. 1998. *Emotional Intelligence at Work: The Untapped Edge for Success*. San Francisco: Jossey-Bass.

White, D. 2002. *Knowledge Mapping and Management*. London: IRM Press.

Whorf, Benjamin Lee. 1964. *Language, Thought and Reality: Selected Writings*. Cambridge: MIT Press.

Index

Livelink, 106, 168, 232
Lockheed Martin, 232
Logan, Robert K., 53, 65, 100, 102, 126, 249
Logan-Stokes Collaboration Tool, 19, 210, 224
Logan-Stokes Collaborative Knowledge Network, 21, 225-38
Logan-Stokes Model of Collaboration, 17, 121-26
Logan-Stokes-Wagner Matrix, 204-05
loyalty, 17, 49, 81, 83, 91, 105, 127, 147, 167-70, 187, 216
LSCKN. *See* Logan-Stokes Collaborative Knowledge Network
Lucier, Charles, 11

M
Manager's Collaboration Quotient, 20, 220-21
Manville, Brook, 92
marketing. *See* sales and marketing
Maslow, A., 141, 158
Mayer, J. D., 136-38, 140
Mayo, George Elton, 61
McClelland, D. C., 141
McGraw-Hill, 232
McGregor, D., 141
McKinsey & Co., 92
McLuhan, Marshall, 16, 25, 37-38, 47, 53, 98-103, 112, 127
meetings, 93, 150, 189, 200
   collaborative, 192, 199-202
   face-to-face, 27, 92-93, 113, 124, 192, 195, 201-03, 206, 216, 226, 229
   virtual, 114, 146, 195, 201-07
Mertins, Kai, 36
Michigan Gaming Board, 69
Microsoft, 58, 252

MIS, 6, 30, 42, 45, 59, 62, 65, 111, 161-62
Mills Corporation, 69
Mitnick, James, 24-25, 109, 145-47, 157, 165-67, 198
motivation, 4, 8, 14, 17-21, 34, 36, 48, 52-53, 61, 107, 122, 129, 132-33, 140-47, 154-56, 158, 163-65, 169, 171-73, 177-78, 182-84, 188-89, 191-92, 197-98, 201-02, 209, 211-20, 228, 251
Motorola, 35
MQ. *See* motivation
Myers-Briggs, 136

N
NASA, 158
Nasser, Jacque, 24
National Safety Council, 232
National Semiconductor, 187, 243
Netscape, 23, 37, 56, 74, 89, 158, 250
Nonaka, I., 16, 40, 65, 71, 77, 85-86, 91, 126, 226-27, 229, 259
non-profit organizations and collaboration, 95, 158, 193-94
Northrop Grumman, 168, 206-07

O
objectives. *See* tactical objectives
obstacles to collaboration, 11-13
online training, 21, 109, 164-65, 227, 232-37
openness, 111, 136, 150, 170-72, 187, 231
Open Text, 106, 109, 166, 168, 232, 270
Oracle, 28
Organizational Collaboration Quotient, 20, 210, 222-23
Otis Elevator Company, 104-05,